E·l·e·g·a·n·c·e
With Ease

E·l·e·g·a·n·c·e
With Ease

Scorpion Publishing Group
Cincinnati, Ohio

Scorpion Publishing Group
P.O.Box 14694
Cincinnati, OH 45250
Phone: 606-846-4388
Facsimile: 606-846-5078

London Office:
Victoria House,
Victoria Road,
Buckhurst Hill,
Essex,
England
Phone: 01-310-9350

ISBN 0-943877-00-8 (Previously numbered 1-86806-018-7)
Revised edition 1987
Previously titled THE NEW MYRNA ROSEN COOKBOOK

Library of Congress Catalog Card Number: 87-62279

Cover Photographs © Jeff Friedman, Cincinnati, OH
Cover Design: Siebert Design, Cincinnati, OH

Edited By Ann Bryce and Linda Thomas

Printed and bound by Colorcraft Ltd.

For
RONNIE, DESIRÉE & DEAN
who gave me the inspiration and
who have always been there
when I needed them

I grew up in a large family that, in addition to entertaining frequently, was always known for its culinary expertise. My recollections begin with my grandmother, Leah Chait, a descendant of Russian emigrants who settled in Johannesburg. Assisted by her five daughters, one of whom is my mother, Mercia, my grandmother ran a thriving restaurant in a city recognized for its international cuisine. My grandmother's desire to cultivate an appreciation for the rich culinary traditions which originated from Russia and Poland, is evidenced by the fact that all of my aunts and uncles also excel in cooking.

My own cooking skill is a result of many factors, not the least of which is my mother, a superb cook who possesses the uncanny ability of being able to read a recipe and reliably predict its outcome. I remember numerous incidents when she would merely look at a recipe and say, "This can never work as it is." Then she would just add or delete enough of the correct ingredients to create a result which was spectacular.

My cooking is also influenced by having lived on three continents, Africa, Europe, and North America, where I enjoyed experimenting with the various traditional cuisines. Johannesburg, a melting pot of Dutch, English, and Jewish settlers, as well as numerous other nationalities, provided me with a broad sampling of international cooking styles and recipes. The European's unique attitude toward good food led to a number of recipes originating from Switzerland, France, Italy, and Germany. While travelling extensively within various countries in these and other continents, I paid particular attention in both restaurants and homes to each dish—the way it was prepared and the way it was presented.

My husband Ronnie and I have always been very sociable. Wherever we have lived, we have enjoyed having company to our home for dinner. Perhaps partly because of this desire to entertain, and of course my love for cooking, I always seemed to be teaching my friends and neighbors to cook. This initiated the idea of holding some informal cooking lessons, and before I realized it, we had converted our children's play room into a second kitchen, and I was directing a very large cooking school. The recipes from these classes became the basis for my first book which is now in its tenth printing.

Due to our involvement with Thoroughbred horses, we reside in Lexington, Kentucky, a mecca for the horse industry. People from around the world are regularly attracted to this area, affording me a unique opportunity to cook and entertain frequently. From small dinner parties to pre-Derby occasions for which I have personally catered for over 400 guests, we enjoy entertaining friends, clients, acquaintances, and celebrities, many of whom have travelled from distant countries.

To say that I enjoy cooking is quite an understatement. In many ways, I feel a great part of my life revolves around cooking. Good food is a love of mine. I love creating it, and I get tremendous satisfaction from seeing people enjoy it.

My favorite things to make are all kinds of desserts, because I can be very innovative. I love to make foods look beautiful, and with desserts, you can create some very exotic dishes.

I hope you enjoy the beautiful photographs in this book, but more importantly, I hope you *use* the recipes within it, because if you do, I know that you will experience the same level of satisfaction and success that I have enjoyed. You will be able to see how easy it is to make elegant foods, and you will gain confidence, knowing that whatever recipe you choose, the dish will be captivating.

Bon Appetit,

Myrna Rosen

Myrna Rosen

Contents

REFERENCE TO PHOTOGRAPHS 8

APPETIZERS & HORS D'OEUVRES 11
    Cold 12
    Hot 18

SOUPS 31

FISH & SEAFOOD 39

POULTRY 55

MEAT DISHES 65
    Beef 66
    Veal 74
    Lamb 76

VEGETABLES, PASTA & SIDE DISHES 81

SALADS 89

DESSERTS 95
    Hot 96
    Cold 103

CAKES 113
    Baking Tips & Cake Decorations 114

TARTS & PIES 135

SMALL CAKES & BISCUITS 145

BREAD & SCONES 161

TRADITIONAL JEWISH DISHES 165
    Passover 176

WEIGHTS & MEASURES 179

INDEX 180

Reference to Photographs

	Photo Page	Recipe Page
Appetizers & Hors d'oeuvres		
Aioli Dip with Crudités in Ice Mould	14	12
Cantonese Chicken Wings	27	23
Cheese Strata	26	22
Mexican Pizza	26	19
Quiche, Terry's Fabulous	34	28
Smoked Salmon Pâté	27	13
Tuna Melt	35	18
Soups & Salads		
Chicken Gumbo	34	32
Clam Chowder	35	33
Exotic Waldorf Salad	f. cover	92
Lobster Bisque	f. cover	32
Spinach & Water Chestnut Salad	34	93
Main Courses (Fish & Seafood, Poultry, Meat Dishes)		
Duck Montmorency	f. cover	60
Duck with Figs	62	60
Fish en Croûte	42	44
Pineapple Ginger Fish	50	45
Prawn (Shrimp) Brochette	51	52
Rib Roast Sauce with Green Peppercorn Sauce	78	66
Roast Beef and Yorkshire Pudding with Horseradish Sauce	f. cover	67
Sole aux Pommes	51	41
Sole Véronique	f. cover	41
Whole Baked Fish with Herbs	f. cover	41
Vegetables and Side Dishes		
Broccoli with Mushroom Sauce	78	82
Corn Pudding	79	85
Green Beans with Almonds	78	83
Harvard Beets	78	84
Wild Rice with Mushrooms and Water Chestnuts	79	86
Desserts		
Baked Apples with Caramel Sauce	99	96
Chocolate Mousse Fancy Cake	98	111
Chocolate Truffles	154	112
Crème Caramel, Mercia's	98	110
Crêpes Suzette	98	102
Lemon Cream Puff Ring	106	105
Lemon Florentine	b. cover	105
Marshmallow Ring with Cream and Berries	99	108
Pavlova, Mercia's Foolproof	b. cover	110
Souffled Crêpes with Custard	b. cover	103
White Chocolate Mousse with Raspberry Sauce	118-119	108
Cakes		
Black Forest Cherry Cake	126	130
Caramel Crunch Cake	b. cover	116
Chocolate Raspberry Roulade	b. cover	129
Lemon Cheese Gâteau	155	125
Lemon Upside-down Cake	154	120
Marble Cheese Cake	147	124
Quick Orange-glazed Cake	155	117
Tarts, Pies & Cookies		
Banana Cream Pie	146	140
Butterflies	146	148
French Silk Tart	138	141
Fruit Tart	98	142
Koeksusters	147	150
Linzer Cookies	155	153
Meringues with Coffee Cream and Walnuts	154	151
Mille Feuilles	154	149
Petits Fours Made Easy	155	148
Thumbprints	155	157
Decorating Tips		
Butter Rose	35	114
Chocolate Cabbage Leaves	118	114
Traditional Jewish Dishes		
Chicken Soup	171	166
Flaumen Brisket with Prunes	171	169
Gefilte Fish	170	168
Kitke or Challah	170	175
Kreplach	171	166
Teiglach	170	174
Upside-down Noodle Kugel	170	173

Foreword & Acknowledgements

The overwhelming response to my first book, Cooking with Myrna Rosen, as well as my continual enjoyment in experimenting with new and exciting culinary ideas, led to the publication of this book.

You will find each of the recipes to contain metric and American measurements, as well as, interchangeable ingredients, so that irrespective of where you live, you can have confidence in the over 300 tried and tested recipes included herein.

I am deeply grateful to the following people, whose combined interest, support and talents have made this book possible:

My husband RONNIE, whose love, pride and confidence in me have been a continual source of inspiration

My parents, MERCIA and MAURICE FINE, who helped me in so many ways. In particular I would like to thank my mother for her advice and assistance with the recipes, as well as with the preparation of the food for the photographs. Without her love, encouragement and

hard work, I could not have achieved my goal

My children, DESIRÉE and DEAN, for their love and support during the preparation of this, book

SUSAN BRODNAX, for her help in converting measurements, and assistance in arranging, and typing the recipes

LINDA THOMAS, whose command of the English language was evident in editing revisions

JEFF FRIEDMAN, who took the beautiful photographs used on the cover, LORI SIEBERT who designed the cover, and GAGE INTERIORS who provided props and accessories for the cover photographs.

Finally, to JEFF STAPLES for using his numerous skills in overseeing the publication of this revised edition.

Myrna Rosen

September 1987

Appetizers & Hors d'oeuvres

COLD

Aioli Dip with Crudités in Ice Mould 12
Hummous 12
Vegetable Cream Cheese Dip 12
Spinach & Vegetable Dip 12
Guacamole 13
Liver Pâté 13
Smoked Salmon Pâté 13
Shrimp Pâté 13
Pink Salmon Pâté 16
Salmon Mould with Cucumber Sauce 16
Lobster Cocktail 16
Tarragon Crab Salad 16
Party Egg Mould with Sour Cream & Caviar 17
Smoked Salmon (Lox) & Cream Cheese Mould 17

HOT

Eight-Layer Mexican Dip with Taco Sauce 18
Artichoke Dip 18
Tuna Melt 18
Mushrooms in French Loaf 19
Mexican Pizza 19
Quick 'n Easy Pizza Loaf 19
Curry Puffs 20
Sausage Rolls 20
Greek Cheese Pastries 21
Polynesian Chicken Fingers 21
Mushrooms Stuffed with Crab & Artichokes 21
Cheese Strata 22
Samoosas 22
Salmon Croquettes with Mushroom Sauce 22
Escargots in Mushroom Caps 23
Oysters Supreme 23
Peri-Peri Chicken Livers 23
Cantonese Chicken Wings 23
Terry's Italian-style Artichokes 24
Artichoke & Shrimp Casserole 24
Spoonbread Soufflé with Seafood Sauce 24
Tuna Crêpe Casserole 25
Savoury Salmon or Tuna Roll 25
Asparagus Tart 28
Curried Chicken in Phyllo 28
Terry's Fabulous Quiche 28
Ricotta Cheese & Artichoke Pie 29
Tuna Fish Strudel 29
Asparagus & Tuna Pie 29
Tuna Soufflé 30
Snoek & Sweetcorn Soufflé 30
Crab & Asparagus Crêpes Gratinée 30

Cold

Aioli Dip with Crudités in Ice Mould

METRIC	AMERICAN
4 cloves garlic, peeled	4 cloves garlic, peeled
1 whole egg & 1 yolk	1 whole egg & 1 yolk
5 ml (1 t) prepared mustard	1 teaspoon Dijon mustard
15 ml (1 T) white wine or vinegar / lemon juice	1 tablespoon white wine or vinegar / lemon juice
2 ml (½ t) salt	½ teaspoon salt
Dash of cayenne pepper	Dash of cayenne pepper
250 ml (1 C) olive or sunflower oil	1 cup olive or vegetable oil

METHOD Place all ingredients except oil in a blender and blend until smooth. Add oil in a thin, steady stream until a thick mayonnaise is formed. Cover and refrigerate.

Serve chilled with crudités (a selection of fresh vegetables such as carrots, celery sticks, radishes, broccoli, cauliflower florets, cherry tomatoes, green pepper strips, mushrooms, etc).

Makes 375 ml / 1½ cups

ICE MOULD Half-fill a bundt tin or plastic mould with water. Place flowers or rose radishes on top of the water and freeze until solid. Continue to add a cup of water at a time, allowing it to freeze after each addition, until the tin is full – this may take up to 2 days.

Unmould onto a bed of crushed ice, fill the centre with crudités and if desired, place more crudités around the mould on the crushed ice.

PHOTOGRAPH ON PAGE 14

Hummous

METRIC	AMERICAN
1 x 425 g tin chickpeas, drained	1 x 15 oz can garbonza beans, drained
45 ml (3T) fresh lemon juice	3 tablespoons fresh lemon juice
2 cloves garlic	2 cloves garlic
5 ml (1 t) salt	1 teaspoon salt
2 ml (½ t) black pepper	½ teaspoon black pepper
125 ml (½ C) tehina (sesame seed paste)	½ cup sesame seed paste

GARNISH	GARNISH
45 ml (3 T) olive oil	3 tablespoons olive oil
Chopped parsley	Chopped parsley
Cayenne pepper	Red pepper
Olives	Olives

METHOD Combine ingredients in a food processor or blender. To garnish, drizzle with olive oil, sprinkle with parsley and pepper and dot with olives. Serve with pita, nachos, tortilla chips or crisps, as a dip.

Makes 500 ml / 2 cups

Vegetable Cream Cheese Dip

METRIC	AMERICAN
250 g cream cheese	8 oz cream cheese
250 ml (1 C) sour cream	1 cup sour cream
250 ml (1 C) mayonnaise	1 cup mayonnaise
1 packet vegetable soup mix	1 envelope vegetable soup mix

METHOD Combine all ingredients and blend well. Refrigerate for several hours. Serve with crudités (selection of raw vegetables).

Makes 750 ml / 3 cups

Spinach & Vegetable Dip

METRIC	AMERICAN
250 ml (1 C) sour cream	1 cup sour cream
250 ml (1 C) plain yoghurt	1 cup plain yoghurt
500 g frozen spinach, drained & chopped	1 lb frozen spinach, drained & chopped
1 envelope vegetable soup mix	1 envelope vegetable soup mix

METHOD Mix sour cream with yoghurt to form creamy consistency. Add remaining ingredients and mix together well. Refrigerate for 2 hours before serving. Serve with crudités.

Makes 1 litre / 4 cups

Guacamole

METRIC	AMERICAN
2 ripe, medium-sized avocados, peeled & pips removed	2 ripe, medium-sized avocados, peeled & seeds removed
4 cloves garlic	4 cloves garlic
2 ml (½ t) salt	½ teaspoon salt
2 ml (½ t) crushed red or cayenne pepper	½ teaspoon crushed red or cayenne pepper
125 ml (½ C) mayonnaise	½ cup mayonnaise
Dash of Worcestershire sauce	Dash of Worcestershire sauce
15 ml (1 T) lemon juice	1 tablespoon lemon juice

METHOD Blend all ingredients in a blender or using the steel blade of a food processor. Cover and chill for several hours.

Serve with crisps (chips), nachos or tortilla chips.

Makes 500 ml / 2 cups

Liver Pâté

METRIC	AMERICAN
500 g chicken livers	1 lb chicken livers
1 stick celery, with leaves	1 stick celery, with leaves
Few bay leaves	Few bay leaves
Few peppercorns	Few peppercorns
2 ml (½ t) salt	½ teaspoon salt
2–3 onions, sliced	2–3 onions, sliced
2 cloves garlic, chopped	2 cloves garlic, chopped
60 ml (¼ cup) oil & 30 ml (2 T) chicken fat *	4 tablespoons oil & 2 tablespoons chicken fat*
4 hard-boiled eggs	4 hard-boiled eggs
15 ml (1 T) sherry	1 tablespoon sherry
15 ml (1 T) brandy	1 tablespoon cognac
Pepper to taste	Pepper to taste

* Or instead of oil and fat, use 125 g (½ cup) butter or margarine

METHOD Wash livers thoroughly under cold water. Place celery, bay leaves, peppercorns and salt in a small saucepan of boiling water and boil for 10 minutes. Add livers and continue to boil for approximately 3 minutes. Drain and remove livers.

Sauté onion and garlic in oil or butter. Mince the fried onions with the liver and 2 hard-boiled eggs. Stir in the sherry and brandy (cognac). Add pepper to taste; adjust seasoning.

Spoon into an oiled mould and refrigerate until ready to serve. Unmould and decorate with remaining sliced hard-boiled eggs.

CHEF'S TIP For an extra-creamy texture, add 125 ml (½ cup) cream or non-dairy creamer to the ingredients.

Serves 8 to 10

Smoked Salmon Pâté

METRIC	AMERICAN
500 g smoked salmon	1 lb lox
60 g butter, softened	4 tablespoons butter, softened
15 ml (1 T) oil	1 tablespoon oil
Juice of ½ lemon	Juice of ½ lemon
125 ml (½ C) cream	½ cup cream
Freshly ground black pepper	Freshly ground black pepper
Few drops of Tabasco	Few drops of Tabasco
GARNISH	**GARNISH**
Caviar (optional)	Caviar (optional)
Sprigs of fresh parsley	Sprigs of fresh parsley

METHOD Combine 250 g (½ lb) of the salmon with the butter in a food processor or blender. Add oil and lemon juice and blend until light and fluffy. Pour in cream; continue to process until well blended. Add pepper and Tabasco to taste. Using remaining salmon, line bottom and sides of 4 ramekins. Fill with mixture and allow to set in refrigerator.

Invert onto serving platter. Top with caviar (if desired) and surround with parsley sprigs. Serve with buttered wholewheat toast points (slices of toast buttered and cut into triangles).

Serves 4 PHOTOGRAPH ON PAGE 27

Shrimp Pâté

METRIC	AMERICAN
1 onion, diced	1 onion, diced
125 g butter	½ cup butter
2 x 120 g tins shrimp, drained or 500 g fresh, boiled shrimp	2 x 4½ oz cans shrimp, drained or 1 lb fresh, boiled popcorn shrimp
2 ml (½ t) black pepper	½ teaspoon black pepper
Juice of ½ lemon	Juice of ½ lemon
30 ml (2 T) mayonnaise	2 tablespoons mayonnaise
125 g cream cheese	4 oz cream cheese
Crushed garlic powder to taste	Garlic powder to taste

METHOD Sauté onion in butter. Place in food processor with shrimp. Add remaining ingredients, process and adjust seasonings if necessary.

Serve with thinly sliced wholewheat bread, or with shrimp chips which have been fried in hot oil and drained on absorbent paper. (These are available in packages from Chinese or Oriental stores.)

Serves 6

Overleaf: Crudités in Ice Mould

Pink Salmon Pâté

METRIC	AMERICAN
1 x 440 g tin pink salmon, drained	1 x 15½ oz can pink salmon, drained
125 mℓ (½ C) mayonnaise	½ cup mayonnaise
125 mℓ (½ C) sour cream	½ cup sour cream
125 – 175 g smoked salmon (lax)	4 – 6 oz lox
30 mℓ (2 T) butter, melted	2 tablespoons butter, melted
Pepper to taste	Pepper to taste
1 x 100 g jar salmon roe	1 x 3½ oz jar salmon roe
Salt to taste (if necessary)	Salt to taste (if necessary)

GARNISH	GARNISH
Freshly chopped dill	Freshly chopped dill

METHOD Place all ingredients, except roe and dill, in food processor or blender and process. Carefully fold in roe.

Pour or spoon mixture into mould and refrigerate until ready to serve. Sprinkle with freshly chopped dill.

Serves 12

Salmon Mould with Cucumber Sauce

METRIC	AMERICAN
1 envelope gelatine	1 envelope unflavored gelatin
60 mℓ (¼ C) cold water	¼ cup cold water
125 mℓ (½ C) boiling water	½ cup boiling water
125 mℓ (½ C) mayonnaise	½ cup mayonnaise
125 mℓ (½ C) sour cream	½ cup sour ceam
15 mℓ (1 T) lemon juice	1 tablespoon lemon juice
5 mℓ (1 t) Worcestershire sauce	1 teaspoon Worcestershire sauce
2 x 212 g tins salmon	2 x 7½ oz cans salmon
10 mℓ (2 t) finely grated onion	2 teaspoons finely grated onion
2 sticks celery, diced	2 sticks celery, diced
125 mℓ (½ C) finely diced cucumber	½ cup finely diced cucumber
2 mℓ (½ t) salt	½ teaspoon salt
Few drops Tabasco	Few drops Tabasco

CUCUMBER SAUCE	CUCUMBER SAUCE
250 mℓ (1 C) sour cream	1 cup sour cream
250 mℓ (1 C) finely chopped cucumber	1 cup finely chopped cucumber
2 mℓ (½ t) dill (dried or fresh)	½ teaspoon dillweed or fresh, chopped dill
Salt & pepper to taste	Salt & pepper to taste

METHOD Soften gelatine in cold water, then dissolve in boiling water. Stir in mayonnaise, sour cream, lemon juice and Worcestershire sauce. Skin and debone salmon; fold into mixture with remaining ingredients. Spoon into an oiled mould, cover and refrigerate until firm.

Unmould and serve with Cucumber Sauce and crackers. Sprinkle with freshly chopped dill or parsley.

CUCUMBER SAUCE Combine all ingredients well. Chill until ready to serve.

Serves 12

Lobster Cocktail

METRIC	AMERICAN
4 crayfish tails	4 lobster tails
250 mℓ (1 C) mayonnaise	1 cup mayonnaise
125 mℓ (½ C) tomato sauce	½ cup ketchup
5 mℓ (1 t) vinegar	1 teaspoon vinegar
5 mℓ (1 t) Worcestershire sauce	1 teaspoon Worcestershire sauce
Few drops Tabasco	Few drops Tabasco
1 mℓ (¼ t) salt	¼ teaspoon salt

GARNISH	GARNISH
Sliced hard-boiled eggs	Sliced hard-boiled eggs
Olives	Olives
Paprika	Paprika

METHOD Boil crayfish (lobster) tails in salted water for 25 minutes. Shell and cut into bite-size chunks; set aside. Combine remaining ingredients and chill well.

Place crayfish (lobster) on a bed of shredded lettuce. Spoon sauce over and garnish with slices of hard-boiled egg, olives and paprika.

CHEF'S TIP For Avocado Ritz, serve the crayfish (lobster) mixture in halved avocado pears.

Serves 4

Tarragon Crab Salad

METRIC	AMERICAN
500 g crab meat	1 lb crab meat
125 mℓ (½ C) mayonnaise	½ cup mayonnaise
Juice of ½ lemon	Juice of ½ lemon
10 mℓ (2 t) Worcestershire sauce	2 teaspoons Worcestershire sauce
2 mℓ (½ t) dried tarragon	½ teaspoon dried tarragon
15 mℓ (1 T) prepared mustard	1 tablespoon prepared mustard
Dash of brandy	Dash of brandy
Paprika	Paprika

METHOD Combine all ingredients except crab and paprika. Refrigerate for several hours to allow flavours to blend. Fold in crab meat. Arrange on lettuce leaves and sprinkle with paprika.

Serves 4

Party Egg Mould with Sour Cream & Caviar

METRIC	AMERICAN
MOULD	MOULD
18 hard-boiled eggs, mashed	18 hard-boiled eggs, mashed
125 mℓ (½ C) mayonnaise	½ cup mayonnaise
1 stick celery, finely diced	1 stick celery, finely diced
15 mℓ (1 T) prepared mustard	1 tablespoon Dijon mustard
10 mℓ (2 t) Worcestershire sauce	2 teaspoons Worcestershire sauce
1 pickled cucumber, finely diced	1 pickle, finely diced
5 mℓ (1 t) salt (or to taste)	1 teaspoon salt (or to taste)
2 mℓ (½ t) pepper	½ teaspoon pepper
½ mℓ (⅛ t) cayenne pepper	⅛ teaspoon cayenne pepper
10 mℓ (2 t) gelatine	2 teaspoons gelatin
60 mℓ (¼ C) boiling water	¼ cup boiling water
TOPPING	TOPPING
250 mℓ (1 C) sour cream	1 cup sour cream
1 x 99 g jar caviar	1 x 3½ oz jar caviar

METHOD Combine and mix together all ingredients for mould, except gelatine and boiling water. Soften gelatine in small amount of cold water, then dissolve in boiling water. Combine with egg mixture and set aside.

Mix 15 mℓ (1 tablespoon) oil with 15 mℓ (1 tablespoon) water; use this mixture to rinse out mould. Press egg mixture into mould and refrigerate for 6–8 hours or overnight. Unmould, spoon sour cream over and top with caviar.

Serve with wholewheat toast points (wholewheat toast cut diagonally into four triangles) or melba toast.

Serves 12 to 15

Smoked Salmon (Lox) & Cream Cheese Mould

METRIC	AMERICAN
250 g thinly sliced smoked salmon	8 oz thinly sliced lox
1 kg cream cheese	2 lb cream cheese
125 mℓ (½ C) milk	½ cup milk
Pinch of salt	Pinch of salt
Dash of white pepper	Dash of white pepper
1 envelope gelatine	1 envelope unflavored gelatin
60 mℓ (¼ C) cold water	¼ cup cold water
60 mℓ (¼ C) boiling water	¼ cup boiling water
30 mℓ (2 T) chopped spring onion	2 tablespoons chopped green onion
GARNISH	GARNISH
1 tomato, sliced	1 tomato, sliced
1 green pepper, sliced	1 green pepper, sliced
1 onion, sliced into rings	1 purple onion, sliced into rings

METHOD Rinse a 5-cup ring mould with 15 mℓ (1 tablespoon) oil and 15 mℓ (1 tablespoon) water. Line mould with slices of smoked salmon (lox). (It is not necessary to cover the surface of the mould completely with salmon, as it looks attractive if the cream cheese mixture is visible when it is unmoulded.)

Blend cream cheese with milk and season with salt and pepper to taste. Soften gelatine in cold water, then add boiling water to dissolve. Cool, stir into cheese mixture and add spring (green) onions .

Pour cheese mixture into mould and allow to set in refrigerator, or leave overnight. Unmould onto a platter. Garnish with tomato and green pepper slices and onion rings. Serve with bagels or melba toast.

CHEF'S TIP This makes a delightful brunch dish.

Serves 12 to 15

Hot

Eight-Layer Mexican Dip

METRIC	AMERICAN
1 large onion, diced	1 large onion, diced
500 g beef mince	1 lb ground beef
1 x 440 g tin red kidney beans, mashed or puréed in food processor	1 x 15½ oz can refried beans
Taco sauce*	Taco sauce*
1 x 250 g tin black olives, sliced	1 x 8 oz can black olives, sliced
Diced green pepper	Diced green pepper
Grated Cheddar cheese	Grated Cheddar cheese
500 mℓ Guacamole (recipe on p 13)	2 cups Guacamole (recipe on p 13)
Sour cream	Sour cream

* If you cannot obtain commercially prepared taco sauce, make your own using the recipe below

METHOD Lightly brown onion and meat; simmer for 25–30 minutes. In a paella (casserole) dish place one layer each of beans, browned meat mixture, taco sauce, olives, green pepper and Cheddar cheese.

Bake in 180°C (350°F) oven until hot (about 30 minutes). Top with Guacamole and sour cream. Serve with tortilla chips, nachos, or potato crisps (chips).

Serves 12

Taco Sauce

METRIC	AMERICAN
1 x 850 g tin tomatoes, drained & chopped	1 x 1 lb 12 oz can tomatoes, drained & chopped
1 onion, diced	1 onion, diced
5 mℓ (1 t) chilli powder	1 teaspoon chili powder
1 x 90 g tin green chillis	1 x 3 oz can green chilis
2 mℓ (½ t) salt	½ teaspoon salt
2 mℓ (½ t) pepper	½ teaspoon pepper
2 mℓ (½ t) crushed garlic powder	½ teaspoon garlic powder

METHOD Combine all ingredients in a saucepan and stir to mix well. Bring to the boil, then reduce heat and simmer for 20 minutes, stirring occasionally.

Cover and refrigerate. Heat before serving.

Makes 750 mℓ–1 ℓ / 3–4 cups

Artichoke Dip

METRIC	AMERICAN
2 x 400 g tins artichoke hearts	2 x 14 oz cans artichoke hearts
250 mℓ (1 C) mayonnaise	1 cup mayonnaise
100 g grated Parmesan cheese	1 cup grated Parmesan cheese
Dash of crushed garlic powder	Dash of garlic powder
Paprika	Paprika

METHOD Drain artichoke hearts and tear with a fork. Combine with mayonnaise, Parmesan cheese and garlic powder.

Spoon into a greased crock-pot or small, deep oven-proof dish (approximately 15 cm / 6 inches in diameter). Sprinkle with paprika and bake in 180°C (350°F) oven, until lightly browned. Serve with crackers.

Makes 1 litre / 4 cups

Tuna Melt

METRIC	AMERICAN
2 x 185 g tins tuna, drained	2 x 6½ oz cans solid white albacore tuna, drained
1 small tomato, diced	1 small tomato, diced
15 mℓ (1 T) finely diced onion	1 tablespoon finely diced onion
15 mℓ (1 T) finely diced green pepper	1 tablespoon finely diced green pepper
125 mℓ (½ C) finely diced celery	½ cup finely diced celery
Salt & pepper to taste	Salt & pepper to taste
Mayonnaise to moisten	Mayonnaise to moisten
2 pita breads	2 pita breads
Butter or margarine	Butter or margarine
4 cheese slices	4 cheese slices

METHOD Mix together tuna, tomato, onion, green pepper and celery. Season with salt and pepper and add mayonnaise.

Split each pita bread in two, brush with butter or margarine and place under grill (broiler) until golden brown. Place a scoop of tuna mixture on each one. Top with a slice of cheese and grill (broil) until cheese melts.

Serves 4   PHOTOGRAPH ON PAGE 35

Mushrooms in French Loaf

METRIC	AMERICAN
1 French loaf	1 loaf French bread
60 g butter	4 tablespoons butter
500 g mushrooms, sliced	1 lb mushrooms, sliced
125 mℓ (½ C) white wine	½ cup white wine
1 spring onion, chopped	1 green onion, chopped
5 mℓ (1 t) coarsely ground black pepper	1 teaspoon coarsely ground black pepper
15 mℓ (1 T) cornflour mixed to a paste with milk	1 tablespoon cornstarch mixed to a paste with milk
250 mℓ (1 C) cream	1 cup heavy cream
1 egg, slightly beaten	1 egg, slightly beaten
100 g grated Jarlsberg, Swiss or Monterey Jack cheese	1 cup grated Jarlsberg, Swiss or Monterey Jack cheese
Salt to taste	Salt to taste

METHOD Slice off top of French loaf lengthwise and scoop out. Melt butter; add sliced mushrooms and cook for 2–3 minutes. Add wine, onion and pepper and continue to simmer over low heat for 3–5 minutes. Add cornflour paste and stir until thickened.

Remove from heat and stir in cream. Stir a little of the hot mixture into the egg, then add egg to hot mushroom mixture. Return to heat and stir for 1 minute. Add half of the grated cheese and season to taste with salt. Cool. (If the mixture seems too thin, tear some of the scooped-out bread into small pieces and add to mixture to thicken.)

Spoon mixture into French loaf, sprinkle with remaining cheese and bake at 200°C (400°F) for approximately 20 minutes or until piping hot.

Serves 6 to 8

Mexican Pizza

METRIC	AMERICAN
TORTILLAS	TORTILLAS
420 g (3½ C) flour	3½ cups all purpose flour
5 mℓ (1 t) salt	1 teaspoon salt
2 mℓ (½ t) baking powder	½ teaspoon baking powder
75 g margarine	⅓ cup butter
325 mℓ (1⅓ C) warm milk	1⅓ cups warm milk
FILLING	FILLING
Cheese slices	Cheese slices
Diced tomato	Diced tomato
Diced green pepper	Diced green pepper
Diced onion	Diced onion
Butter for frying	Butter for frying

METHOD To prepare tortillas combine flour, salt and baking powder. Grate or cut in margarine or butter until mixture resembles breadcrumbs. Stir in milk and mix well. Turn dough onto smooth surface and knead very well (approximately 3 minutes).

Divide into 10 equal portions and roll as thinly as possible into circles about 20 cm (8 inches) in diameter. Cut each circle in half.

Heat a non-stick pan over medium heat; cook tortillas for 2 minutes on each side or until lightly brown, being careful not to let them wrinkle. Pat lightly with spatula while browning the second side.

Place slices of cheese on one tortilla half-circle. Sprinkle with diced tomato, green pepper and onion. Cover with another tortilla and fry in butter over medium heat until crisp and golden, turning over carefully with a spatula and adding more butter if necessary. Cut in half and serve.

Serves 10   PHOTOGRAPH ON PAGE 26

Quick 'n Easy Pizza Loaf

METRIC	AMERICAN
300 g grated Swiss or Cheddar cheese	3 cups grated Swiss or Cheddar cheese
1 medium tomato, chopped	1 medium tomato, chopped
200 mℓ (¾ C) mayonnaise	¾ cup mayonnaise
60 mℓ (¼ C) chopped spring onion	¼ cup chopped green onion
1 large rye bread or French loaf	1 large loaf rye or French bread
1 x 50 g tin flat anchovy fillets	1 x 2 oz can flat anchovy fillets

METHOD Stir together cheese, tomato, mayonnaise and onion. Slice bread three-quarters the way through. Fill every alternate slice with the mixture and place an anchovy fillet in the middle. Wrap in foil.

Bake at 180°C (350°F) for 25–30 minutes, or until the cheese has melted. Cut through unfilled slices when serving.

CHEF'S TIP This makes a piquant accompaniment to cocktails.

Serves 8

Puff Pastry

METRIC	AMERICAN
500 g (4 C) flour*	3¾ cups all purpose flour
5 mℓ (1 t) salt	1 teaspoon salt
450 g butter	2 cups butter
375 mℓ (1½ C) iced water	1½ cups iced water
30 mℓ (2 T) lemon juice	2 tablespoons lemon juice

* This measurement differs from the American

METHOD Sift flour and salt together. Rub one third of the butter into the flour, then mix into a dough with the water and lemon juice.

Working on a floured board, roll dough out into a large rectangle (about ½ cm / ¼ inch thick). Spread two thirds of the dough with a quarter of the remaining butter. Fold the unbuttered section over the centre section, then fold over the remaining section to cover.

Give the dough a quarter turn to bring the open edge towards you, then roll out again to ½ cm (¼ inch) thickness. Spread with a quarter of the remaining butter, fold as before and chill for 20 minutes. Repeat this procedure twice again, using remaining butter.

The pastry is now ready to be used, or may be wrapped in wax paper and refrigerated for 12–24 hours. It may also be deep-frozen indefinitely.

Makes 1 kg / 2 lb

Curry Puffs

METRIC	AMERICAN
500 g puff pastry*	1 lb puff pastry*
FILLING	**FILLING**
1 onion, finely diced	1 onion, finely diced
15 mℓ (1 T) oil	1 tablespoon oil
500 g beef mince	1 lb ground beef
30 mℓ (2 T) vinegar	2 tablespoons vinegar
30 mℓ (2 T) apricot jam	2 tablespoons apricot preserves
125 mℓ (½ C) water	½ cup water
5 mℓ (1 t) salt	1 teaspoon salt
½ beef bouillon cube	½ beef bouillon cube
15 mℓ (1 T) flour	1 tablespoon flour
30 mℓ (2 T) curry powder	2 tablespoons curry powder
5 mℓ (1 t) cumin	1 teaspoon cumin

* Use ready-made pastry or see recipe on this page

METHOD To prepare filling, fry onion in oil until golden brown. Add meat and brown, then add vinegar, apricot jam

(apricot preserves), water, salt and bouillon cube. Stir well and simmer over low heat for 1 hour.

Sprinkle flour, curry powder and cumin over meat and stir until mixture thickens. Remove from heat; cool thoroughly.

Roll pastry out and cut into rounds 8 cm (3 inches) in diameter. Place a generous spoonful of meat in each centre and pinch edges of pastry together very well. Fry in hot oil over medium heat until golden and drain on paper towels.

CHEF'S TIP These puffs may be fried early in the day and reheated in the oven before serving.

Makes 32

Sausage Rolls

METRIC	AMERICAN
2 x 400 g packets puff pastry*	2 lb puff pastry*
750 g beef mince	1½ lb ground beef
7 mℓ (1½ t) salt	1½ teaspoons salt
125 mℓ (½ C) fresh bread-crumbs	½ cup fresh breadcrumbs
½ chicken bouillon cube, crushed	½ chicken bouillon cube, crushed
1 small potato, peeled & grated	1 small potato, peeled & grated
1 small onion, peeled & grated	1 small onion, peeled & grated
GLAZE	**GLAZE**
1 egg, beaten	1 egg, beaten

* Use ready-made puff pastry or see recipe on this page

METHOD Roll out pastry into a rectangle on a lightly floured board. (If using ready-made rolled pastry, roll out a little more than it already is.)

Using wet hands, shape meat mixture into a sausage approximately 2,5 cm (1 inch) thick and place along width of the pastry. Wet edge of pastry, roll up and cut off this filled strip. Cut strip into 5 cm (2 inch) pieces. Continue in this manner, using up all the meat mixture and pastry.

Brush with beaten egg, place on greased baking tray and bake in 220°C (425°F) oven for approximately 25 minutes, or until golden brown.

Makes 60

Greek Cheese Pastries

METRIC	AMERICAN
400 g puff pastry*	1 lb puff pastry*

FILLING	FILLING
250 g feta cheese	8 oz feta cheese
125 g Ricotta cheese	4 oz Ricotta cheese
100 g grated Cheddar cheese	1 cup grated Cheddar cheese
1 egg, beaten	1 egg, beaten
Salt & pepper to taste	Salt & pepper to taste
2 mℓ (½ t) freshly chopped fennel, mint or dill	½ teaspoon freshly chopped fennel, mint or dill

GLAZE	GLAZE
1 egg, beaten	1 egg, beaten

* Use ready-made pastry or see recipe on p 20

METHOD Combine all ingredients for filling and mix well. Roll pastry out fairly thinly, then cut into rounds 8 cm (3 inches) in diameter. Brush edges of pastry rounds with water and place a spoonful of filling in each centre. Fold over and seal well.

Brush with glaze and bake at 200°C (400°F) for 10–15 minutes.

Makes 32

Polynesian Chicken Fingers

METRIC	AMERICAN
4 – 6 skinned & deboned chicken breasts, cut into fingers	4–6 skinned & deboned chicken breasts, cut into fingers
Salt, pepper & crushed garlic powder to season	Salt, pepper & garlic powder to season
Flour for coating	Flour for coating
3 eggs, lightly beaten	3 eggs, lightly beaten
Dessicated coconut	Flaked coconut
Oil for frying	Oil for frying

DIP SAUCE*	DIP SAUCE*
1 small onion, diced	1 small onion, diced
1 clove garlic, crushed	1 clove garlic, crushed
5 mℓ (1 t) finely diced fresh ginger (or ground ginger)	1 teaspoon finely diced gingerroot (or ground ginger)
15 mℓ (1 T) margarine	1 tablespoon margarine
15 mℓ (1 T) curry powder	1 tablespoon curry powder
10 mℓ (2 t) brown sugar	2 teaspoons brown sugar
20 mℓ (4 t) flour	4 teaspoons flour
250 mℓ (1 C) strong chicken stock	1 cup strong chicken stock
1 mℓ (¼ t) salt	¼ teaspoon salt

* May be prepared in advance

METHOD Season chicken fingers with salt, pepper and garlic powder. Coat in flour and dip in beaten egg, then roll in coconut.

Heat oil and deep fry a few fingers at a time, turning heat down as soon as chicken is added, as the coconut burns easily. Cook over medium heat until golden brown. Drain on absorbent paper.

DIP SAUCE Sauté onion, garlic and ginger in margarine until lightly browned. Stir in curry powder and brown sugar. Add flour, then slowly add chicken stock, stirring constantly until thickened. If it becomes too thick, add a little boiling water. Add salt.

Blend in a food processor or blender until smooth. Serve hot or cold with the chicken fingers.

CHEF'S TIP The plum sauce served with Roast Rack of Spring Lamb (p 77) also makes a nice dip for these chicken fingers.

Makes 28 to 42

Mushrooms Stuffed with Crab & Artichokes

METRIC	AMERICAN
500 g fresh button mushrooms	1 lb fresh button mushrooms
1 small onion, diced	1 small onion, diced
30 mℓ (2 T) butter	2 tablespoons butter
125 g cream cheese	4 oz cream cheese
80 mℓ (⅓ C) milk	⅓ cup milk
50 g grated Cheddar cheese	½ cup grated Cheddar cheese
2 mℓ (½ t) paprika	½ teaspoon paprika
5 mℓ (1 t) chopped parsley	1 teaspoon chopped parsley
1 x 185 g tin artichoke hearts, drained & diced	1 x 6 ½ oz jar marinated artichoke hearts, drained & diced
250 g thawed crab meat	½ lb thawed crab meat
200 mℓ (¾ C) fresh bread-crumbs	¾ cup fresh breadcrumbs
Salt & pepper to taste	Salt & pepper to taste
Grated Parmesan cheese	Grated Parmesan cheese

METHOD Remove stems from mushrooms and dice. Sauté onion in butter. Add mushroom stems and cook for an additional 2–3 minutes.

Add cream cheese, milk, Cheddar cheese, paprika and parsley. Stir over low heat until well blended. Stir in artichokes, crab meat, seasonings and 125 mℓ (½ cup) bread-crumbs. Blend well.

Stuff mushroom caps with mixture. Place caps in a greased ovenware dish and sprinkle with Parmesan cheese and remaining breadcrumbs. Bake at 200°C (400°F) for 15–20 minutes or until sizzling.

Makes about 30

Cheese Strata

METRIC	AMERICAN
8 slices pre-sliced white bread	8 slices pre-sliced white bread
Butter	Butter
250 g grated Cheddar cheese	2½ cups grated Cheddar cheese
4 eggs, lightly beaten	4 eggs, lightly beaten
625 mℓ (2½ C) milk	2½ cups milk
5 mℓ (1 t) salt	1 teaspoon salt
1 mℓ (¼ t) dry mustard	¼ teaspoon dry mustard

METHOD Trim crusts from bread. Butter bread on both sides. Cut each slice in half and alternate layers of bread with cheese in deep ovenware dish, ending with a cheese layer.

Combine remaining ingredients and pour over the layers. Cover and chill for 6 hours or overnight. Bake in a *bain-marie* (placed in a pan of water) at 160°C (325°F) for 1 hour or until firm.

Serves 6 to 8   PHOTOGRAPH ON PAGE 26

Samoosas

METRIC	AMERICAN
DOUGH	DOUGH
420 g (3½ C) flour	3½ cups all purpose flour
5 mℓ (1 t) salt	1 teaspoon salt
5 mℓ (1 t) baking powder	1 teaspoon baking powder
80 mℓ (⅓ C) oil	⅓ cup oil
300 mℓ (1¼ C) warm water	1¼ cups warm water
FILLING	FILLING
15 mℓ (1 T) oil	1 tablespoon oil
5 mℓ (1 t) finely grated fresh ginger	1 teaspoon finely grated ginger-root
1 onion, diced	1 onion, diced
2 green chillis, diced	2 green or red chilis, diced
1 carrot, peeled & grated	1 carrot, peeled & grated
2 cloves garlic, crushed	2 cloves garlic, crushed
125 g (½ C) peas	½ cup peas
2 potatoes, boiled & diced	2 potatoes, boiled & diced
2 mℓ (½ t) salt	½ teaspoon salt
1 mℓ (¼ t) pepper	¼ teaspoon pepper
2 mℓ (½ t) cumin	½ teaspoon cumin
5 mℓ (1 t) curry powder	1 teaspoon curry powder
2 mℓ (½ t) ground coriander	½ teaspoon ground coriander
125 mℓ (½ C) water	½ cup water

METHOD To prepare dough, combine flour, salt and baking powder. Stir in oil and water and mix well. Turn out onto a smooth surface and knead very well. Cover and allow to 'rest' for ½ hour.

Divide dough in half. Roll out paper thin. Cut into strips 7,5 cm (3 inches) wide and 25 cm (10 inches) long.

FILLING Heat oil in frying pan. Add ginger, onion, chillis, carrot and garlic. Sauté for a few minutes, then add peas, potatoes, seasonings and spices. Finally, add water and simmer for 10 minutes. Allow to cool thoroughly.

TO COOK Place a spoonful of filling at the top of each strip and fold into a triangle four times, until filling is enclosed. Place samoosas, a few at a time, into deep, hot oil. Fry until golden brown and drain on absorbent paper.

CHEF'S TIP If you wish, add 250 g (½ lb) minced (ground) beef to the filling. First brown the meat, then add to other ingredients and simmer for 30–40 minutes (instead of 10 minutes).

Makes 32

Salmon Croquettes with Mushroom Sauce

METRIC	AMERICAN
CROQUETTES	CROQUETTES
2 x 213 g tins pink salmon, drained	1 x 15½ oz can pink salmon, drained
½ medium onion, grated	½ medium onion, grated
2 eggs	2 eggs
125 mℓ (½ C) fresh breadcrumbs	½ cup fresh breadcrumbs
60 g butter, melted	4 tablespoons butter, melted
Salt, pepper, crushed garlic powder & paprika to taste	Salt, pepper, garlic powder & paprika to taste
Chopped celery, green pepper & pimento (optional)	Chopped celery, green pepper & pimento (optional)
Crushed salty crackers or potato crisps	Crushed salty crackers or potato chips
Oil & butter for frying	Oil & butter for frying
MUSHROOM SAUCE	MUSHROOM SAUCE
250 g mushrooms	½ lb mushrooms
Chopped spring onions (optional)	Chopped green onions (optional)
60 g butter	4 tablespoons butter
30 mℓ (2 T) flour	2 tablespoons flour
500 mℓ (2 C) milk	2 cups milk
Salt & pepper to taste	Salt & pepper to taste

METHOD To prepare croquettes, mix together all ingredients except the crackers and crisps (potato chips). Shape into croquettes and roll in the crushed crackers or chips. Fry in oil and butter until golden brown.

MUSHROOM SAUCE Sauté mushrooms and chopped onions in butter. Stir in flour and milk to make a fairly thick white sauce. Season with salt and pepper. Serve with the croquettes.

CHEF'S TIP As an alternative, heat a can of cream of mushroom or celery soup and serve instead of the sauce.

Serves 4

Escargots in Mushroom Caps

METRIC	AMERICAN
24 tinned snails	2 dozen canned escargots
125 g butter	½ cup butter
5 mℓ (1 t) minced parsley	1 teaspoon minced parsley
3 cloves garlic, crushed	3 cloves garlic, crushed
Dash of salt	Dash of salt
Pinch of pepper	Pinch of pepper
Few drops Worcestershire sauce	Few drops Worcestershire sauce
Few drops lemon juice	Few drops lemon juice
24 fresh black mushroom caps	2 dozen fresh black mushroom caps
Breadcrumbs (about 250 mℓ)	Breadcrumbs (about 1 cup)

METHOD Drain snails (escargots) and rinse under cold water. Pat dry. Soften butter and mix with parsley, garlic, salt, pepper, Worcestershire sauce and lemon juice. Place a little of this mixture on each mushroom cap, top with a snail, then cover with another blob of butter mixture.

Sprinkle with breadcrumbs and place in an ovenware dish. Cover tightly with foil and bake in a 200°C (400°F) oven for 15–20 minutes.

CHEF'S TIP To make the mushrooms lie flat, slice the tips off their curved sides.

Makes 24

Oysters Supreme

METRIC	AMERICAN
24 shelled fresh oysters (or 2 x 375 g tins drained select oysters)	24 shelled fresh oysters (or 2 x 12 oz cans drained select oysters)
20 mℓ (4 t) butter	1½ tablespoons butter
15 mℓ (1 T) white wine	1 tablespoon white wine
2 mℓ (½ t) crushed garlic powder or 5 mℓ (1 t) crushed garlic	½ teaspoon garlic powder or 1 teaspoon crushed garlic
2 mℓ (½ t) coarsely ground black pepper	½ teaspoon coarsely ground black pepper
Few drops Tabasco	Few drops Tabasco
20 mℓ (4 t) lemon juice	4 teaspoons lemon juice
30 mℓ (2 T) chopped fresh parsley (or dried parsley)	2 tablespoons chopped fresh parsley (or dried parsley)
Croûtons*	Croûtons*

* preferably garlic-flavoured

METHOD Place 3 oysters in each of 8 individual oven-proof dishes, ramekins or seafood shells. In a small saucepan melt butter; add wine, garlic or garlic powder, black pepper, Tabasco, lemon juice and parsley. Stir well.

Spoon 15 mℓ (1 tablespoon) of this mixture over oysters in each dish. Crush croûtons and sprinkle over the oysters. Dot with additional butter and place under the griller (broiler) for 6–8 minutes, until crisp and golden.

Serves 8

Peri-Peri Chicken Livers

METRIC	AMERICAN
500 g chicken livers	1 lb chicken livers
Oil for frying	Oil for frying
250 g fresh mushrooms, sliced (optional)	½ lb fresh mushrooms, sliced (optional)
2 onions, halved & sliced	2 onions, halved & sliced
Salt & pepper to taste	Salt & pepper to taste
2 mℓ (½ t) peri-peri powder	½ teaspoon cayenne pepper or Mexican crushed red pepper
Flour for coating	Flour for coating

GARNISH	GARNISH
2 hard-boiled eggs, quartered	2 hard-boiled eggs, quartered
Sprigs of parsley or watercress	Sprigs of parsley or watercress

METHOD Rinse chicken livers thoroughly under cold water. Drain well on absorbent paper. Heat oil and cook mushrooms until golden brown. Remove and set aside. Fry onions until lightly browned and set aside.

Season chicken livers with salt, pepper and peri-peri (cayenne or crushed red pepper), dip in flour and then fry, using more oil if necessary, until crisp and golden brown. Add mushrooms and onion and adjust seasoning.

Place on a heated serving platter and surround with quarters of hard-boiled egg and sprigs of parsley or watercress.

Serves 4 to 6

Cantonese Chicken Wings

METRIC	AMERICAN
1 kg chicken wings	2 lb chicken wings
125 mℓ (½ C) soy sauce	½ cup soy sauce
1 x 200 mℓ jar peach baby food	1 large jar apricot & tapioca baby food
60 mℓ (¼ C) apricot jam	¼ cup apricot preserves
10 mℓ (2 t) ground ginger	2 teaspoons ground ginger
1 clove garlic, crushed	1 clove garlic, crushed

METHOD Cut wings and spread open on foil-covered baking tray. Combine remaining ingredients and spread over chicken. Marinate overnight.

Bake uncovered in a 160°C (325°F) oven for 50–60 minutes.

Serves 8 to 10   PHOTOGRAPH ON PAGE 27

Terry's Italian-style Artichokes

METRIC	AMERICAN
6 artichokes	6 artichokes
200 mℓ (¾ C) olive oil	¾ cup olive oil
6 cloves garlic, crushed	6 cloves garlic, crushed
125 mℓ (½ C) grated Parmesan cheese	½ cup grated Parmesan cheese
250 mℓ (1 C) fresh bread-crumbs	1 cup fresh breadcrumbs

METHOD Trim the artichokes by cutting off the sharp edges of the leaves with a pair of scissors. Boil in salted water for 45 minutes–1 hour. Drain well; open out the leaves and place on a baking sheet.

Combine olive oil, garlic and cheese; sprinkle over artichokes. Sprinkle with breadcrumbs, cover with foil and bake in 180°C (350°F) oven for 20 minutes.

Serves 6

Artichoke & Shrimp Casserole

METRIC	AMERICAN
500 g fresh mushrooms, sliced	1 lb fresh mushrooms, sliced
Butter for sautéing	Butter for sautéing
Salt & pepper	Salt & pepper
90 g butter (for white sauce)	6 tablespoons butter (for white sauce)
45 mℓ (3 T) flour	3 tablespoons flour
375 mℓ (1½ C) milk, scalded	1½ cups milk, scalded
250 mℓ (1 C) cream	1 cup cream
125 mℓ (½ C) sherry	½ cup sherry
30 mℓ (2 T) Worcestershire sauce	2 tablespoons Worcestershire sauce
2 x 400 g tins artichoke hearts, drained & cut into halves	2 x 14 oz cans artichoke hearts, drained & cut into halves
1 kg cooked, peeled prawns	2 lb cooked, peeled shrimp
Grated Parmesan cheese	Grated Parmesan cheese

METHOD Sauté mushrooms in small amount of butter, season with salt and pepper and set aside.

Make a white sauce by melting the butter, stirring in flour over low heat and then adding the scalded milk and the cream. Stir constantly over low heat until smooth and creamy. Stir in sherry and Worcestershire sauce.

Grease an oven-proof casserole dish and layer artichokes, prawns (shrimp), mushrooms and white sauce. Top with Parmesan cheese. Bake at 190°C (375°F) for 45–60 minutes. Serve over rice.

Serves 8

Spoonbread Soufflé with Seafood Sauce

METRIC	AMERICAN
SPOONBREAD SOUFFLÉ	SPOONBREAD SOUFFLÉ
250 mℓ (1 C) mealie meal or corn meal	1 cup corn meal
250 mℓ (1 C) water	1 cup water
750 mℓ (3 C) milk, scalded	3 cups milk, scalded
4 eggs, separated	4 eggs, separated
5 mℓ (1 t) salt	1 teaspoon salt
45 mℓ (3 T) melted butter, cooled	3 tablespoons melted butter, cooled
15 mℓ (1 T) baking powder	1 tablespoon baking powder
SEAFOOD SAUCE	SEAFOOD SAUCE
500 g prawns or crayfish, boiled, shelled & cut up	1 lb shrimp or lobster, boiled, shelled & cut up
1 onion, diced	1 onion, diced
125 g butter	1 stick butter
175 g mushrooms, sliced	6 oz mushrooms, sliced
30 mℓ (2 T) flour	2 tablespoons flour
375 mℓ (1½ C) milk	1½ cups milk
125 mℓ (½ C) cream	½ cup cream
5 mℓ (1 t) dry mustard	1 teaspoon dry mustard
30 mℓ (2 T) sherry	2 tablespoons sherry
50 g grated Cheddar cheese	½ cup grated Cheddar cheese
Pinch of salt	Pinch of salt
Dash of pepper	Dash of pepper

METHOD Mix mealie meal or corn meal and water together. Stir into scalded milk and cook over low heat, stirring constantly, until thick (about 3 minutes). Remove from heat and cool. Beat egg yolks with salt and melted butter and add to the mealie meal (corn meal) mixture, mixing well. Fold in baking powder, then stiffly beaten egg whites.

Turn into a lightly greased deep, round oven-proof dish and bake for 45–55 minutes at 180°C (350°F) until puffed and firm to touch. (Do not open oven before time.) Serve soufflé immediately, accompanied by Seafood Sauce.

SEAFOOD SAUCE Prepare seafood. Sauté onion in butter until golden; add mushrooms and cook for 2–3 minutes. Stir in flour and make a smooth, medium-thick sauce by adding milk and cream. Stir in mustard, sherry, cheese, salt and pepper. Add seafood and serve.

CHEF'S TIP This soufflé may also be served as a dessert, by substituting strawberry sauce for the seafood sauce (recipe on p 102).

Serves 6 to 8

Tuna Crêpe Casserole

METRIC	AMERICAN
CRÊPE BATTER	CRÊPE BATTER
3 eggs	*3 eggs*
625 mℓ (2½ C) cold water	*2½ cups cold water*
180 g (1½ C) flour	*1½ cups flour*
Pinch of salt	*Pinch of salt*
2 mℓ (½ t) baking powder	*½ teaspoon baking powder*
FILLING	FILLING
1 large onion, chopped	*1 large onion, chopped*
1 green pepper, seeded & diced	*1 green pepper, seeded & diced*
60 g butter	*4 tablespoons butter*
125 g fresh mushrooms or tinned mushrooms	*¼ lb fresh mushrooms or 1 x 4 oz can mushrooms*
2 x 185 g tins tuna or salmon (undrained)	*2 x 6½ oz cans tuna or salmon (undrained)*
250 mℓ (1 C) cream	*1 cup cream*
30 mℓ (2 T) cornflour mixed with 125 mℓ(½ C) milk	*2 tablespoons cornstarch mixed with ½ cup milk*
Dash of cayenne pepper	*Dash of cayenne pepper*
Salt & black pepper to taste	*Salt & black pepper to taste*
15 mℓ (1 T) lemon juice	*1 tablespoon lemon juice*
SAUCE	SAUCE
60 g butter	*4 tablespoons butter*
30 mℓ (2 T) flour	*2 tablespoons all purpose flour*
500–625 mℓ (2–2½ C) milk	*2–2½ cups milk*
50 g grated Cheddar cheese	*½ cup grated Cheddar cheese*
Salt & black pepper to taste	*Salt & black pepper to taste*

METHOD To prepare batter, beat eggs with cold water. Sift together flour, salt and baking powder; beat in egg mixture. Strain. Grease a pan approximately 15 cm (6 inches) in diameter with oil or non-stick spray.

Spoon in about 15 mℓ (1 tablespoon) batter and rotate pan to cover base evenly. (The crêpes need only be cooked on one side.) Turn out onto a clean cloth and stack one on top of another. Set aside until ready to use.

FILLING Sauté onion and green pepper in butter until slightly golden. Add sliced mushrooms and simmer for 5 minutes. Add tuna or salmon and juice, cream and milk / cornflour (cornstarch) mixture. Mix in seasonings and lemon juice and stir until thickened.

Place a spoonful of filling on each crêpe, roll up envelope fashion, closing sides, and place in greased oven-proof dish.

SAUCE Melt butter, stir in flour and then slowly add milk. Stir in grated Cheddar cheese, season with salt and black pepper.

Spoon sauce over crêpes and bake in 180°C (350°F) oven until hot and bubbly (about 20 minutes).

Serves 12

Savoury Salmon or Tuna Roll

METRIC	AMERICAN
*400 g puff pastry**	*1 lb puff pastry**
1 egg, beaten	*1 egg, beaten*
FILLING	FILLING
1 onion, chopped	*1 onion, chopped*
1 stick celery, chopped	*1 stick celery, chopped*
30 mℓ (2 T) butter	*2 tablespoons butter*
3 baby marrows (small courgettes), grated	*3 small zucchini, grated*
30 mℓ (2 T) thick cream	*2 tablespoons thick cream*
60 mℓ (¼ C) milk	*¼ cup milk*
30 mℓ (2 T) cornflour, thickened to a paste with a little milk	*2 tablespoons cornflour, thickened to a paste with a little milk*
1 x 200 g tin salmon or tuna	*1 x 7½ oz can salmon or tuna*
2 mℓ (½ t) black pepper	*½ teaspoon black pepper*
2 mℓ (½ t) salt	*½ teaspoon salt*
50 g grated Cheddar cheese	*½ cup grated Cheddar cheese*

* *Use ready-made pastry or see recipe on p 20*

METHOD Prepare filling. Fry onion and celery in butter for several minutes; add grated courgettes (zucchini), cream and milk. Simmer gently for 5 minutes and thicken with cornflour (cornstarch) paste. Add drained and flaked salmon or tuna, seasonings and cheese. Cool thoroughly.

Roll out pastry into a rectangle (about ½ cm / ¼ inch thick). Spread filling along edge of pastry. Moisten one edge of pastry with water and roll up.

Place on baking sheet. Cut slits in top of roll about 2,5 cm (1 inch) apart. Brush with beaten egg and bake for 25–30 minutes in a 200°C (400°F) oven.

Serves 8

Overleaf (foreground, l to r) *Mexican Pizza and Cantonese Chicken Wings.* Rear (l to r) *Cheese Strata and Smoked Salmon Pâté*

Asparagus Tart

METRIC	AMERICAN
PASTRY	PASTRY
250 g (2 C) flour	2 cups flour
Pinch of salt	Pinch of salt
10 ml (2 t) baking powder	2 level teaspoons baking powder
250 g margarine	1 cup margarine
1 egg	1 egg
125 ml (½ C) iced water	½ cup iced water
ASPARAGUS FILLING	ASPARAGUS FILLING
1 x 410 g tin asparagus cuts	1 x 13½ oz can asparagus cuts
60 g butter	4 tablespoons butter
45 ml (3 T) flour	3 tablespoons flour
100 g grated Cheddar cheese	1 cup grated Cheddar cheese
125 ml (½ C) cream	½ cup cream
Pinch of salt	Pinch of salt
1 egg, beaten	1 egg, beaten
GARNISH	GARNISH
Caraway seeds	Caraway seeds
Anchovy fillets	Anchovy fillets

METHOD Sift dry ingredients together. Rub in margarine until mixture resembles breadcrumbs. Knead into dough with egg and water. Roll out the dough to fit a 23 cm (9 inch) pie dish. Pour in filling and bake at 230°C (450°F) for 10 minutes, then turn oven down to 200°C (400°F) and bake for 20 minutes.

FILLING Drain asparagus, reserving juice. Melt butter and add flour, mixing well. Stir in asparagus juice. Add grated cheese, cream and salt and stir over medium heat until sauce thickens. Add beaten egg; fold in asparagus. Pour into pastry shell, sprinkle top with caraway seed and decorate with anchovies.

Serves about 12

Curried Chicken in Phyllo

METRIC	AMERICAN
2 chicken breasts boiled, skinned & deboned	2 chicken breasts boiled, skinned & deboned
30 ml (2 T) butter or margarine	2 tablespoons butter or margarine
1 small onion, finely chopped	1 small onion, finely chopped
40 ml (2 T & 2 t) flour	2 rounded tablespoons flour
7 ml (1½ t) curry powder	1½ teaspoons curry powder
250 ml (1 C) cream or non-dairy creamer	1 cup cream or non-dairy creamer
2 ml (½ t) salt	½ teaspoon salt
50 g chopped walnuts	½ cup chopped walnuts
125 ml (½ C) sultanas (optional)	½ cup golden raisins (optional)
500 g phyllo pastry	1 lb phyllo pastry
375 g butter or margarine, melted	¾ lb butter or margarine, melted

METHOD Dice chicken into small pieces. Melt butter or margarine, add onion and sauté lightly. Add flour and curry powder. Stir in cream or non-dairy creamer and cook until smooth. Add salt. Stir in nuts and raisins. Remove from heat and cool thoroughly.

Using 3 sheets of phyllo, brush inbetween each layer with melted butter or margarine. Cut in half lengthwise, then cut each half again crosswise into 6 equal sections (making 12 altogether). Position spoonfuls of filling on each, then fold over into triangles (like samoosas), enclosing filling completely.

Place on a greased baking sheet and brush with butter or margarine. Bake in 200°C (400°F) oven until golden brown (about 10 minutes).

Makes 50

Terry's Fabulous Quiche

METRIC	AMERICAN
PASTRY	PASTRY
250 g (2 C) flour	2 cups flour
30 ml (2T) sugar	2 tablespoons sugar
125 g butter	8 tablespoons butter
1 egg + 1 yolk, slightly beaten	1 egg + 1 yolk, slightly beaten
5 ml (1 t) vanilla essence	1 teaspoon vanilla extract
FILLING	FILLING
6 eggs	6 eggs
30 ml (2 T) melted butter	2 tablespoons melted butter
20 ml (4 t) flour	1½ tablespoons flour
375 ml (1½ C) cream	1½ cups heavy cream
125 ml (½ C) milk	½ cup milk
6 rashers cooked bacon, crumbled	6 slices cooked bacon, crumbled
1 onion, diced & sautéed	1 onion, diced & sautéed
Pinch of salt	Pinch of salt
Dash of pepper	Dash of pepper
Ground nutmeg to taste	Ground nutmeg to taste
50 g grated Swiss cheese	½ cup grated Swiss cheese

METHOD To prepare pastry, mix flour and sugar, then grate butter into flour mixture and knead into a dough with egg and vanilla. Pat dough into a greased 23 cm (9 inch), deep quiche dish (or use a loose-bottomed pan).

FILLING Beat together eggs, butter, flour, cream and milk. Press crumbled bacon into crust and sprinkle with onion. Carefully spoon in custard mixture. Sprinkle with salt, pepper, nutmeg and cheese.

Bake at 180°C (350°F) for 40 minutes, or until an inserted knife comes out clean.

CHEF'S TIP Diced smoked salmon (lox) may be used instead of bacon. For a well-baked crust, bake dough blind for 15 minutes.

Serves 8 to 10   PHOTOGRAPH ON PAGE 34

Ricotta Cheese & Artichoke Pie

METRIC	AMERICAN
30 mℓ (2 T) chopped spring onion	2 tablespoons chopped green onion
15 mℓ (1 T) olive oil	1 tablespoon olive oil
500 g Ricotta cheese	1 lb Ricotta cheese
100 g grated Cheddar cheese	1 cup grated Cheddar cheese
200 mℓ (¾ C) grated Parmesan cheese	¾ cup grated Parmesan cheese
3 eggs & beaten egg for glaze	3 eggs & beaten egg for glaze
5 mℓ (1 t) dried tarragon	1 teaspoon dried tarragon
2 mℓ (½ t) freshly ground black pepper	½ teaspoon freshly ground black pepper
500 g phyllo pastry	1 lb phyllo pastry
Melted butter	Melted butter
1 x 450 g tin artichokes, halved & drained	1 x 16 oz can artichokes, halved & drained

METHOD Fry onion in olive oil. Place all three cheeses in food processor. Add eggs, tarragon and pepper and process. Line a 20 cm (8 inch) springform pan with 5 layers of phyllo pastry, brushing each layer with melted butter and allowing pastry to overlap sides.

Place half of the cheese mixture on pastry, then half of the artichokes. Add a few more layers of pastry; again layer cheese and artichokes. Fold over the overlapping pastry. Brush with additional beaten egg and bake at 200°C (400°F) for 30 minutes.

Serves 8

Tuna Fish Strudel

METRIC	AMERICAN
1 large onion, chopped	1 large onion, chopped
1 green pepper, seeded & diced	1 green pepper, seeded & diced
60 g butter	2 oz butter
125 g mushrooms, sliced	4 oz mushrooms, sliced
2 x 185 g tins tuna (with liquid)	2 x 6½ oz cans tuna fish (with liquid)
250 mℓ (1 C) cream	1 cup cream
Dash of cayenne pepper	Dash of cayenne pepper
Salt & black pepper to taste	Salt & black pepper to taste
20 mℓ (4 t) cornflour, mixed to paste with a little cold milk	4 teaspoons cornstarch, mixed to a paste with a little cold milk
500 g phyllo pastry	1 lb phyllo pastry
Melted butter for brushing pastry	Melted butter for brushing pastry
120 g (1 C) dry breadcrumbs	1 cup dry breadcrumbs

METHOD Sauté onion and green pepper in butter until slightly golden. Add mushrooms and simmer for 5 minutes. Add tuna and juice, cream, seasonings and cornflour (cornstarch) paste, and stir until thickened.

Brush one phyllo sheet with melted butter; sprinkle with breadcrumbs. Repeat this process, layering the pastry until you have 6 layers. Place half of the fish mixture about 2,5 cm (1 inch) from the edge of the long side of the phyllo, fold in the sides and roll up as you would for a Swiss (jelly) roll.

Using the remaining fish mixture, make a second strudel in the same way. Make little slits in the top of each strudel, to allow steam to escape. (If you wish, you may freeze the strudels at this stage.)

To bake, place on buttered baking sheets, sprinkle with a little water and bake in 180°C (350°F) oven for 25 minutes, then turn off oven completely and leave for another 10–15 minutes, allowing the phyllo to become very crispy. Cut into thick slices and serve.

Makes 2 strudels & serves 8 to 12

Asparagus & Tuna Pie

By courtesy of Auntie Hilda

METRIC	AMERICAN
PASTRY	PASTRY
120 g (1 C) flour	1 cup flour
10 mℓ (2 t) baking powder	2 teaspoons baking powder
5 mℓ (1 t) sugar	1 teaspoon sugar
Pinch of salt	Pinch of salt
60 g butter	4 tablespoons butter
125 mℓ (½ C) milk	½ cup milk
FILLING	FILLING
2 onions, chopped	2 onions, chopped
60 g butter	4 tablespoons butter
Salt & pepper	Salt & pepper
1 x 185 g tin tuna	1 x 6½ oz can tuna fish
1 x 410 g tin asparagus cuts (reserve juice)	1 x 13½ oz can asparagus cuts (reserve juice)
50 g grated Cheddar cheese	½ cup grated Cheddar cheese
60 mℓ (¼ C) thick cream	¼ cup thick cream
1 egg	1 egg

METHOD To prepare pastry, sift together dry ingredients, rub in butter and blend into a dough with milk. Press into a 23 cm (9 inch) pie dish.

FILLING Simmer onions in butter until tender; season with salt and pepper. Drain tuna and mix in a bowl with the drained asparagus cuts, fried onions, grated cheese, cream, egg and a little asparagus juice.

Pour asparagus mixture into pie dish and sprinkle additional grated cheese on top. Bake in 220°C (425°F) oven for 20 minutes.

Serves 8 to 10

Tuna Soufflé

METRIC	AMERICAN
1 onion, chopped	1 onion, chopped
125 g mushrooms, sliced	4 oz mushrooms, sliced
60 g butter	4 tablespoons butter
1 x 185 g tin tuna	1 x 6½ oz can tuna
1 x 290 g tin asparagus soup	1 x 10 oz can asparagus soup
3 eggs, separated	3 eggs, separated
125 mℓ (½ C) milk	½ cup milk
200 mℓ (¾ C) fresh bread-crumbs	¾ cup fresh breadcrumbs
30–45 mℓ (2–3 T) cream	2–3 tablespoons cream
2 mℓ (½ t) salt	½ teaspoon salt
1 mℓ (¼ t) pepper	¼ teaspoon pepper
45 mℓ (3 T) grated Cheddar cheese	3 tablespoons grated Cheddar cheese
125 mℓ (½ C) crushed potato crisps	½ cup crushed potato chips

METHOD Sauté onion and mushrooms in butter. Flake tuna and mix together all the ingredients except egg whites, cheese and potato crisps (potato chips).

Beat the egg whites stiffly and fold gently into the mixture. Top with the cheese and potato crisps (chips). Bake at 180°C (350°F) for 45 minutes. Serve immediately.

Serves 4

Snoek & Sweetcorn Soufflé

METRIC	AMERICAN
3 eggs, separated	3 eggs, separated
100 g grated Cheddar cheese	1 cup grated Cheddar cheese
500 mℓ (2 C) white sauce (recipe below)	2 cups white sauce (recipe below)
500 g smoked snoek, flaked	1 lb smoked white fish, tuna fish or salmon, flaked
30 mℓ (2 T) thick cream	2 tablespoons thick cream
2 mℓ (½ t) salt	½ teaspoon salt
1 mℓ (¼ t) pepper	¼ teaspoon pepper
2 mℓ (½ t) dry mustard	½ teaspoon dry mustard
2 onions, chopped & sautéed in butter	2 onions, chopped & sautéed in butter
1 x 420 g tin creamed sweetcorn*	1 x 15½ oz can creamed corn*
Cayenne pepper	Cayenne pepper

WHITE SAUCE	WHITE SAUCE
30 mℓ (2 T) butter	2 tablespoons butter
30 mℓ (2 T) flour	2 tablespoons flour
500 mℓ (2 C) milk	2 cups milk

* 1 tin (can) drained asparagus cuts may be used instead of corn

METHOD Make the white sauce by melting butter over low heat and stirring in flour. Remove from heat and add milk slowly, stirring constantly, until thick and smooth.

Add egg yolks and grated cheese to white sauce. Add the fish, then the cream, salt, pepper and mustard. Mix in sautéed onions; fold in corn or asparagus. Add stiffly beaten egg whites to mixture.

Pour into soufflé dish. Top with additional grated Cheddar cheese and sprinkle with cayenne pepper. Bake at 180°C (350°F) for 30–40 minutes.

Serves 8

Crab & Asparagus Crêpes Gratinée

METRIC	AMERICAN
CRÊPE BATTER	CRÊPE BATTER
See recipe for Cheese Blintzes on p 173	*See recipe for Cheese Blintzes on p 173*
FILLING	FILLING
500 g crab meat	1 lb lump crab meat
1 x 450 g tin asparagus spears, drained & juice reserved	1 x 16 oz can asparagus spears, drained & juice reserved
SAUCE	SAUCE
60 g butter	4 tablespoons butter
30 mℓ (2 T) flour	2 tablespoons flour
125 mℓ (½ C) vermouth	½ cup vermouth
125 mℓ (½ C) cream	½ cup heavy cream
TOPPING	TOPPING
Grated Parmesan cheese	Grated Parmesan cheese
Butter	Butter

METHOD Prepare crêpes as for recipe on p 173. Place some crab meat and two asparagus spears on each crêpe. Roll up and arrange in a buttered ovenware dish.

SAUCE Melt butter over low heat and stir in flour. Remove from heat and add asparagus juice a little at a time, stirring constantly until smooth and thick.

Return to heat and cook for a few minutes, stirring constantly. Add vermouth and cream and heat through, but do not allow to boil.

Pour sauce over crêpes, sprinkle thickly with Parmesan cheese and dot with butter. Place under grill (broiler) until lightly browned and sizzling.

Serves 12

Soups

Fab Crab Soup 32
Chicken Gumbo 32
Lobster Bisque 32
Creamy Seafood Soup 33
Clam Chowder 33
Crusted Creamy Oyster Soup 33
Easy Minestrone 36
Cream of Broccoli & Mushroom Soup 36
Chinese Soup 36
Bean & Barley Soup 36
Koppel Lentil Soup 37
Vichyssoise 37
Curried Butternut Soup 37
Corn Chowder 37

Fab Crab Soup

METRIC	AMERICAN
2 x 300 g tins cream of tomato soup	3 x 6½ oz cans cream of tomato soup
500 mℓ (2 C) milk	2 cups milk
250 mℓ (1 C) cream	1 cup cream
Dash of ground black pepper	Dash of ground black pepper
60–125 mℓ (¼–½ C) sherry	¼–½ cup sherry
500 g boiled & diced crab meat or crayfish	1 lb boiled & diced crab meat or lobster
1 x 425 g tin tomatoes, chopped	1 x 15 oz can tomatoes, chopped

METHOD Warm tomato soup, milk and cream over medium heat. Season with pepper to taste. Several minutes before serving add sherry, seafood and tomatoes.

Serves 6

Chicken Gumbo

METRIC	AMERICAN
1 chicken	1 chicken
1 onion	1 onion
2–3 carrots	2–3 carrots
2 sticks celery	2 sticks celery
Few bay leaves	Few bay leaves
Few peppercorns	Few peppercorns
15 mℓ (3 t) salt	3 teaspoons salt
2 mℓ (½ t) pepper	½ teaspoon pepper
1 x 425 g tin tomatoes	1 x 15 oz can tomatoes
1 chicken bouillon cube	1 chicken bouillon cube
250 g frozen or canned okra, drained	8 oz frozen or canned okra, drained
500 mℓ (2 C) cooked rice	2 cups cooked rice

ROUX	ROUX
1 large onion, diced	1 large onion, diced
2–3 sticks celery, diced	2–3 sticks celery, diced
1 green pepper, seeded & diced	1 green pepper, seeded & diced
5 mℓ (1 t) crushed garlic	1 teaspoon crushed garlic
60 mℓ (¼ C) oil	¼ cup oil
2 mℓ (½ t) chilli powder	½ teaspoon chili powder
5 mℓ (1 t) dry mustard	1 teaspoon dry mustard
2 mℓ (½ t) cayenne pepper	½ teaspoon cayenne pepper
5 mℓ (1 t) paprika	1 teaspoon paprika
5 mℓ (1 t) crushed garlic powder	1 teaspoon garlic powder
45 mℓ (3 T) flour	3 tablespoons flour

METHOD Cover chicken with water. Add onion, carrots, celery, bay leaves, peppercorns, salt and pepper. Bring to the boil, then simmer for 1–2 hours, or until chicken is tender.

Skin and debone the chicken, dice meat and set aside. Strain chicken stock and measure 2½ litres (10 cups). Set aside.

ROUX Sauté onion, celery, green pepper and garlic in oil for 3–4 minutes. Stir in chilli powder, mustard, cayenne pepper, paprika, garlic powder and flour.

Gradually add chicken stock, tomatoes and bouillon cube, stirring constantly until the mixture comes to a boil. Add diced chicken and okra and simmer gently for another 15 minutes. Stir in rice and adjust seasonings.

Serves 8   PHOTOGRAPH ON PAGE 34

Lobster Bisque

METRIC	AMERICAN
2 whole crayfish	2 whole lobsters
1,5 ℓ (6 C) water	6 cups water
1 chicken bouillon cube, crushed	1 chicken bouillon cube, crushed
125 g butter	½ cup butter
3 sticks celery, diced	3 sticks celery, diced
1 large onion, diced	1 large onion, diced
2 carrots, sliced	2 carrots, sliced
125 mℓ (½ C) flour	½ cup flour
2 mℓ (½ t) cayenne pepper	½ teaspoon cayenne pepper
15 mℓ (1 T) paprika	1 tablespoon paprika
30–45 mℓ (2–3 T) sherry	2–3 tablespoons sherry
250 mℓ (1 C) milk	1 cup milk
250 mℓ (1 C) cream	1 cup heavy or whipping cream
Salt to taste	Salt to taste

METHOD Break off the tails and claws of the crayfish (lobsters) and split the bodies in half. Clean the insides and the heads (reserve the creamy coral and set aside).

Place all the parts in a large pot and cover with the water*. Add crushed chicken bouillon cube and cook gently for 10–15 minutes, or until lobster is bright red. Remove the tails and large claws from the saucepan, allowing the stock to continue cooking over low heat for another 20 minutes. Remove the meat from the tails and claws; dice and set aside.

Using another pot, melt butter and sauté the celery, onion and carrot until tender but not brown. Stir in flour, cayenne pepper and paprika. Strain the stock and stir slowly into the vegetable mixture over low heat, until smooth and thickened. Add creamy coral from head.

Purée the mixture in a blender or food processor. Return to pot over low heat and add sherry, milk and cream. Add diced lobster and salt to taste and serve. Alternatively, this bisque may be prepared in advance and refrigerated for a day or two before serving. It also freezes well.

*CHEF'S TIP It is a good idea to freeze the skin and / or bones from other fish which you may have used and add these to the stock when boiling the lobster. This will enhance the flavour and result in a really good, strong court bouillon.

Serves 6

Creamy Seafood Soup

METRIC	AMERICAN
1 onion, finely diced	1 onion, finely diced
1 stick celery, finely diced	1 stick celery, finely diced
125 g butter	½ cup butter
125 g mushrooms, sliced	¼ lb mushrooms, sliced
60 mℓ (¼ C) flour	4 tablespoons flour
1 ℓ (4 C) milk	4 cups milk
1 x 420 g tin creamed sweetcorn	1 x 17 oz can creamed corn
15 mℓ (1 T) diced pimento	1 tablespoon diced pimento
250 g peeled, deveined prawns	½ lb peeled, deveined shrimp
1 x 305 g tin lobster bisque	1 x 10¾ oz can lobster bisque
1 x 225 g tin oysters (optional)	1 x 8 oz can oysters (optional)
5 mℓ (1 t) salt	1 teaspoon salt
2 mℓ (½ t) pepper	½ teaspoon pepper
Few drops Tabasco	Few drops Tabasco
125 mℓ (½ C) dry sherry	½ cup dry sherry
250 mℓ (1 C) cream	1 cup cream

METHOD Sauté onion and celery in butter for a few minutes. Add mushrooms and cook for 2–3 minutes. Stir in flour, then slowly add milk, stirring constantly until well blended.

Add sweetcorn (corn), pimento, prawns (shrimp), lobster bisque, oysters and seasonings. Just before serving, stir in sherry and cream.

Serves 6 to 8

Clam Chowder

METRIC	AMERICAN
1 large onion, diced	1 large onion, diced
125 g butter	½ cup butter
45 mℓ (3 T) flour	3 tablespoons flour
250 mℓ (1 C) chicken stock	1 cup chicken stock
250 mℓ (1 C) milk	1 cup milk
1 x 296 mℓ bottle clam juice*	1 x 10 fl oz bottle clam juice*
2 potatoes, parboiled & diced	2 potatoes, parboiled & diced
2 x 285 g tins chopped clams, undrained	2 x 10½ oz cans chopped clams, undrained
5 mℓ (1 t) salt	1 teaspoon salt
Dash of pepper	Dash of pepper
250 mℓ (1 C) cream	1 cup cream
Freshly chopped parsley	Freshly chopped parsley

* If bottled clam juice is unobtainable, use an additional 250 mℓ (1 cup) chicken stock

METHOD Sauté onion in butter. Stir in flour, then slowly add chicken stock, milk and clam juice, stirring constantly. Add potatoes, chopped clams, salt and pepper. Simmer for 10–15 minutes. Stir in cream and sprinkle with chopped parsley to serve.

CHEF'S TIP If the soup is not as thick as you would like it, thicken with a little cornflour (cornstarch) mixed to a paste with cold water, before adding the cream.

Serves 6 to 8 PHOTOGRAPH ON PAGE 35

Crusted Creamy Oyster Soup

METRIC	AMERICAN
500 mℓ (2 C) strong chicken stock*	2 cups strong chicken stock*
12 shucked oysters (reserve liquid)	12 shucked oysters (reserve liquid)
Pinch of dried dill	Pinch of dillweed
2 mℓ (½ t) dried thyme	½ teaspoon dried thyme
250 mℓ (1 C) cream	1 cup heavy or whipping cream
Salt & freshly ground black pepper to taste	Salt & freshly ground black pepper to taste
30 mℓ (2 T) chopped spring onion	2 tablespoons chopped green onion
6 x 10 cm rounds of puff pastry	6 x 4 inch rounds of puff pastry
1 egg, beaten	1 egg, beaten

* Prepare by combining crushed chicken bouillon cubes with boiling water

METHOD Combine chicken stock, oyster liquid, dill and thyme in saucepan and cook until reduced to half. Add cream; season to taste. Chill thoroughly.

Dice oysters and divide among 6 ramekins. Sprinkle with chopped onion. Spoon cream mixture over oysters.

Brush edges of pastry with beaten egg, place over the top of the ramekins and seal around sides. Brush pastry surface with egg and bake in 200°C (400°F) oven for 25 minutes, or until puffed and golden.

Serves 6

Overleaf (foreground, l to r) Chicken Gumbo and Clam Chowder Centre (l to r) Terry's Fabulous Quiche, Tuna Melt and a Butter Rose (see Decorations on p 114). At the back Spinach & Water Chestnut Salad

Easy Minestrone

METRIC	AMERICAN
30 ml (2 T) oil	2 tablespoons oil
2 onions, chopped	2 onions, chopped
1 clove garlic, crushed	1 clove garlic, crushed
2 sticks celery, diced	2 sticks celery, diced
2 carrots, peeled & grated	2 carrots, peeled & grated
½ cabbage, finely shredded	½ cabbage, finely shredded
1 packet vegetable soup mix	1 package vegetable soup mix
1 large soup bone (optional)	1 large soup bone (optional)
1 ½ l (6 C) water	6 cups water
2 chicken bouillon cubes	2 chicken bouillon cubes
Salt to taste	Salt to taste
2 ml (½ t) pepper	½ teaspoon pepper
1 x 425 g tin tomato purée	1 x 15 oz can tomato purée
1 x 425 g tin butter beans	1 x 16 oz can great northern butter beans
1 x 420 g tin spaghetti rings in tomato sauce	1 x 16 oz can spaghetti O's
Grated Parmesan cheese	Grated Parmesan cheese

METHOD Heat oil in large saucepan. Add onions, garlic, celery, carrots and cabbage and fry until limp. Add soup mix, soup bone, water, bouillon cubes and seasonings and simmer for ½–¾ hour.

Mix in tomato purée, beans and spaghetti rings and cook for another 15 minutes. Adjust seasoning and serve with Parmesan cheese sprinkled on top.

Serves 8 to 10

Cream of Broccoli & Mushroom Soup

METRIC	AMERICAN
1 chicken bouillon cube	1 chicken bouillon cube
10 ml (2 t) instant vegetable stock	1 envelope instant vegetable stock
500 ml (2 C) boiling water	2 cups boiling water
90 g butter	6 tablespoons butter
500 g fresh mushrooms, sliced	1 lb fresh mushrooms, sliced
500 g fresh broccoli, chopped*	1 lb fresh broccoli, chopped*
60 ml (¼ C) flour	4 tablespoons flour
500 ml (2 C) milk	1 cup milk
250 ml (1 C) cream	1 cup half & half**
Pinch of salt	1 cup cream
Dash of black pepper	Pinch of salt
	Dash of black pepper

* Before chopping broccoli be sure to remove the tough outer skin – loosen at the end of the stem and pull upwards
** When using metric measurements do not use half & half

METHOD Dissolve bouillon cube and vegetable stock in boiling water. Set aside. Melt butter in a separate saucepan. Add mushrooms and broccoli to butter. Cook for 5 minutes, then remove from heat.

Stir in flour. Slowly add chicken and vegetable stock and return to low heat. Stir in milk and cream (or milk, half and half and cream). Cook, stirring constantly until thickened. Season to taste with salt and black pepper.

CHEF'S TIP If you prefer to use either mushrooms or broccoli instead of the combination, use 1 kg (2 lb) of the one vegetable.

Serves 8

Chinese Soup

METRIC	AMERICAN
2 l (8 C) clear chicken soup	8 cups clear chicken soup
1 x 420 g tin creamed sweetcorn	1 x 17 oz can creamed corn
250 g crabmeat	½ lb crabmeat
Chopped spring onions	Chopped green onions

METHOD Combine all ingredients, except onions. Heat to boiling point and serve sprinkled with the chopped onions.

Serves 6 to 8

Bean & Barley Soup

METRIC	AMERICAN
125 ml (½ C) barley	½ cup barley
1 x 425 g tin butter beans	1 x 15½ oz can great northern beans
2 slices shin & 2 soup bones	2 slices shank & 2 soup bones
2 leeks, diced	2 leeks, diced
2 onions, diced	2 onions, diced
3–4 carrots, diced	3–4 carrots, diced
2 sticks celery, diced	2 sticks celery, diced
1 parsnip, diced	1 parsnip, diced
1 turnip, diced	1 turnip, diced
15 ml (1 T) chopped parsley	1 tablespoon chopped parsley
15 ml (3 t) salt	3 teaspoons salt
Pepper to taste	Pepper to taste
2 chicken bouillon cubes	2 chicken bouillon cubes
Few drops yellow food colouring	Few drops yellow food color

METHOD Place all ingredients in a large saucepan and cover with water. Bring to the boil; skim the top of the soup. Lower heat and simmer for approximately 6 hours. Adjust seasoning.

Serves 8 to 10

Koppel Lentil Soup

METRIC	AMERICAN
250 g macon or bacon, diced	½ lb Kosher beef fry or bacon, diced
4–5 litres water	16–20 cups water
250 g bolo meat	½ lb soup meat
3–4 meaty soup bones	3–4 meaty soup bones
2 onions, diced	2 onions, diced
3 carrots, grated	3 carrots, grated
400 g lentils, soaked overnight in cold water	2 cups lentils, soaked overnight in cold water
3 parsnips, diced	3 parsnips, diced
3 turnips, diced	3 turnips, diced
2–3 sticks celery, diced	2–3 sticks celery, diced
2–3 potatoes, diced	2–3 potatoes, diced
10–15 mℓ (2–3 t) salt	2–3 teaspoons salt
2 mℓ (½ t) pepper	½ teaspoon pepper
2–3 cloves garlic, diced	2–3 cloves garlic, diced
2 chicken or beef bouillon cubes	2 chicken or beef bouillon cubes

METHOD Sauté macon (Kosher beef fry) or bacon and garlic in large cooking pot. Add water to pot as well as meat, soup bones and all vegetables except potatoes. Bring to the boil.

Turn down heat and simmer for 5-6 hours, adding the potatoes one hour before serving. Add seasonings 30 minutes before soup is ready.

Serve with a variety of sliced German sausages or spicy sausages.

Serves 12

Vichyssoise

METRIC	AMERICAN
125 g butter	½ cup butter
1 onion, diced	1 onion, diced
2 cloves garlic, crushed	2 cloves garlic, crushed
2 leeks, sliced	2 leeks, sliced
1,5 ℓ (6 C) strong chicken stock*	6 cups strong chicken stock*
2 large potatoes, peeled & diced	2 large potatoes, peeled & diced
15 mℓ (1 T) finely chopped parsley	1 tablespoon finely chopped parsley
375 mℓ (1½ C) cream	1½ cups heavy or whipping cream
Salt & freshly ground black pepper to taste	Salt & freshly ground black pepper to taste

GARNISH	GARNISH
Freshly chopped parsley	Freshly chopped parsley

* May be made with chicken bouillon cubes and boiling water

METHOD Using a deep saucepan, melt butter and sauté onion and garlic just until limp, but not brown. Add leeks and cook until soft. Add chicken stock, potatoes and parsley and bring to the boil. Turn heat down to low and allow to simmer for 1 hour.

Pour the soup in batches into a food processor and blend until smooth. Stir in cream and season to taste with salt and pepper. Chill thoroughly. Garnish with parsley to serve.

Serves 6

Curried Butternut Soup

METRIC	AMERICAN
2 leeks, thinly sliced	2 leeks, thinly sliced
2 onions, diced	2 onions, diced
60 g butter	4 tablespoons butter
15 mℓ (1 T) curry powder	1 tablespoon curry powder
2 butternut squash	2 butternut squash
4 potatoes, quartered	4 potatoes, quartered
2–2½ ℓ (8–10 C) water	8–10 cups water
2 chicken bouillon cubes	2 chicken bouillon cubes
Salt & pepper to taste	Salt & pepper to taste

METHOD Cook leeks and onions in butter until glassy. Add curry powder. Peel squash, remove seeds and dice the flesh. Add to saucepan with potatoes and water to cover. Add seasonings and simmer for 1 hour.

Liquidise, heat and serve.

Serves 8

Corn Chowder

METRIC	AMERICAN
1 x 410 g tin whole kernel corn	1 x 13½ oz can whole kernel corn
1 x 420 g tin creamed sweetcorn	1 x 13½ oz can creamed corn
500 mℓ (2 C) milk	2 cups milk
15 mℓ (1 T) butter	1 tablespoon butter
1 vegetable bouillon cube	1 vegetable bouillon cube
Salt, pepper & ground nutmeg to taste	Salt, pepper & ground nutmeg to taste
Chopped parsley	Chopped parsley

METHOD Place corn, milk, butter and bouillon cube in a saucepan. Bring to the boil, then reduce heat and simmer for 10 minutes. Season to taste with salt, pepper and nutmeg. Garnish with chopped parsley.

CHEF'S TIP As a variation, add diced potato and allow to cook in the soup.

Serves 4

Fish & Seafood

Trout Almondine **40**
Stuffed Trout—Southern Style **40**
Broiled Kingklip, Halibut or Swordfish **40**
Sole Véronique **41**
Sole aux Pommes **41**
Whole Baked or Barbecued Fish with Herbs **41**
Marinade for Barbecued Fish **44**
Fish en Croûte **44**
Haddock Pie **44**
Pineapple Ginger Fish **45**
Whole Poached Salmon with Caper Sauce **45**
Cape Malay Pickled Fish **46**
Gravilax **46**
Broiled Scallops **47**
Sweet & Sour Prawns **47**
Spaghetti with Scallops **47**
Grilled Crayfish **48**
Shrimp Creole **48**
Chinese Vegetables with Prawns **48**
Lobster & Prawn Thermidor **49**
Moules Marinière **49**
Marinated Seafood **49**
Prawn Brochette **52**
Lobster Américaine **52**
Bombay Prawn Jambalaya **52**
Garlic Prawns **53**
Schezuan Shrimp **53**
Spaghetti with White Clam Sauce **53**

Trout Almondine

METRIC	AMERICAN
4 fresh trout	4 fresh trout
Salt & black pepper	Salt & black pepper
Seafood spice	Old bay seasoning
Milk	Milk
Flour for coating	Flour for coating
125 g butter	½ cup butter
15 mℓ (1 T) oil	1 tablespoon oil
50 g flaked almonds	½ cup flaked almonds
Juice of ½ lemon	Juice of ½ lemon
15 mℓ (1 T) chopped parsley	1 tablespoon chopped parsley

METHOD Clean trout and season with salt, black pepper and seafood spice (old bay seasoning). Dip first in milk, then flour; sauté in butter and oil until crisp and golden. Remove from pan and keep warm.

Add almonds to pan and cook until golden. Add lemon juice and parsley; pour over trout. Serve with boiled new potatoes sprinkled with parsley, and a French salad.

Serves 4

Stuffed Trout – Southern Style

METRIC	AMERICAN
4 fresh trout	4 fresh trout
Juice of 1 lemon	Juice of 1 lemon
Salt & pepper	Salt & pepper
Flour	Flour
Mixture of butter & oil for frying	Mixture of butter & oil for frying

STUFFING	STUFFING
60 g butter	4 tablespoons butter
1 onion, finely diced	1 onion, finely diced
250 g fresh mushrooms, coarsely chopped	½ lb fresh mushrooms, coarsely chopped
125 g peeled prawns, diced	¼ lb cleaned shrimp, diced
125 g crab meat	¼ lb crab meat
500 g (2 C) crumbled cornbread or breadcrumbs	2 cups crumbled cornbread or breadcrumbs
15 mℓ (1 T) milk	1 tablespoon milk
30 mℓ (2 T) cream	2 tablespoons cream
5 mℓ (1 t) dried thyme	1 teaspoon dried thyme
Salt & pepper	Salt & pepper

GARNISH	GARNISH
Sliced lemon	Sliced lemon
Freshly chopped parsley	Freshly chopped parsley

METHOD Rinse fish well. Pat dry and remove tail and fins with sharp scissors, cutting out all the smaller bones. Working on inside of fish, loosen at tail end and using your fingers, push the flesh away from the bone all the way up on both sides, then remove bone. Pull the small side bones out. Sprinkle fish with lemon juice and season with salt and pepper.

STUFFING Sauté onion in butter for 2–3 minutes. Add mushrooms and cook a few minutes longer. Add prawns (shrimp) and crab meat and cook for another 2 minutes. Stir in cornbread (or breadcrumbs), milk, cream and thyme. Remove from heat. Season to taste with salt and pepper.

Place a generous amount of stuffing in each trout. Roll in flour and fry in butter and oil until crisp and golden. Serve garnished with a lemon twist and sprinkled with finely chopped parsley.

Serves 4

Broiled Kingklip, Halibut or Swordfish

METRIC	AMERICAN
6 kingklip steaks	6 halibut or swordfish steaks
Juice of ½ lemon	Juice of ½ lemon
5 mℓ (1 t) salt	1 teaspoon salt
5 mℓ (1 t) pepper	1 teaspoon pepper
5 mℓ (1 t) paprika	1 teaspoon paprika
5 mℓ (1 t) dried dill	1 teaspoon dillweed
60 mℓ (¼ C) mayonnaise	4 tablespoons mayonnaise
60 g margarine or butter	4 tablespoons margarine or butter

GARNISH	GARNISH
Lemon slices	Lemon slices
Parsley sprigs	Parsley sprigs

METHOD Sprinkle both sides of kingklip, halibut or swordfish with lemon juice, seasonings, paprika and dill. Spread with a very thin layer of mayonnaise. Dot very lightly with butter and place on oiled foil under the griller (broiler) for approximately 7–10 minutes (do not turn).

Serve at once, topped if desired with a round of herb butter (see below) and garnished with a twist of lemon and parsley sprigs.

HERB BUTTER It is a good idea to top any grilled or broiled fish with herb butter, which may be made as follows: Soften a quantity of butter, add a few herbs of your choice and spread onto foil in a layer 1 cm (½ inch) thick. Refrigerate and cut into rounds with a small biscuit (cookie) cutter.

Serves 6

Sole Véronique

METRIC	AMERICAN
4 large sole or flounder	4 large sole or flounder
5 mℓ (1 t) salt	1 teaspoon salt
Pepper to taste	Pepper to taste
2 spring onions, chopped	2 green onions, chopped
250 mℓ (1 C) dry white wine	1 cup dry white wine
Bay leaves & peppercorns to taste	Bay leaves & peppercorns to taste
60 g butter	4 tablespoons butter
10 mℓ (1 level T) flour	1 level tablespoon flour
250 mℓ (1 C) cream	1 cup heavy cream
100 g seedless green grapes, skinned	1 cup seedless green grapes, skinned

METHOD Sprinkle fish with salt and pepper. In a large pan, combine spring (green) onions, wine, bay leaves and peppercorns. Bring to the boil and reduce heat. Add fish and poach for 2–3 minutes. Remove fish carefully, place on an ovenware platter and keep warm.

Continue to boil the liquid, uncovered, until it has reduced to approximately 125 mℓ (½ cup). Remove from heat and strain. Melt butter over low heat; stir in flour. Add stock, stirring constantly until smooth. Add cream and adjust seasonings.

Arrange grapes around fish and pour sauce over fish. Place under grill (broiler) for 2 minutes, or until browned. Serve immediately.

CHEF'S TIP To skin grapes, immerse in boiling water for a few seconds, after which they will peel easily.

Serves 4

Sole aux Pommes

METRIC	AMERICAN
4 large potatoes	4 large potatoes
Butter & milk for mash	Butter & milk for mash
4 fillets sole (approximately 175–250 g each)	4 fillets sole, flounder or orange roughy (approximately ½ lb each)
Salt, pepper & seafood spice to taste	Salt, pepper & old bay seasoning to taste
1 medium onion, diced	1 medium onion, diced
60 g butter	4 tablespoons butter
1 medium tomato, diced	1 medium tomato, diced
1 x 225 g tin sliced mushrooms, drained	1 x 8 oz can sliced mushrooms, drained
30 mℓ (2 T) tomato sauce	2 tablespoons ketchup
125 mℓ (½ C) double cream	½ cup heavy cream

METHOD Scrub potatoes, prick all over and rub with oil. Bake in 180°C (350°F) oven until soft (about 1 hour). Cut tops off potatoes; scoop out pulp (reserving shells) and mash with salt, pepper, and butter, then soften with milk. Keep warm or reheat in microwave before combining with fish.

Season fish with salt, pepper and seafood spice (old bay seasoning). Roll up from tail end and secure with toothpick. Place in greased ovenware dish.

Sauté onion in butter until golden brown. Add tomato and mushrooms and cook for 2–3 minutes. Spoon over fish, dot with tomato sauce and bake uncovered in 200°C (400°F) oven for 15–20 minutes. Remove from oven and pour over most of the cream.

Place a little mashed potato in each potato shell. Remove toothpicks from fish and place 1 fillet in each potato. Arrange filled potatoes on ovenware platter.

Blend remaining sauce in food processor or blender and stir in the rest of the cream, then pour around base of potatoes. Pipe a border of mashed potato around edge and place under grill (broiler) until golden brown.

Serves 4   PHOTOGRAPH ON PAGE 51

Whole Baked or Barbecued Fish with Herbs

METRIC	AMERICAN
1 x 2–2,5 kg whole fish (eg kabeljou, stumpnose or red roman)	1 x 4–5 lb whole fish (eg grouper or snapper)
125 g butter or margarine	½ cup butter or margarine
Juice of 1 lemon	Juice of 1 lemon
5 mℓ (1 t) dried dill	1 teaspoon dillweed
5 mℓ (1 t) dried thyme	1 teaspoon dried thyme
5 mℓ (1 t) finely chopped fresh parsley	1 teaspoon finely chopped fresh parsley
1 large tomato, diced	1 large tomato, diced
2–3 spring onions, diced	2–3 green onions, diced
5 mℓ (1 t) salt	1 teaspoon salt
5 mℓ (1 t) black pepper	1 teaspoon black pepper
5 mℓ (1 t) seafood or fish spice	1 teaspoon old bay seasoning
Bay leaves & peppercorns	Bay leaves & peppercorns

METHOD Place fish on a large piece of foil. Smear fish with butter or margarine, then sprinkle with lemon juice, herbs, tomato, onion, seasonings, bay leaves and peppercorns. Cover with the foil, place on a large baking sheet and bake in a 180°C (350°F) oven until cooked (about 1–1½ hours, depending on size of fish). The fish is done if it flakes easily when tested with a fork.

CHEF'S TIP This fish may also be cooked in the foil on the braai or barbecue.

Serves 8 to 10

Overleaf: Fish en Croûte

Marinade for Barbecued Fish

METRIC	AMERICAN
1 small onion, diced	1 small onion, diced
2 spring onions, diced	2 green onions, diced
30 mℓ (2 T) soy sauce	2 tablespoons soy sauce
15 mℓ (1 T) lemon juice or vinegar	1 tablespoon lemon juice or vinegar
15 mℓ (1 T) white wine	1 tablespoon white wine
2 mℓ (½ t) ground black pepper	½ teaspoon ground black pepper

METHOD Mix all ingredients together. Pour over fish and leave for at least 2 hours. Place fish on greased foil to barbecue.

Makes enough for 1 kg / 2 lb fish

Fish en Croûte

METRIC	AMERICAN
3 x 400 g packets ready-made puff pastry*	3 lb ready-made puff pastry*

FILLING	FILLING
1 kg hake, skinned & filleted	2 lb orange roughy, haddock, or tubot, skinned & filleted
Salt, pepper & seafood spice to taste	Salt, pepper & old bay seasoning to taste
125 g butter	½ cup butter
30 mℓ (2 T) oil	2 tablespoons oil
1 onion, finely diced	1 onion, finely diced
30 mℓ (2 T) flour	2 tablespoons flour
250 mℓ (1 C) milk	1 cup milk
50 g grated Cheddar cheese	½ cup grated Cheddar cheese
1 egg, slightly beaten	1 egg, slightly beaten
1 x 225 g tin sliced mushrooms, drained	1 x 8 oz can sliced mushrooms, drained

* Or use recipe on p 20

METHOD First prepare the filling. Season fish with salt, pepper and seafood spice (old bay seasoning). Heat half the butter and the 30 mℓ (2 tablespoons) oil in a pan. Add onion and sauté gently for a few minutes. Add fish to the pan and sauté gently until cooked – just a few minutes. Remove onion and fish from pan and set aside.

Melt remaining butter in pan, stir in flour then add milk, stirring constantly over low heat until thickened. Add cheese to sauce and cook until melted.

Divide cheese sauce in half and set half aside to serve as additional sauce with the dish. Beat a little of the remaining sauce into the egg, then whisk this mixture back into the sauce and cook in the pan for another minute. Add drained mushrooms and gently fold fish and onions into sauce. Adjust seasonings and allow to cool completely. Meanwhile, prepare the pastry case.

PASTRY Roll out dough on a lightly floured board and cut into 2 even rectangles. Using a cardboard facsimile as a guide, cut out two fish shapes, one from each rectangle, one being 2.5cm (1 inch) larger all around.

Place the smaller fish shaped pastry onto a biscuit (cookie tray) which has been lightly greased. Spoon the cooled fish filling evenly along the centre and about 4 cm (1½ inches) from the edges. Brush the edges with water. Top with the other fish-shaped pastry; seal ends together with a fork to form the fins and tail. Press remaining edges together with fingers, sealing well.

Using the point of a sharp knife cut an eye, mouth and scales into the pastry. Be sure not to cut through the pastry, but deeply enough for definition when baked (refer to photograph on p 42).

Brush with beaten egg and bake in a 220°C (425°F) oven for 15 minutes. Turn oven down to 180°C (350°F) and bake for a further 20–25 minutes.

Remove from oven and lift or slide gently onto a serving platter. Slice and serve with the remaining cheese sauce, heated and thinned down with additional milk.

Serves 6 to 8   PHOTOGRAPH ON PAGE 42

Haddock Pie
By courtesy of Aunt Celie

METRIC	AMERICAN
500 g haddock	1 lb Finnan Haddie or smoked white fish
1 onion, diced	1 onion, diced
60 g butter	4 tablespoons butter
30 mℓ (2 T) flour	2 tablespoons flour
375 mℓ (1½ C) milk	1½ cups milk
125 mℓ (½ C) cream	½ cup cream
1 x 420 g tin creamed sweetcorn	1 x 13½ oz can creamed corn
2 eggs	2 eggs
Salt & pepper to taste	Salt & pepper to taste
50 g grated Cheddar cheese	½ cup grated Cheddar cheese

METHOD Boil haddock and flake, discarding skin and bones. If using smoked white fish, simply flake.

Sauté diced onion in butter. Stir in flour, then slowly add milk over low heat, stirring constantly until thickened. Add cream and creamed sweetcorn. Remove from heat.

Beat eggs lightly and fold in. Season to taste with salt and pepper. Pour into a lightly greased ovenware dish, sprinkle with cheese and bake in 180°C (350°F) oven for 25 minutes.

Serves 8

Pineapple Ginger Fish

METRIC	AMERICAN
750 g hake, sole or kingklip	1½ lb orange roughy, haddock
Salt, pepper & seafood spice	or cod
	Salt, pepper & old bay seasoning

BATTER	BATTER
140 g (1 C) self-raising flour	1 cup self-rising flour
1 can beer	1 can beer

SAUCE	SAUCE
1 x 825 g tin pineapple rings	1 large can pineapple rings
(reserve 250 mℓ juice)	(reserve 1 cup juice)
30 mℓ (2 T) brown sugar	2 tablespoons brown sugar
4 pieces preserved ginger	4 pieces stem ginger
60 mℓ (¼ C) ginger syrup	4 tablespoons ginger syrup
(from the preserved ginger)	(from the stem ginger)
2 mℓ (½ t) ground ginger	½ teaspoon ground ginger
15 mℓ (1 T) cornflour	1 tablespoon cornstarch
30 mℓ (2 T) vinegar	2 tablespoons vinegar
15 mℓ (1 T) soy sauce	1 tablespoon soy sauce
30 mℓ (2 T) water	2 tablespoons water
1 mℓ (¼ t) salt	¼ teaspoon salt
250 g plain, unsalted cashew	½ lb plain, unsalted cashew
nuts, fried in oil until crisp	nuts, fried in oil until crisp
& golden	& golden
Oil for frying	Oil for frying

GARNISH	GARNISH
Tinned lychees	Canned lychee nuts

METHOD Cut fish into fingers. Season well with salt, pepper and seafood spice (old bay seasoning).

BATTER Mix flour with enough beer to form the consistency of thick cream (not too thin).

SAUCE Chop 6 of the pineapple rings into small pieces. In a saucepan combine the chopped pineapple, reserved juice, brown sugar, preserved ginger (stem ginger), ginger syrup, ground ginger, cornflour (cornstarch), vinegar, soy sauce and water. Bring to the boil and cook until thickened. Season to taste with salt.

TO COOK Dip fish into batter, allowing excess batter to drain off. Deep fry in hot oil until crisp and golden. Drain on paper towel. Place fish on a large serving platter and surround with remaining pineapple rings.

Sprinkle fish with cashew nuts. Spoon some of the sauce over fish and garnish with lychees (lychee nuts). Serve the remainder of the sauce in a bowl on the side. Serve hot.

CHEF'S TIP To make the batter stick more easily, you may dip the fish in flour or cornflour (cornstarch) before dipping it in the batter.

Serves 6   PHOTOGRAPH ON PAGE 50

Whole Poached Salmon with Caper Sauce

METRIC	AMERICAN
1 x 2,5 kg fresh whole salmon	1 x 6 lb fresh whole salmon
15 mℓ (1 T) salt	1 tablespoon salt
2 mℓ (½ t) pepper	½ teaspoon pepper
Pinch of dried thyme	Pinch of dried thyme
Pinch of dried dill	Pinch of dillweed
1 onion, sliced	1 onion, sliced
2–3 bay leaves	2–3 bay leaves
6 peppercorns	6 peppercorns
250 mℓ (1 C) white wine	1 cup white wine
250 mℓ (1 C) water	1 cup water

CAPER SAUCE	CAPER SAUCE
1 onion	1 onion
30 mℓ (2 T) lemon juice	2 tablespoons lemon juice
5 mℓ (1 t) coarsely ground	1 teaspoon coarsely ground
black pepper	black pepper
250 mℓ (1 C) mayonnaise	1 cup mayonnaise
15 mℓ (1 T) sugar	1 tablespoon sugar
3 cloves garlic	3 cloves garlic
2 mℓ (½ t) salt	½ teaspoon salt
2–3 cucumbers, chopped &	2–3 cucumbers, chopped &
drained	drained
30 mℓ (2 T) chopped parsley	2 tablespoons chopped parsley
45 mℓ (3 T) capers, drained	3 tablespoons capers, drained
250 mℓ (1 C) sour cream	1 cup sour cream

METHOD Wash fish well under cold water. Dry and season with salt, pepper, thyme and dill (dillweed). Place either in fish poacher or place on a double thickness of foil and lay on baking tray. Place sliced onion, bay leaves and peppercorns on top of and underneath fish.

Combine wine and water and pour over fish. Cover tightly or close foil over fish and bake at 200°C (400°F) for 1½ hours, or until fish flakes easily when tested with a fork. Cool and place in refrigerator overnight.

CAPER SAUCE Place first seven ingredients in food processor and blend until smooth. Mix together remaining ingredients, add to the mayonnaise sauce and combine well.

TO SERVE Remove skin from one side of salmon; invert onto serving platter, then remove skin from other side. Decorate with caper sauce and if desired, use slices of radish, carrot, pickled cucumber (pickles) as 'scales' and thin strips of carrot, green pepper, tomato, celery and anchovies as 'tail' and 'fins'.

Serves 16 to 20

Cape Malay Pickled Fish

METRIC	AMERICAN
1,5–2 kg hake, kingklip or any firm white fish suitable for frying	3–4 lb orange roughy, halibut or any firm white fish suitable for frying
Salt & pepper	Salt & pepper
Fish spice	Old bay seasoning
Flour	Flour
3 eggs, beaten	3 eggs, beaten
Oil for frying	Oil for frying

PICKLING SOLUTION	PICKLING SOLUTION
375 mℓ (1½ C) red wine vinegar	1½ cups red wine vinegar
375 mℓ (1½ C) water	1½ cups water
3–4 onions, sliced	3–4 onions, sliced
5 mℓ (1 t) salt	1 teaspoon salt
2 mℓ (½ t) ground ginger	½ teaspoon ground ginger
30 mℓ (2 T) apricot jam	2 tablespoons apricot preserves
30 mℓ (2 T) sugar	2 tablespoons sugar
2–3 bay leaves	2–3 bay leaves
6–8 peppercorns	6–8 peppercorns
30 mℓ (2 T) curry powder	2 tablespoons curry powder
30 mℓ (2 T) sultanas (optional)	2 tablespoons golden raisins (optional)
10 mℓ (2 t) cornflour, mixed to a paste with a little water	2 teaspoons cornstarch, mixed to a paste with a little water

METHOD Season fish lightly with salt, pepper and fish spice (old bay seasoning). Dip into flour, then into beaten egg and fry in hot oil over medium heat until deep golden brown. Drain on absorbent paper.

TO PREPARE PICKLING SOLUTION Combine vinegar and water. Add sliced onions and boil together for 10–15 minutes. Add the remaining ingredients, except cornflour (cornstarch). Lastly, thicken with cornflour (cornstarch) paste. Pour over fried fish and refrigerate for 24 hours before serving.

Serves 12

Gravilax

By courtesy of Sy Baskin

This recipe is from a very dear friend of ours who lives in Chicago and makes the best Gravilax I have ever tasted. He was kind enough to share his special recipe with me. The amounts given are approximate, so use your own judgement where necessary.

METRIC	AMERICAN
2 salmon sides – approximately 2,25 kg (preferably king salmon)	2 salmon sides – approximately 4–5 lb (preferably king salmon)
10 mℓ (2 t) coarse black pepper	2 teaspoons coarse black pepper
5 mℓ (1 t) fine black pepper	1 teaspoon fine black pepper
30 mℓ (2 T) sugar	2 tablespoons sugar
30 mℓ (2 T) coarse (Kosher) salt	2 tablespoons coarse (Kosher) salt
Fresh dill*	Fresh dill*

* Use plenty of fresh dill, some with flower buds on it. (Sy insists this is the key ingredient)

METHOD Place salmon sides, skins down, in a large, flat, shallow pan. Sprinkle with coarse pepper and rub in well, then sprinkle with the fine pepper and also rub in well. Sprinkle with sugar and again rub into the flesh with your fingers. Finally, rub in the coarse salt in the same manner. The fillets should now have a white appearance.

Cut off most of the dill flowers and rub them into the fish, then lay the stalks on the fish fillets – be very generous. Lay some of the stalks underneath the skin and on the bottom of the pan as well.

Place one fillet on top of the other, sandwich-style, with skin sides on the outside. Cover the entire pan with foil and put weights on the foil. (Sy uses telephone directories!)

Place in the refrigerator. Remove every 12 hours, drain fluid from pan and turn the sandwiched fillets upside down. After 1½–2 days there will be no more fluid; however, keep turning the fillets every 12 hours for 5–6 days.

Remove weights and foil. Scrape off the major portion of the dill particles, salt, pepper, etc. To serve, slice very thinly on the diagonal (an electric knife is ideal for this task).

CHEF'S TIP If not consumed within a few days, wrap and store in the freezer. Lax may be refrozen and thawed an unlimited number of times without suffering any adverse effects to its quality or texture.

Serves 20

Broiled Scallops

METRIC	AMERICAN
1 kg scallops	2 lb bay scallops
Salt & pepper to taste	Salt & pepper to taste
Crushed garlic powder to taste	Garlic powder to taste
30 mℓ (2 T) lemon juice	2 tablespoons lemon juice
2 cloves garlic, crushed	2 cloves garlic, crushed
60 g butter, melted	4 tablespoons butter, melted

METHOD Season scallops with salt, pepper and garlic powder. Combine with remaining ingredients. Arrange on foil-lined baking tray and place under broiler for 2–3 minutes. Serve over rice or pasta.

Serves 4

Sweet & Sour Prawns (Shrimp)

METRIC	AMERICAN
1,5 kg prawns, shelled & deveined	3 lb cleaned shrimp
Salt & pepper to taste	Salt & pepper to taste
5 mℓ (1 t) crushed garlic powder	1 teaspoon garlic powder
120 g (1 C) cornflour	1 cup cornstarch
250 mℓ (1 C) peanut oil for frying	1 cup peanut oil for frying

BATTER	BATTER
140 g (1 C) self-raising flour	1 cup self-rising flour
1 can beer	1 can beer

SAUCE	SAUCE
30 mℓ (2 T) brown sugar	2 tablespoons brown sugar
30 mℓ (2 T) white sugar	2 tablespoons white sugar
45 mℓ (3 T) vinegar	3 tablespoons vinegar
60 mℓ (¼ C) tomato sauce	4 tablespoons ketchup
80 mℓ (⅓ C) cold water	5 tablespoons cold water
15 mℓ (1 T) cornflour	1 tablespoon cornstarch
5 mℓ (1 t) finely chopped fresh ginger or 2 mℓ (½ t) ground ginger	1 teaspoon finely chopped ginger-root or ½ teaspoon ground ginger
5 mℓ (1 t) salt	1 teaspoon salt
5 mℓ (1 t) sesame oil	1 teaspoon sesame oil
Few drops red colouring	Few drops red color
Peanut oil for frying	Peanut oil for frying
2 celery sticks, diagonally sliced	2 celery sticks, diagonally sliced
½ green pepper, sliced	½ green pepper, sliced
1 x 410 g tin pineapple chunks (reserve ½ the juice)	1 x 15 oz can pineapple chunks (reserve ½ the juice)

METHOD Season prawns (shrimp) with salt, pepper and garlic powder and set aside.

BATTER Sift flour and add enough beer to form the consistency of thick sour cream. Beat well until smooth. Set aside.

SAUCE Combine sugars, vinegar, tomato sauce, water, cornflour (cornstarch), ginger, salt, sesame oil and food colouring in a saucepan and boil together until thickened. Heat a little peanut oil in a pan (skillet) and stir-fry the celery and green pepper. Add the pineapple chunks and juice. Combine with the thickened sauce and heat through.

TO COOK PRAWNS Dip seasoned prawns (shrimp) in cornflour (cornstarch), then in batter. Drain off excess batter. Heat peanut oil in wok and fry prawns in hot oil for 3–5 minutes, or until golden brown.

TO SERVE Arrange prawns (shrimp) on a large platter. Pour over a little of the heated sauce and serve the remaining sauce in a bowl on the side.

CHEF'S TIPS Fillets of sole or chicken breast fillets may be substituted for the prawns (shrimp) and cooked in the same way.

I sometimes serve this dish as a finger appetizer, in which case I omit the celery, green pepper and pineapple but add about 125 mℓ (½ cup) pineapple juice to the sauce.

Serves 6

Spaghetti with Scallops

METRIC	AMERICAN
250 g spaghetti	½ lb spaghetti
60 g butter	4 tablespoons butter
30 mℓ (2 T) olive oil	2 tablespoons olive oil
4 cloves garlic, crushed	4 cloves garlic, crushed
250 g mushrooms, sliced	½ lb mushrooms, sliced
500 g bay scallops	1 lb bay scallops
15 mℓ (1 T) dry white wine	1 tablespoon dry white wine
15 mℓ (1 T) lemon juice	1 tablespoon lemon juice
Pinch of dried thyme	Pinch of dried thyme
15 mℓ (1 T) fresh parsley, finely chopped	1 tablespoon fresh parsley, finely chopped
Salt & pepper to taste	Salt & pepper to taste
Grated Parmesan cheese	Grated Parmesan cheese

METHOD Cook spaghetti in salted water until tender. Meanwhile, heat butter and oil in a frying pan and add garlic and mushrooms. Sauté until light brown.

Add remaining ingredients, except Parmesan cheese, and sauté for 2–3 minutes, or until scallops are no longer translucent.

Drain spaghetti; toss with additional butter and the Parmesan cheese, then mix in scallop mixture and serve.

Serves 4

Grilled Crayfish (Lobster)

METRIC	AMERICAN
6 live crayfish	6 live lobsters
Juice of ½ lemon	Juice of ½ lemon
125 g butter, melted	½ cup butter, melted
3–4 cloves garlic, crushed	3–4 cloves garlic, crushed

GARNISH	GARNISH
Lemon slices	Lemon slices
Parsley sprigs	Parsley sprigs

METHOD Boil crayfish (lobster) in salted water for 20 minutes. Remove from water; slit the shells down the back and remove veins. Rinse well under cold running water.

Cut crayfish (lobster) open so that both sides remain flat and place on foil-lined tray. Sprinkle lightly with lemon juice and brush with melted butter combined with crushed garlic.

Place under griller (broiler) for 3–5 minutes, brushing frequently with the butter mixture. Serve on a bed of rice, garnished with lemon twists and parsley.

Serves 6

Shrimp Creole

METRIC	AMERICAN
2 kg cooked prawns, peeled	4 lb cooked shrimp, peeled
1 onion, finely diced	1 onion, finely diced
2 cloves garlic, crushed	2 cloves garlic, crushed
1 stick celery, diced	1 stick celery, diced
1 green pepper, diced	1 green pepper, diced
Butter for browning	Butter for browning
30 mℓ (2 T) flour	2 tablespoons flour
2 x 425 g tins tomatoes, diced	2 x 15 oz cans tomatoes, diced
15 mℓ (1 T) parsley, finely chopped	1 tablespoon parsley, finely chopped
7 mℓ (1½ t) salt	1½ teaspoons salt
5 mℓ (1 t) celery salt	1 teaspoon celery seed
1 mℓ (¼ t) peri-peri powder	¼ teaspoon crushed red pepper
1–2 mℓ (¼–½ t) paprika	¼–½ teaspoon paprika
15 mℓ (1 T) lemon juice	1 tablespoon lemon juice
45 mℓ (3 T) Worcestershire sauce	3 tablespoons Worcestershire sauce
125 mℓ (½ C) water	½ cup water

METHOD Brown onion, garlic, celery and green pepper in butter. Stir in flour. When blended, stir in tomatoes, parsley, seasonings, peri-peri powder, paprika, lemon juice and Worcestershire sauce. Add water and simmer over low heat for 8–10 minutes. Finally, add prawns (shrimp) to the sauce. Serve over rice.

Serves 4 to 6

Chinese Vegetables with Prawns (Shrimp)

METRIC	AMERICAN
1 kg prawns, boiled & shelled	2 lb shrimp, boiled & shelled
30–45 mℓ (2–3 T) peanut oil*	2–3 tablespoons peanut oil
3 sticks celery, sliced diagonally in thin pieces	3 sticks celery, sliced diagonally in thin pieces
1 green pepper, seeded & cut into strips	1 green pepper, seeded & cut into strips
1 onion, halved & cut into strips	1 onion, halved & cut into strips
2 carrots, halved & sliced diagonally in thin pieces	2 carrots, halved & sliced diagonally in thin pieces
Piece of cabbage or Bok Choy (Chinese cabbage), sliced (optional)	Piece of cabbage or Bok Choy (Chinese cabbage), sliced (optional)
Broccoli flowerets	Broccoli flowerets
250 mℓ (1 C) tender young peas in the pod (optional)	1 cup snow peas (optional)
1 x 227 g tin sliced water chestnuts, drained	1 x 8 oz can sliced water chestnuts, drained
2–3 cloves garlic, crushed	2–3 cloves garlic, crushed
10 mℓ (2 t) finely diced fresh ginger	2 teaspoons finely diced ginger-root
1 chicken bouillon cube, crushed	1 chicken bouillon cube, crushed
250 mℓ (1 C) boiling water	1 cup boiling water
15 mℓ (1 T) soy sauce	1 tablespoon soy sauce
15 mℓ (1 T) Chinese wine or sherry	1 tablespoon Chinese wine or sherry
10 mℓ (2 t) cornflour mixed to a paste with a little cold water	2 teaspoons cornstarch, mixed to a paste with a little cold water
Salt & pepper to taste	Salt & pepper to taste

* If unavailable, use sunflower oil

METHOD If using uncooked prawns, boil, shell and set aside. Heat oil in wok or non-stick large pan. Add all vegetables, garlic and ginger and stir-fry for 3–4 minutes, or until tender but still crisp.

Dissolve crushed bouillon cube in boiling water and add to vegetables. Add soy sauce, wine or sherry and cornflour (cornstarch) paste, to thicken. Stir until vegetables are glazed. Add prawns (shrimp); season with salt and pepper to taste. Serve with steamed white rice.

CHEF'S TIP This dish may be prepared with Tofu (soy bean curd) instead of prawns (shrimp), or the vegetables may be served as a side dish without the seafood or Tofu – a delicious, simple and very healthy accompaniment. Baby corn cobs may also be added, if desired.

Serves 6 to 8

Lobster & Prawn (Shrimp) Thermidor

METRIC	AMERICAN
2 crayfish tails	2 lobster tails
1 kg prawns, peeled & deveined	2 lb shrimp, shelled & deveined
125 g butter	½ cup butter
1 onion, finely chopped	1 onion, finely chopped
3 cloves garlic, crushed	3 cloves garlic, crushed
500 g fresh mushrooms, sliced & fried in oil	1 lb fresh mushrooms, sliced & fried in oil
2 mℓ (½ t) dried thyme	½ teaspoon dried thyme
2 mℓ (½ t) dried dill	½ teaspoon dillweed
30 mℓ (2 T) flour	2 tablespoons flour
500 mℓ (2 C) chicken stock	2 cups chicken stock
60 mℓ (¼ C) white wine	¼ cup white wine
250 mℓ (1 C) cream	1 cup cream
Salt & black pepper to taste	Salt & black pepper to taste

METHOD Remove crayfish (lobster) meat from shells and dice. Sauté prawns (shrimp) and crayfish in butter for several minutes, until they turn pink. Remove and set aside.

Adding more butter if necessary, sauté onion and garlic, then add mushrooms, thyme and dill (dillweed) and cook for 2–3 minutes. Stir in flour; slowly add chicken stock and wine and cook, stirring constantly, until thickened.

Add cream and seafood and heat thoroughly. Season to taste with salt and black pepper. If necessary, thicken more with a paste of cornflour (cornstarch) and water.

Serve on a bed of buttered noodles or fettucini.

Serves 8

Moules Marinière

METRIC	AMERICAN
1 – 1,5 kg fresh mussels*	2–3 lb fresh mussels*
125 g butter	½ cup butter
1 large onion, finely diced	1 large onion, finely diced
Pinch of dried thyme	Pinch of dried thyme
5 mℓ (1 t) finely chopped fresh parsley	1 teaspoon finely chopped fresh parsley
125 mℓ (½ C) dry white wine	½ cup dry white wine
500 mℓ (2 C) water	2 cups water
125 mℓ (½ C) cream	½ cup cream
Salt & freshly ground black pepper to taste	Salt & freshly ground black pepper to taste

*   Make sure that the shells of the mussels are firmly closed when you buy them, to ensure freshness

METHOD Clean mussels very well in cold water by scrubbing and scraping off the beards.

Melt butter in a large saucepan. Add onion, thyme and parsley and sauté for 2–3 minutes. Add mussels, wine and water and simmer gently until mussels open. (Discard those which do not open.)

Remove mussels from saucepan, reserving the liquid, which is now your stock. Add the cream to the stock, stir in and pour over the mussels. If necessary, the stock may be slightly thickened with 5 mℓ (1 teaspoon) cornflour (cornstarch) mixed to a paste with a little cold water. Season to taste with salt and pepper.

Serve immediately, accompanied by garlic bread.

Serves 4 to 6

Marinated Seafood

METRIC	AMERICAN
500 g squid	1 lb squid
500 g scallops	1 lb scallops
1 green pepper, chopped	1 green pepper, chopped
1 red hot chilli pepper or 5 mℓ (1 t) crushed red pepper or cayenne pepper	1 red hot chili pepper or 1 teaspoon crushed red pepper
1 purple onion, cut into rings	1 purple onion, cut into rings
1 red pepper, seeded, cored & cut into strips	1 red pepper, seeded, cored & cut into strips
2 mℓ (½ t) crushed garlic powder	½ teaspoon garlic powder
5 mℓ (1 t) salt	1 teaspoon salt
2 mℓ (½ t) pepper	½ teaspoon pepper
Juice of 1 lemon	Juice of 1 lemon
2 cloves garlic, crushed	2 cloves garlic, crushed
125 mℓ (½ C) tarragon vinegar	½ cup tarragon vinegar
45 mℓ (3 T) olive oil	3 tablespoons olive oil
125 mℓ (½ C) oil	½ cup oil
15 mℓ (1T) fresh parsley, finely chopped	1 tablespoon fresh parsley, finely chopped

METHOD Clean squid out thoroughly, removing eyes and insides, as well as peeling off all the fine purple skin on the tentacle clusters. Rinse very well, then slice into rings, leaving tentacle clusters whole. Dip scallops and squid into boiling water for 1 minute. Dry off well and place in an earthenware bowl.

Combine squid, scallops, green pepper, chilli pepper, red pepper and onion. Combine remaining ingredients and add. Blend well and toss, then cover and allow to marinate in refrigerator for 24 hours, turning often. Serve cold.

Serves 8

Overleaf: Pineapple Ginger Fish, Sole aux Pommes and Prawn (Shrimp) Brochette

Prawn (Shrimp) Brochette

METRIC	AMERICAN
1 kg prawns	2 lb shrimp
500 mℓ bottled Italian salad dressing	1 x 16 fl oz bottle Italian salad dressing
5 mℓ (1 t) Worcestershire sauce	1 teaspoon Worcestershire sauce
2 mℓ (½ t) crushed garlic powder	½ teaspoon garlic powder
5 mℓ (1 t) dried, mixed herbs	1 teaspoon Italian seasoning
2 mℓ (½ t) peri-peri powder (optional)	½ teaspoon crushed red pepper (optional)
Button mushrooms	Black mushrooms
Green peppers, cut roughly into squares	Green peppers, cut roughly into squares
Baby onions	Baby onions
Cherry tomatoes	Cherry tomatoes

METHOD Devein prawns (shrimp) and remove shells. Combine salad dressing with Worcestershire sauce, garlic powder, herbs and peri-peri powder (crushed red pepper) and marinate seafood in this mixture overnight.

Thread prawns (shrimp) onto skewers, alternating with mushroooms, green pepper squares, onions and tomatoes. Grill (broil) on each side for 2–3 minutes, basting frequently with the marinade.

Serve on a bed of rice or buttered pasta. Pour over a mixture of melted butter, crushed garlic and lemon juice.

Serves 6   PHOTOGRAPH ON PAGE 51

Lobster Américaine

METRIC	AMERICAN
4 lobsters or crayfish weighing approximately 500 g each	4 lobsters weighing approximately 1 lb each
15 mℓ (1 T) oil	1 tablespoon oil
60 g butter	4 tablespoons butter
1 large onion, finely diced	1 large onion, finely diced
2 cloves garlic, crushed	2 cloves garlic, crushed
30 mℓ (2 T) brandy	2 tablespoons brandy or cognac
250 mℓ (1 C) dry white wine	1 cup dry white wine
1 x 425 g tin whole tomatoes	1 x 14½ oz can whole tomatoes
1 x 227 g tin tomato purée	1 x 8 oz can tomato sauce
2 mℓ (½ t) salt	½ teaspoon salt
Dash of pepper	Dash of pepper
1 mℓ (¼ t) cayenne pepper	¼ teaspoon cayenne pepper
1 chicken bouillon cube, crushed	1 chicken bouillon cube, crushed
2 mℓ (½ t) dried tarragon	½ teaspoon dried tarragon
2 mℓ (½ t) dried parsley	½ teaspoon dried parsley
Beurre manié*	Beurre manié*
125 mℓ (½ C) cream	½ cup cream

* 125 g (½ cup) butter creamed with 30 mℓ (2 tablespoons) flour

METHOD Break off head and claws of lobster and set aside.

Boil tails in salted water for 20 minutes. Remove meat from shells, slice and set aside. Crush lobster heads and claws.

Heat oil and butter in a saucepan, add onion and crushed garlic and sauté over medium heat for 2–3 minutes. Add crushed lobster, then add brandy and ignite. Stir in wine, tomatoes, tomato purée (or sauce), salt, pepper, cayenne pepper, crushed bouillon cube, tarragon and parsley and simmer over gentle heat for about 30–40 minutes.

Strain, then return to heat. Add beurre manié to the sauce, a little at a time, until desired thickness is achieved. Bring to the boil and remove from heat. Stir in cream.

Melt about 60 mℓ (4 tablespoons) butter in a large pan. Add sliced lobster, then add the sauce. Combine gently, heat through and serve on a bed of rice or pasta.

Serves 4

Bombay Prawn Jambalaya

METRIC	AMERICAN
1 large onion, chopped	1 large onion, chopped
125 g butter	½ cup butter
1–1,5 kg prawns, deveined & peeled	2–3 lb shrimp, deveined & peeled
30 mℓ (2 T) brandy	2 tablespoons cognac
5–10 mℓ (1–2 t) curry powder	1–2 teaspoons curry powder
250 mℓ (1 C) cream	1 cup cream
125 mℓ (½ C) white wine or chicken stock	½ cup white wine or chicken stock
2 mℓ (½ t) salt	½ teaspoon salt
2 mℓ (½ t) black pepper	½ teaspoon black pepper
375 mℓ (1½ C) rice boiled with 5 mℓ (1 t) butter	1½ cups rice boiled with 1 teaspoon butter
1 x 410 g tin pineapple chunks, drained (or slices of fresh pineapple)	1 x 15½ oz can pineapple chunks, drained (or slices of fresh pineapple)
Grapes	Grapes
Melon & spanspek balls	Melon & cantaloupe balls
1 banana, sliced	1 banana, sliced
1 mango, sliced	1 mango, sliced
Dessicated coconut	Shredded coconut

METHOD Sauté onion in butter. Add prawns (shrimp) and cook for a further 3–5 minutes. Flambé with brandy (cognac). Remove shrimp and set aside. Stir in curry powder, cream, wine or chicken stock and seasonings. Cook until thickened. Return shrimp to mixture.

Spoon rice onto serving platter; top with seafood mixture and surround with some or all of the fruit. Spoon sauce over prawns (shrimp) and fruit. Sprinkle with coconut.

Serves 6 to 8

Garlic Prawns (Shrimp)

METRIC	AMERICAN
45 mℓ (3 T) sunflower oil or olive oil	3 tablespoons sunflower oil or olive oil
45 mℓ (3 T) butter	3 tablespoons butter
1 kg medium prawns (deveined but not shelled)	2 lb medium shrimp (deveined but not shelled)
4 cloves garlic, crushed	4 cloves garlic, crushed
30 mℓ (2 T) lemon juice	2 tablespoons lemon juice
30 mℓ (2 T) cream sherry	2 tablespoons cream sherry
2 mℓ (½ t) paprika	½ teaspoon paprika
2 mℓ (½ t) cayenne pepper	½ teaspoon Mexican crushed red pepper
Salt to taste	Salt to taste
Finely chopped fresh parsley	Finely chopped fresh parsley

METHOD Heat oil and butter in a large pan or copper casserole dish. Add prawns (shrimp) and sauté over high heat for about 3 minutes. Add garlic, lemon juice, sherry, paprika, pepper and salt to taste. Heat through. Sprinkle with parsley and serve immediately.

Serves 4

Schezuan Shrimp

METRIC	AMERICAN
1 kg prawns, shelled & deveined	2 lb shrimp, shelled & deveined
1 onion, quartered & sliced	1 onion, quartered & sliced
2 sticks celery, diagonally sliced	2 sticks celery, diagonally sliced
1 carrot, cut into julienne strips	1 carrot, cut into julienne strips
1 green pepper, seeded & cut into strips	1 green pepper, seeded & cut into strips
250 g snow peas*	½ lb snow peas
1 x 227 g tin water chestnuts, drained & sliced	1 x 8 oz can water chestnuts, drained & sliced
Peanut oil for frying	Peanut oil for frying
SAUCE	**SAUCE**
30 mℓ (2 T) sherry	2 tablespoons sherry
45 mℓ (3 T) soy sauce	3 tablespoons soy sauce
30 mℓ (2 T) tomato sauce	2 tablespoons tomato ketchup
2 mℓ (½ t) crushed Mexican red pepper or cayenne pepper	½ teaspoon red pepper flakes
10 mℓ (2 t) cornflour	2 teaspoons cornstarch
250 mℓ (1 C) chicken stock	1 cup chicken stock
2 mℓ (½ t) finely grated fresh ginger	½ teaspoon finely grated ginger-root
3 cloves garlic, crushed	3 cloves garlic, crushed
10 mℓ (2 t) sugar	2 teaspoons sugar

* *Snow peas are tender young peas in the pod*

METHOD Combine sauce ingredients in a small bowl and set aside.

Stir-fry all vegetables with oil in wok for 1–2 minutes. Remove and set aside. Add prawns (shrimp) to wok and cook for a few minutes, or until pink and tender.

Add vegetables and sauce ingredients. Cook until thickened. Serve with Chinese Fried Rice (recipe on p 86).

Serves 4

Spaghetti with White Clam Sauce

METRIC	AMERICAN
500 g spaghetti	1 lb spaghetti
125 g butter (for spaghetti)	½ cup butter (for spaghetti)
SAUCE	**SAUCE**
1 onion, chopped	1 onion, chopped
4 cloves garlic, crushed	4 cloves garlic, crushed
125 g butter or 60 mℓ (4 T) olive oil	½ cup butter or 4 tablespoons olive oil
250 g frozen clam meat*	½ lb frozen clam meat*
15 mℓ (1 T) chopped parsley	1 tablespoon chopped parsley
250 mℓ (1 C) chicken stock	1 cup chicken stock
Pinch of salt	Pinch of salt
Freshly ground black pepper to taste	Freshly ground black pepper to taste
2 mℓ (½ t) dried origanum	½ teaspoon dried oregano
2 mℓ (½ t) dried thyme	½ teaspoon dried thyme
15 mℓ (1 T) cornflour	1 tablespoon cornstarch

* *If frozen clam meat is not available, use tinned (canned) clam meat together with juices*

METHOD Boil spaghetti in salted water for 20–25 minutes, while making clam sauce.

SAUCE Sauté onion and garlic in butter or olive oil. Add clams and cook for 5 minutes. If clams are frozen, cook until done. Add chopped parsley, chicken stock, seasonings and herbs.

Mix cornflour (cornstarch) to a paste with cold water. Stir into sauce and cook until thickened.

TO SERVE Drain cooked spaghetti well and toss with butter. Pour clam sauce over spaghetti, toss lightly and serve immediately.

Serves 4 to 6

Poultry

Apricot Chicken *56*
Honey-glazed Chicken *56*
Chicken Breasts Normandy *56*
Hungarian Chicken Paprikash *57*
Teriyaki Chicken *57*
Chicken with Zucchini (Courgettes) & Tarragon *57*
Chicken Parisienne *58*
Marinade for Barbecued or Oven-roasted Chicken *58*
Chinese Stir-fried Chicken *58*
Tandoori Chicken *59*
Peri-Peri Chicken with Pineapple *59*
Smoked Turkey *59*
Duck with Figs *60*
Duck Montmorency *60*
Duck à l'Orange *61*
Duck in Clay *61*

Apricot Chicken

METRIC	AMERICAN
2 chickens	2 frying chickens
5 mℓ (1 t) salt	1 teaspoon salt
5 mℓ (1 t) pepper	1 teaspoon pepper
5 mℓ (1 t) crushed garlic powder	1 teaspoon garlic powder
Flour for coating	Flour for coating
Oil for frying	Oil for frying
1 x 250 mℓ bottle French dressing	1 x 8 fl oz bottle French dressing
1 package onion soup	1 envelope onion soup mix
1 x 450 g tin apricot jam	1 x 12 oz jar apricot preserves
1 x 410 g tin apricots, undrained	1 x 16 oz can apricots, undrained
15 mℓ (1 T) soy sauce	1 tablespoon soy sauce

METHOD Cut chickens into portions and season with salt, pepper and garlic powder. Coat lightly with flour and fry in oil until nicely browned. Place in a single layer in an oven-ware dish.

Combine the French dressing, onion soup, apricot jam (preserves), apricots and soy sauce. Pour this mixture over the chicken and bake covered in 180°C (350°F) oven for ¾–1 hour. Uncover and continue to bake until brown and tender. Serve on rice with almonds.

Serves 8

Honey-glazed Chicken

METRIC	AMERICAN
6 chicken breasts	6 chicken breasts
Salt & pepper	Salt & pepper
80 mℓ (⅓ C) honey	⅓ cup honey
15 mℓ (1 T) Worcestershire sauce	1 tablespoon Worcestershire sauce
30 mℓ (2 T) butter or margarine	2 tablespoons butter or margarine
15 mℓ (1 T) prepared mustard	1 tablespoon prepared mustard
Dash of Tabasco	Dash of Tabasco

METHOD Season chicken breasts with salt and pepper. Heat honey, Worcestershire sauce, butter or margarine, mustard and Tabasco in a small saucepan until the fat has melted. Mix well and brush chicken breasts with some of the mixture.

Arrange chicken breasts skin-side up in a shallow baking dish. Bake uncovered at 190°C–200°C (375°F–400°F) for approximately 45 minutes, or until tender. Five minutes before end of cooking time, pour over the remaining glaze. Serve with rice.

Serves 6

Chicken Breasts Normandy

METRIC	AMERICAN
8 chicken breasts, skinned & deboned	8 chicken breasts, skinned & deboned
Salt & coarsely ground black pepper	Salt & coarsely ground black pepper
30 mℓ (2 T) flour	2 tablespoons flour
Butter or margarine for frying	Butter or margarine for frying
1 onion, finely chopped	1 onion, finely chopped
1 Granny Smith apple, peeled & diced	1 Granny Smith apple, peeled & diced
30 mℓ (2 T) Calvados	2 tablespoons apple brandy
125 mℓ (½ C) apple cider	½ cup apple cider
125 mℓ (½ C) chicken stock	½ cup chicken stock
125 mℓ (½ C) cream	½ cup cream
5 mℓ (1 t) cornflour mixed to a paste with cold water	1 teaspoon cornstarch mixed to a paste with cold water

GARNISH	GARNISH
1 apple, peeled, cored & sliced into rings	1 apple, peeled, cored & sliced into rings
Butter	Butter
Cinnamon or nutmeg	Cinnamon or nutmeg

METHOD Flatten breasts with mallet. Season with salt and pepper; sprinkle with flour. Melt butter or margarine in large frying pan (skillet) and brown breasts. Remove and keep warm.

Sauté onion and apple for 2–3 minutes. Add Calvados / apple brandy, apple cider and chicken stock and bring to the boil.

Return chicken to pan and simmer over gentle heat until chicken is tender. Add cornflour (cornstarch), then stir in cream. Adjust seasoning.

GARNISH Sauté apple rings in butter, sprinkle with cinnamon or nutmeg and use to garnish each breast.

Serves 8

Hungarian Chicken Paprikash

METRIC	AMERICAN
2 chickens, cut into portions	2 chickens, cut into portions
Oil or butter for frying	Oil or butter for frying
2 onions, chopped	2 onions, chopped
1 green pepper, chopped	1 green pepper, chopped
5 mℓ (1 t) salt	1 teaspoon salt
60 mℓ (4 T) paprika	4 tablespoons paprika
30 mℓ (2 T) tomato paste	2 tablespoons tomato paste
1 chicken bouillon cube, crushed	1 chicken bouillon cube, crushed
¾–1 ℓ (3–4 C) boiling water	3–4 cups boiling water
250 mℓ (1 C) sour cream	1 cup sour cream
10 mℓ (2 t) cornflour	2 teaspoons cornstarch

METHOD Brown chicken portions in oil or butter. Remove and set aside. Sauté onion and green pepper for a few minutes. Return chicken and all remaining ingredients, except cream and cornflour (cornstarch), to saucepan and simmer over gentle heat until chicken is tender; or place in a casserole dish and bake in a 180°C (350°F) oven for 45 minutes–1 hour.

Combine cream and cornflour (cornstarch). Stir in and cook until thickened. Serve over pasta.

Serves 8

Teriyaki Chicken

METRIC	AMERICAN
8 chicken breasts, skinned & deboned	8 chicken breasts, skinned & deboned
200 mℓ (¾ C) soy sauce	¾ cup soy sauce
60 mℓ (¼ C) dry sherry	¼ cup dry sherry
60 mℓ (¼ C) lemon juice	¼ cup lemon juice
30 mℓ (2 T) brown sugar	2 tablespoons brown sugar
30 mℓ (2 T) honey	2 tablespoons honey
15 mℓ (1 T) finely grated fresh ginger*	1 tablespoon finely grated fresh ginger-root*
2 large cloves garlic, crushed (or 5 mℓ / 1 t crushed garlic powder)	2 large cloves garlic, crushed (or 1 teaspoon garlic powder)
1 spring onion, diced	1 green onion, diced

GARNISH	GARNISH
Tinned pineapple rings	Canned pineapple rings

*   Alternatively, use 5 mℓ (1 teaspoon) powdered ginger

METHOD Prick chicken breasts all over with a sharp knife. Combine remaining ingredients and marinate for at least 4 hours, but preferably overnight. Grill (broil) until done, about 10 minutes on each side. Be sure not to overcook, as the chicken must be moist and juicy inside.

Decorate each serving with a pineapple ring which has been dipped in the marinade and grilled (broiled).

Serve with rice boiled with a pinch of saffron, then mixed with diced and sautéed onion and green pepper, 2 slices pineapple, diced and 30 mℓ (2 tablespoons) pine nuts.

CHEF'S TIP This chicken is ideally suited to a braai or barbecue, particularly as it may be prepared well in advance. You can also freeze the marinated chicken and cook it at a later stage.

Serves 6 to 8

Chicken with Zucchini (Courgettes) & Tarragon

METRIC	AMERICAN
2 chickens, cut into portions	2 chickens, cut into portions
5 mℓ (1 t) each salt, pepper & crushed garlic powder	1 teaspoon each salt, pepper & garlic powder
Dash of cayenne pepper	Dash of cayenne pepper
2 mℓ (½ t) paprika	½ teaspoon paprika
2 large onions, coarsely diced	2 large onions, coarsely diced
1 large green pepper, coarsely diced	1 large green pepper, coarsely diced
2–3 tomatoes, coarsely diced	2–3 tomatoes, coarsely diced
3 large courgettes (baby marrows), sliced	3 large zucchini, sliced
500 g fresh mushrooms, sliced	1 lb fresh mushrooms, sliced
2 carrots, sliced	2 carrots, sliced
1 chicken bouillon cube	1 chicken bouillon cube
250 mℓ (1 C) water	1 cup water
15 mℓ (1 T) dried tarragon	1 tablespoon dried tarragon
5–6 potatoes, peeled & halved	5–6 potatoes, peeled & halved

METHOD Season chicken with salt, pepper and spices. Combine all the vegetables except potatoes and place half the mixed vegetables in a roasting pan or large ovenware dish. Place the chicken on top and cover with remaining vegetable mixture.

Crush the chicken bouillon cube and sprinkle over the top. Pour over water and sprinkle with tarragon. Cover and bake at 180°C (350°F) for 45 minutes.

Uncover and add potatoes, placing them on top of the chicken. Turn oven temperature up to 200°C (400°F) and bake for another 30–45 minutes.

Serves 8

Chicken Parisienne

METRIC	AMERICAN
8 chicken breasts, skinned & deboned	8 chicken breasts, skinned & deboned
Salt & black pepper	Salt & black pepper
Seasoning salt	Seasoned salt
Crushed garlic powder	Garlic powder
Oil or butter for frying	Oil or butter for frying
250 g mushrooms, sliced	½ lb mushrooms, sliced
125 mℓ (½ C) white wine	½ cup white wine
125 mℓ (½ C) chicken stock	½ cup chicken stock
Pinch of dried tarragon	Pinch of dried tarragon
15 mℓ (1 T) cornflour	1 tablespoon cornstarch
30 mℓ (2 T) cold milk	2 tablespoons cold milk
125 mℓ (½ C) cream	½ cup cream

GARNISH	GARNISH
Freshly chopped parsley	Freshly chopped parsley

METHOD Season chicken breasts, then brown in oil or butter in large frying pan (skillet). Remove chicken and set aside. Add mushrooms to pan and cook for 3 minutes. Add wine, chicken stock and tarragon and bring to the boil.

Return chicken to pan and allow to simmer gently until tender. Combine cornflour (cornstarch) and milk. Add to chicken and cook over gentle heat until thickened. Stir in cream and heat thoroughly.

Serve on a bed of rice and garnish with freshly chopped parsley.

Serves 8

Marinade for Barbecued or Oven-roasted Chicken

METRIC	AMERICAN
100 g (½ C) brown sugar	½ cup brown sugar
125 mℓ (½ C) vinegar	½ cup vinegar
125 mℓ (½ C) tomato sauce	½ cup ketchup
3 cloves garlic, crushed	3 cloves garlic, crushed
125 mℓ (½ C) soy sauce	½ cup soy sauce
5 mℓ (1 t) Tabasco	1 teaspoon Tabasco
15 mℓ (1 T) Worcestershire sauce	1 tablespoon Worcestershire sauce
1 onion, grated	1 onion, grated
5 mℓ (1 t) paprika	1 teaspoon paprika
Salt & pepper	Salt & pepper

METHOD Combine all the ingredients. Allow to simmer for 10–15 minutes. Cool before using. Marinate chickens overnight, then barbecue or oven roast.

Makes enough to marinate 2 chickens

Chinese Stir-fried Chicken

METRIC	AMERICAN
4 chicken breasts, skinned, deboned & cubed	4 chicken breasts, skinned, deboned & cubed
30 mℓ (2 T) soy sauce	2 tablespoons soy sauce
15 mℓ (1 T) sherry	1 tablespoon sherry
15 mℓ (1 T) sesame oil*	1 tablespoon sesame oil
Peanut oil for frying*	Peanut oil for frying
1 large onion, sliced lengthwise	1 large onion, sliced lengthwise
1 green pepper, sliced in strips	1 green pepper, sliced in strips
2 sticks celery, sliced diagonally	2 sticks celery, sliced diagonally
2 carrots, sliced in julienne strips	2 carrots, sliced in julienne strips
1 x 227 g tin water chestnuts, drained & sliced	1 x 8 oz can water chestnuts, drained & sliced
½ head Chinese cabbage, shredded (optional)	½ head Chinese cabbage, shredded (optional)
250 mℓ (1 C) bean sprouts, fresh or canned**	1 cup bean sprouts, fresh or canned**
Broccoli flowerets	Broccoli flowerets

THICKENING SAUCE	THICKENING SAUCE
30 mℓ (2 T) soy sauce	2 tablespoons soy sauce
10 mℓ (2 t) cornflour	2 teaspoons cornstarch
250 mℓ (1 C) chicken stock, cooled	1 cup chicken stock, cooled

* If unavailable, use sunflower oil
** Bamboo shoots may be substituted

METHOD Prepare chicken and set aside. Combine soy sauce, sherry and sesame oil and marinate chicken in this mixture for at least 1 hour. Drain.

While the chicken is marinating, combine ingredients for thickening sauce. Set aside until required.

Heat peanut oil in wok and brown chicken, then remove from wok and set aside. Add more oil to the wok and stir-fry onion, green pepper, celery and carrots for 2–3 minutes. Add the water chestnuts, cabbage, bean sprouts and broccoli; stir-fry for another 2–3 minutes.

Return chicken to wok with thickening sauce. Cook until thickened. Serve with Chinese Fried Rice (recipe on p 86).

Serves 8

Tandoori Chicken

METRIC	AMERICAN
2 spring chickens*	2 spring chickens*
200 mℓ (¾ C) yoghurt	¾ cup yoghurt
10 mℓ (2 t) salt	2 teaspoons salt
5 mℓ (1 t) crushed garlic powder	1 teaspoon garlic powder
7 mℓ (1½ t) cumin	1½ teaspoons cumin
Juice of 1 large lemon	Juice of 1 large lemon
4 cloves garlic, crushed	4 cloves garlic, crushed
2 mℓ (½ t) cayenne pepper	½ teaspoon cayenne pepper
5 mℓ (1 t) freshly grated ginger or ground ginger	1 teaspoon freshly grated ginger-root or ground ginger
10 mℓ (2 t) ground coriander	2 teaspoons ground coriander
15 mℓ (1 T) paprika	1 tablespoon paprika

* Traditionally, the chicken is skinned and then basted with clarified butter. I prefer it cooked with the skin, in its own fat

METHOD Split chickens down the back. Combine remaining ingredients to make a marinade. Marinate chickens in the mixture for at least 1 hour, or overnight. Pour off marinade and reserve.

Place on a rack in a roasting pan on the bottom shelf of a 200°C (400°F) oven and roast for 1¼–1½ hours, turning and basting frequently with the remaining marinade. Serve with curried rice mixed with nuts and raisins (recipe on p 86).

CHEF'S TIP Tandoori Chicken is particularly good cooked in a rotisserie, over an open fire, or on a barbecue.

Serves 8

Peri-Peri Chicken with Pineapple

METRIC	AMERICAN
2 chickens, cut into portions	2 chickens, cut into portions
5 mℓ (1 t) peri-peri powder	1 teaspoon crushed red pepper flakes
Juice of ½ lemon	Juice of ½ lemon
10 mℓ (2 t) salt	2 teaspoons salt
15 mℓ (1 T) oil	1 tablespoon oil
4 cloves garlic, crushed	4 cloves garlic, crushed
Flour	Flour
Oil for frying	Oil for frying
1 fresh pineapple, halved	1 fresh pineapple, halved
1 x 470 g tin pineapple chunks, with juice	1 x 20 oz can pineapple chunks, with juice

METHOD Make a paste with the peri-peri powder (red pepper flakes), lemon juice, salt, oil and garlic. Rub well into the chicken, including the area underneath the breast skin. Leave to stand for at least 1 hour, to allow spices to permeate the meat.

Sprinkle with flour and brown in frying pan in a little oil. Transfer to a casserole dish and arrange in a single layer.

Scoop flesh out of the fresh pineapple, reserving the shells. Combine fresh and tinned pineapple and juice. Pour over the chicken.

Bake covered in a 180°C (350°F) oven for 35 minutes. Uncover and bake for a further 15–20 minutes.

Accompany with rice served in pineapple shells. Spoon pineapple sauce from the chicken over the rice.

Serves 8

Smoked Turkey

METRIC	AMERICAN
1 x 4–5 kg turkey	1 x 10–12 lb turkey
Water to cover turkey	Water to cover turkey

BRINE	BRINE
375 mℓ (1½ C) pickling salt	1½ cups pickling salt
200 g (1 C) sugar	1 cup sugar
6 whole cloves	6 whole cloves
10 mℓ (2 t) coarsely ground black pepper	2 teaspoons coarsely ground black pepper
4 bay leaves, crumbled	4 bay leaves, crumbled
15 mℓ (3 t) saltpeter	3 teaspoons saltpeter
3 cloves garlic, crushed	3 cloves garlic, crushed
10 mℓ (2 t) ground coriander	2 teaspoons ground coriander

METHOD Place turkey in large earthenware dish. Cover with water, then remove turkey and stir all remaining ingredients into the water. Return turkey to brine mixture and leave in refrigerator for 2–3 days, turning occasionally.

Smoke in smoke pot overnight.

Serves 20

Duck with Figs

METRIC	AMERICAN
2 ducks	2 ducks
Salt & pepper	Salt & pepper
5 mℓ (1 t) ground ginger	1 teaspoon ground ginger
Crushed garlic powder	Garlic powder
2 onions, whole	2 onions, whole
1 x 410 g tin figs (reserve juice)	1 x 15½ oz can figs (reserve juice)

SAUCE	SAUCE
500 mℓ (2 C) water	2 cups water
7 mℓ (1½ t) gravy powder	1½ teaspoons gravy mix or browner
30 mℓ (2 T) cornflour	2 tablespoons cornstarch
1 chicken bouillon cube, crushed	1 chicken bouillon cube, crushed
45 mℓ (3 T) tomato sauce	3 tablespoons tomato ketchup
30 mℓ (2 T) soy sauce	2 tablespoons soy sauce
45 mℓ (3 T) sugar	3 tablespoons sugar
250 mℓ (1 C) orange juice	1 cup orange juice
Juice from figs	Juice from figs
30 mℓ (2 T) brandy	2 tablespoons brandy
30 mℓ (2 T) berry liqueur	2 tablespoons berry liqueur

METHOD Season ducks with salt, pepper, ginger and garlic powder and place 1 whole onion in each cavity. Place on roasting rack and roast in a 200°C (400°F) oven for 1–1¼ hours, until golden brown.

Cool and cut into serving portions, then arrange in a casserole dish. Pour fat out of roasting pan and make sauce as follows.

SAUCE Pour water into pan. Dissolve gravy powder and cornflour (cornstarch) in cold water and add to pan with chicken cube, tomato sauce (tomato ketchup), soy sauce, sugar, orange juice, juice from figs, brandy and berry liqueur. Stir until mixture boils. Strain and pour a portion of the sauce over ducks.

Bake uncovered in a slow oven (150°C / 300°F) for ¾ hour, basting occasionally and turning ducks if necessary. Add figs 5–10 minutes before serving. Serve remaining heated sauce on the side.

CHEF'S TIP This dish may be prepared in the morning and left to marinate until ready to bake.

Serves 8   PHOTOGRAPH ON PAGE 62

Duck Montmorency

METRIC	AMERICAN
2 ducks	2 ducks
Salt & pepper	Salt & pepper
Ground ginger	Ground ginger
Crushed garlic powder	Garlic powder
2 whole onions	2 whole onions
1 x 410 g tin red or black cherries (reserve syrup)	1 x 15½ oz can red or black cherries (reserve syrup)

SAUCE	SAUCE
500 mℓ (2 C) water	2 cups water
5 mℓ (1 t) gravy powder	1 teaspoon gravy mix or browner
10 mℓ (2 t) cornflour	2 teaspoons cornstarch
½ chicken bouillon cube, crushed	½ chicken bouillon cube, crushed
45 mℓ (3 T) tomato sauce	3 tablespoons tomato ketchup
15 mℓ (1 T) soy sauce	1 tablespoon soy sauce
Syrup from cherries	Syrup from cherries
Juice of 1 or 2 oranges	Juice of 1 or 2 oranges
30–45 mℓ (2–3 T) sugar	2–3 tablespoons sugar
Salt & pepper to taste	Salt & pepper to taste
30 mℓ (2 T) Kirsch	2 tablespoons Kirsch
30 mℓ (2 T) brandy	2 tablespoons brandy

METHOD Season ducks with salt, pepper, ginger and garlic powder and place 1 whole onion in each cavity. Place on roasting rack over roasting pan and bake on the bottom shelf of a 200°C (400°F) oven, until golden brown (about 1 hour), turning over once half-way through the cooking time.

Remove from oven; when cool enough, cut into portions and arrange in a single layer in a casserole dish. Pour the fat from the duck out of the pan and make the sauce as follows.

SAUCE Pour water into the roasting pan. Dissolve gravy powder and cornflour (cornstarch) in cold water and add to pan with crushed chicken cube, tomato sauce (tomato ketchup), soy sauce, syrup from cherries, orange juice, sugar, salt and pepper to taste, Kirsch and brandy.

Stir constantly until mixture boils, scraping the bottom of the pan as you do so. Taste and adjust seasonings or add sugar if necessary.

Strain sauce and pour over the duck portions. Bake, uncovered, in a slow oven (150°C / 300°F) for ¾–1 hour, basting occasionally and turning the portions.

Remove from oven, arrange cherries on top and return to oven for a further 10 minutes, to heat the fruit.

CHEF'S TIP This dish may be prepared in the morning and baked just before required.

Serves 8

Duck à l'Orange

METRIC	AMERICAN
2 ducks	2 ducks
Salt & black pepper	Salt & black pepper
Crushed garlic powder	Garlic powder
Ground ginger	Ground ginger
Seasoning salt	Seasoned salt

SAUCE	SAUCE
750 ml (3 C) chicken stock*	3 cups chicken stock*
15 ml (1 T) tomato sauce	1 tablespoon tomato ketchup
5 ml (1 t) salt	1 teaspoon salt
Dash of pepper	Dash of pepper
15 ml (1 T) cornflour	1 tablespoon cornstarch
5 ml (1 t) gravy powder	1 teaspoon gravy mix or browner
60 ml (4 T) brown sugar	4 tablespoons brown sugar
15 ml (1 T) soy sauce	1 tablespoon soy sauce
250 ml (1 C) orange juice	1 cup orange juice
125 ml (½ C) Curaçao or Van der Hum	½ cup Grand Marnier or Triple Sec
15 ml (1 T) brandy	1 tablespoon brandy
6 oranges, peeled & sliced	6 oranges, peeled & sliced

* For instant chicken stock, dissolve 1 chicken bouillon cube in boiling water

METHOD Season ducks with salt, pepper and spices. Place on wire rack over a roasting pan, and roast in 180°C (350°F) oven for 1¼–1½ hours, until golden brown. Remove from oven; cool and cut into quarters (or serving portions). Place in a single layer in a large, shallow casserole dish. (Do not overlap pieces.)

SAUCE Pour off fat from roasting pan. Add to drippings in the pan the chicken stock, tomato sauce (ketchup), salt and pepper. Stir in the cornflour (cornstarch) which has been mixed to a smooth paste with a little cold water, then add the gravy powder (gravy mix), brown sugar and soy sauce.

Heat gravy in roasting pan on top of stove, scraping the bottom of the pan and stirring constantly until thickened. Add orange juice, liqueur and brandy. Adjust seasoning to taste.

Strain some of the sauce over the duck portions. Arrange orange slices on top and bake at 180°C (350°F) for approximately 30 minutes or until tender, basting occasionally with sauce. Heat and serve the remaining sauce on the side.

CHEF'S TIP Do not drown the duck with the sauce; you need only pour over enough to cover the bottom of the dish. If necessary, add more at a later stage.

Serves 8

Duck in Clay

METRIC	AMERICAN
1 x 2–2½ kg duck	1 x 4–5 lb duck
5 ml (1 t) salt	1 teaspoon salt
2 ml (½ t) pepper	½ teaspoon pepper
5 ml (1 t) ground ginger	1 teaspoon ground ginger
5 ml (1 t) crushed garlic powder	1 teaspoon garlic powder
30 ml (2 T) honey	2 tablespoons honey
125 ml (½ C) soy sauce	½ cup soy sauce
125 ml (½ C) frozen orange juice	½ cup frozen orange juice

BAKER'S CLAY	BAKER'S CLAY
500 g (4 C) flour	4 cups flour
250 ml (1 C) salt	1 cup salt
325 ml (1⅓ C) water	1⅓ cups water

METHOD Season duck with salt, pepper, ginger and garlic powder. Combine honey, soy sauce and orange juice and marinate duck in this mixture overnight. Place duck on a rack over a roasting pan and roast in 180°C (350°F) oven for 1½ hours.

BAKER'S CLAY Mix flour and salt together in a medium-sized bowl. Add 250 ml (1 cup) water and continue mixing until crumbly. Add the remaining water and knead until smooth and leathery. Take time to mix thoroughly. Add additional water sparingly, only if dough remains very dry.

Place duck on double-thickness foil. Use a small, empty can (such as a frozen orange juice can) or cut off a piece of the cardboard roll used for holding paper towels, and place in neck cavity of duck.

Cover duck with the foil and then wrap in the clay, seam side underneath. Position 2 cherries in clay as eyes. Place on baking tray or cookie sheet and bake in 260°C (500°F) oven for 1 – 2 hours.

Open clay by hitting sharply with a hammer and pull back foil. Serve with sauce made with the drippings in the pan, as for Duck à l'Orange.

Serves 4

Overleaf: Duck with Figs

Meat Dishes

BEEF

Rib Roast with Green Peppercorn Sauce............. 66
Beef en Croûte with Béarnaise Sauce 66
Steak Diane 67
Roast Beef & Yorkshire Pudding with
Horseradish Sauce 67
Roast Beef with Herb Sauce 67
Fillet Chasseur 68
Barbecued Brisket 68
Barbecued Beef Ribs........................... 68
Barbecued Short Ribs 68
Steak on a Stick............................... 69
Marinades for Steak........................... 69
Pickling Solution for Corned Beef or Tongue 69
Glazed Corn Beef.............................. 70
Beef Goulash 70
Braised Beef in Red Wine 70
Beef Stew with Dumplings 71
Curried Meat Pies 71
Fricadelles 72
Cottage Pie 72
Stuffed Cabbage 72
Tostados..................................... 73
Hot 'n Spicy Texas Chili 73
Quick Spaghetti Bolognaise 73

VEAL

Veal Myrna 74
Quick 'n Easy Veal Chops....................... 74
Escalopes à la Crème 74
Veal & Mushroom Casserole 75
Tasty Veal Chops 75
Veal Délicieuse................................ 75
Veal Goulash with Spaetzle 76

LAMB

Simple Madras Curry 76
Roast Rack of Spring Lamb 77
Braised Lamb Chops with Lima Beans 77
Lamp in Mustard Sauce 80
Shashlik..................................... 80
Barbecue Lamb en Croûte 80

Beef

Rib Roast with Green Peppercorn Sauce

METRIC

2 kg prime rib or rib roast
5 mℓ (1 t) salt
5 mℓ (1 t) black pepper
5 mℓ (1 t) crushed garlic powder
5 mℓ (1 t) seasoning salt
2 mℓ (½ t) ground ginger
2 mℓ (½ t) cayenne pepper
2 onions, sliced
Oil for roasting

SAUCE
60 mℓ (¼ C) sherry
15 mℓ (1 T) brandy
250 mℓ (1 C) cream or non-dairy creamer
15 mℓ (1 T) soy sauce
5 mℓ (1 t) cornflour
60 mℓ (¼ C) water
1 x 50 g tin green peppercorns, drained

AMERICAN

4 lb prime rib or rib roast
1 teaspoon salt
1 teaspoon black pepper
1 teaspoon garlic powder
1 teaspoon seasoned salt
½ teaspoon ground ginger
½ teaspoon cayenne pepper
2 onions, sliced
Oil for roasting

SAUCE
¼ cup sherry
1 tablespoon brandy
1 cup cream or non-dairy creamer
1 tablespoon soy sauce
1 level teaspoon cornstarch
¼ cup water
1 x 1¾ oz can green peppercorns, drained

METHOD Place meat on a large piece of foil and season with salt, pepper, garlic powder, seasoning salt, ginger and cayenne pepper. Press onion into the seasonings that remain on the foil and then insert pieces of onion into the meat between the bone and meat, and between the fat and meat. Wrap in foil and refrigerate for a few hours, or preferably overnight.

Place in a roasting pan, pour over 30–45 mℓ (2–3 tablespoons) oil and roast uncovered in a 200°C (400°F) oven for 1¼–1½ hours, or until a fork can be inserted into the meat easily, but some of the juices are still pink. (If the fork does not go in fairly easily, the meat is still very rare.)

SAUCE Combine all sauce ingredients in a small saucepan and cook until thickened, stirring constantly. Serve separately on the side.

Serves 8 to 10   PHOTOGRAPH ON PAGE 78

Beef en Croûte with Béarnaise Sauce

METRIC

1 whole fillet (2–2,5 kg)
Salt & pepper
Crushed garlic powder
Seasoning salt
Ground ginger
125 mℓ (½ C) oil
500 g puff pastry

BÉARNAISE SAUCE
15 mℓ (1 T) chopped spring onion
5 mℓ (1 t) chopped fresh parsley
2 peppercorns, crushed
30 mℓ (2 T) tarragon vinegar
125 mℓ (½ C) dry white wine
4 egg yolks
225 g butter
1 mℓ (¼ t) salt
1 mℓ (¼ t) black pepper
Dash of cayenne pepper

AMERICAN

1 whole tenderloin (4–5 lb)
Salt & pepper
Garlic powder
Seasoned salt
Ground ginger
½ cup oil
1 lb puff pastry

BÉARNAISE SAUCE
1 tablespoon chopped green onion
1 teaspoon chopped fresh parsley
2 peppercorns, crushed
2 tablespoons tarragon vinegar
½ cup dry white wine
4 egg yolks
1 cup butter
¼ teaspoon salt
¼ teaspoon black pepper
Dash of cayenne pepper

METHOD Wipe fillet (tenderloin) and season with salt, pepper, garlic powder, seasoning salt (seasoned salt) and ginger.

Pour oil into a roasting pan and allow to get very hot in 230°C (450°F) oven. Place the meat in the pan and roast for 35 minutes. Turn halfway through roasting period. Remove from oven and allow to cool completely.

Roll out pastry until it is big enough to encase the whole piece of meat. Place meat on top of pastry and enclose completely. Place seam side down on baking sheet. Use left-over scraps of pastry to shape leaves and arrange these along the centre of the pastry.

Place on a baking tray and bake on the centre shelf of a 230°C (450°F) oven, until pastry is golden brown (approximately 35–40 minutes). Serve with Béarnaise Sauce.

BÉARNAISE SAUCE Combine onion, parsley and peppercorns with the vinegar and white wine in a saucepan. Cook until liquid is reduced to about 125mℓ (½ cup).

Beat egg yolks very well, then slowly add the hot liquid to the yolks, beating all the time. Place in a double boiler and beat with a wire whisk, until mixture is light and fluffy.

Remove from heat; add butter gradually, beating all the time, until mixture is thick. Season to taste with salt, black pepper and cayenne pepper.

Serves 8

Steak Diane

METRIC	AMERICAN
1 kg fillet or any other steak	2 lb fillet or any other steak
1 large onion or 45 mℓ (3 T) diced spring onions	1 large onion or 3 tablespoons diced green onions
60 g butter	4 tablespoons butter
250 g fresh mushrooms or 1 x 250 g tin button mushrooms, drained	½ lb fresh mushrooms or 1 x 8 oz can button mushrooms, drained
45 mℓ (3 T) A-1 Sauce	3 tablespoons A-1 Sauce
1 packet mushroom soup mix	1 package dry mushroom soup
125 mℓ (½ C) sherry	½ cup sherry
45 mℓ (3 T) Worcestershire sauce	3 tablespoons Worcestershire sauce
Salt & pepper to taste	Salt & pepper to taste
15 mℓ (1 T) sugar	1 tablespoon sugar
2 cloves garlic, crushed	2 cloves garlic, crushed
Juice of ½ lemon	Juice of ½ lemon
Freshly chopped parsley	Freshly chopped parsley

METHOD Grill (broil), fry or barbecue steaks, as desired. Set aside and keep warm.

Brown onion in butter. Add mushrooms and sauté. Add remaining ingredients, except parsley. Simmer for 5 minutes. Stir in parsley and pour over steak.

CHEF'S TIP The sauce may be prepared in advance and reheated before serving.

Serves 4

Roast Beef & Yorkshire Pudding with Horseradish Sauce

METRIC	AMERICAN
1 fillet or 2–2,5 kg piece of Scotch fillet	1 tenderloin or 4–5 lb New York strip
2–3 cloves garlic, slivered	2–3 cloves garlic, slivered
500 mℓ bottled Italian salad dressing	1 x 16 fl oz bottle Italian salad dressing

HORSERADISH SAUCE	HORSERADISH SAUCE
125 mℓ (½ C) cream or non-dairy cream	½ cup cream or non-dairy cream
2 mℓ (½ t) salt	½ teaspoon salt
2 mℓ (½ t) sugar	½ teaspoon sugar
30 mℓ (2 T) prepared white horseradish	2 tablespoons prepared white horseradish
5 mℓ (1 t) wine vinegar	1 teaspoon wine vinegar

METHOD Cut small slits in the meat and insert the slivers of garlic. Pour the salad dressing over and marinate overnight in the refrigerator.

Drain well, place in a roasting pan with 125 mℓ (½ cup) of the marinade and roast uncovered in a 200°C (400°F) oven for ¾ hour, (for fillet / tenderloin). The Scotch fillet or New York strip must be roasted for 50–60 minutes. Serve with Yorkshire Pudding (recipe on p 85) and Horseradish Sauce.

HORSERADISH SAUCE Whip cream until thick and fold in remaining ingredients.

Serves 8 to 10

Roast Beef with Herb Sauce

METRIC	AMERICAN
2–2,5 kg Scotch fillet	4–5 lb New York strip
10 mℓ (2 t) dry mustard	2 teaspoons dry mustard
3–4 cloves garlic, slivered	3–4 cloves garlic, slivered
7 mℓ (1½ t) salt	1½ teaspoons salt
2 mℓ (½ t) ground ginger	½ teaspoon ground ginger
3,5 mℓ (¾ t) crushed garlic powder	¾ teaspoon garlic powder
2 mℓ (½ t) white pepper	½ teaspoon white pepper
2 mℓ (½ t) seasoning salt	½ teaspoon seasoned salt
125 mℓ (½ C) oil	½ cup oil

SAUCE	SAUCE
500 g black mushrooms, sliced	1 lb black mushrooms, sliced
Butter or oil for sautéing	Butter or oil for sautéing
Salt, black pepper & crushed garlic powder	Salt, black pepper & garlic powder
2 mℓ (½ t) dried mixed herbs	½ teaspoon Italian seasoning
5 mℓ (1 t) flour	1 teaspoon flour
5 mℓ (1 t) dry mustard	1 level teaspoon mustard powder
30 mℓ (2 T) sherry	2 tablespoons sherry
15 mℓ (1 T) brandy	1 tablespoon brandy or cognac
250 mℓ (1 C) sour cream or non-dairy cream	1 cup sour cream or non-dairy cream

METHOD Rub entire surface of meat with mustard. Insert some of the garlic under the fat of the meat and the remainder in slits made in the meat with a sharp knife. Season with salt, ginger, garlic powder, pepper and seasoning salt. Wrap in foil and refrigerate overnight.

Pour over 125 mℓ (½ cup) oil and roast uncovered on bottom shelf of 200°C (400°F) oven, for 1¼ hours.

SAUCE Sauté mushrooms in butter or oil until soft. Add salt, black pepper, garlic powder and mixed herbs (Italian seasoning). Blend flour and mustard with sherry and brandy and add to mushrooms. Cook until thickened. Add cream, heat through and serve separately with the roast beef.

CHEF'S TIP The sauce may be made in advance and reheated gently before serving.

Serves 8 to 10

Fillet Chasseur

METRIC	AMERICAN
4 thick slices fillet	4 thick slices tenderloin
Salt & pepper	Salt & pepper

SAUCE	SAUCE
2 onions, chopped	2 onions, chopped
2 cloves garlic, crushed	2 cloves garlic, crushed
30 mℓ (2 T) oil	2 tablespoons oil
15 mℓ (1 T) flour	1 tablespoon flour
½ chicken bouillon cube, crushed	½ chicken bouillon cube, crushed
375 mℓ (1½ C) water	1½ cups water
125 mℓ (½ C) white wine	½ cup white wine
15 mℓ (1 T) tomato purée	1 tablespoon tomato purée
1 x 225 g tin sliced mushrooms, drained	1 x 8 oz can sliced mushrooms, drained
Salt & pepper to taste	Salt & pepper to taste
Dried origanum to taste	Dried oregano to taste
5 mℓ (1 t) gravy powder	1 teaspoon gravy mix
5 mℓ (1 t) cornflour	1 teaspoon cornstarch

METHOD Season steaks with salt and pepper. Grill (broil) or fry in a hot pan with a small amount of oil until cooked to your satisfaction. Pour over heated sauce (which may be made ahead of time) and serve.

SAUCE Sauté onion and garlic in oil until lightly browned. Stir in flour. Add crushed chicken bouillon cube, water, wine and tomato purée, stirring constantly. Add mushrooms, salt, pepper and origanum (oregano).

Mix gravy powder and cornflour (cornstarch) to a paste with cold water. Stir in and cook until thickened.

Serves 4

Barbecued Brisket

METRIC	AMERICAN
2–2,5 kg fresh brisket	4–5 lb fresh brisket
Salt & pepper	Salt & pepper
Crushed garlic powder	Garlic powder
Paprika	Paprika
500 mℓ (2 C) tomato sauce	2 cups tomato ketchup
250 mℓ (1 C) water	1 cup water
100 g (½ C) brown sugar	½ cup brown sugar
30 mℓ (2 T) Worcestershire sauce	2 tablespoons Worcestershire sauce
Few drops Tabasco	Few drops Tabasco
2 whole onions	2 whole onions

METHOD Place meat in roasting pan. Season with salt, pepper, garlic powder and paprika. Brown in a 230°C (450°F) oven for approximately 30–45 minutes.

Combine tomato sauce (tomato ketchup), water, sugar, Worcestershire sauce and Tabasco. Pour over meat and add onions. Cover and return to 160°C (325°F) oven for 2 hours or until tender.

Remove meat from gravy; cool and slice. Spoon fat off gravy and return meat to pan. Heat and serve.

Serves 8

Barbecued Beef Ribs

METRIC	AMERICAN
1,5 kg beef ribs	3 lb beef ribs
45 mℓ (3 T) brown sugar	3 tablespoons brown sugar
7 mℓ (1½ t) salt	1½ teaspoons salt
1 x 440 g tin brown or red beans	1 x 16 oz can brown or red beans
60 mℓ (4 T) honey or apricot jam	4 tablespoons honey or apricot preserves
125 mℓ (½ C) tomato sauce	½ cup tomato ketchup
15 mℓ (1 T) brandy	1 tablespoon brandy
15 mℓ (1 T) Worcestershire sauce	1 tablespoon Worcestershire sauce

METHOD Combine brown sugar and salt and rub into meat. Combine remaining ingredients, pour over the ribs and allow to marinate for 5 hours.

Roast covered at 180°C (350°F) for 2 hours, or until tender. Uncover and roast for a further 30 minutes.

Serves 4

Barbecued Short Ribs

METRIC	AMERICAN
2 kg beef short ribs	4 lb beef short ribs
10 mℓ (2 t) salt	2 teaspoons salt
1 large onion, diced	1 large onion, diced
200 g (1 C) brown sugar	1 cup brown sugar
30 mℓ (2 T) prepared mustard	2 tablespoons prepared mustard
2 cloves garlic, crushed	2 cloves garlic, crushed
1 x 300 g tin tomato purée	1 x 10 oz can tomato purée
500 mℓ (2 C) tomato sauce	2 cups tomato sauce
200 mℓ (¾ C) vinegar	¾ cup vinegar
30 mℓ (2 T) Worcestershire sauce	2 tablespoons Worcestershire sauce

METHOD Brown ribs under griller (broiler). Pour off the fat. Combine all remaining ingredients and add to meat. Cover and bake at 180°C (350°F) for 2 hours.

Uncover and bake for a further 30–40 minutes, basting often, until browned and glazed.

Serves 8

Steak on a Stick

METRIC	AMERICAN
1 kg steak, cubed	2 lb steak, cubed
125 mℓ (½ C) soy sauce	½ cup soy sauce
60 mℓ (¼ C) oil	¼ cup oil
Juice of ½ lemon	Juice of ½ lemon
2 spring onions, diced	2 green onions, diced
2 cloves garlic, crushed or	2 cloves garlic, crushed or
5 mℓ (1 t) garlic powder	1 teaspoon garlic powder
5 mℓ (1 t) coarsely ground black	1 teaspoon coarsely ground
pepper	black pepper
2 mℓ (½ t) ground ginger	½ teaspoon ground ginger
15 mℓ (1 T) brown sugar	1 tablespoon brown sugar
Cherry tomatoes, baby onions,	Cherry tomatoes, baby onions,
green pepper squares &	green pepper squares &
button mushrooms	button mushrooms

METHOD Combine soy sauce, oil, lemon juice, spring onion (green onion), garlic or garlic powder, black pepper, ginger and sugar. Marinate steak in this mixture for several hours, preferably overnight.

Thread marinated steak cubes onto skewers, alternating with tomatoes, onions, green pepper and mushrooms. Grill (broil) or barbecue.

Makes sufficient for 8 skewers

Marinades for Steak

Barbecue Marinade

METRIC	AMERICAN
30 mℓ (2 T) oil	2 tablespoons oil
2 onions, diced	2 onions, diced
250 mℓ (1 C) tomato sauce	1 cup tomato ketchup
125 mℓ (½ C) Worcestershire	½ cup Worcestershire sauce
sauce	½ cup brown sugar
100 g (½ C) brown sugar	½ teaspoon garlic powder
2 mℓ (½ t) crushed garlic	1–2 cups water
powder	1 cup prepared barbecue sauce
250–500 mℓ (1–2 C) water	1 tablespoon prepared mustard
250 mℓ (1 C) prepared barbecue	½–1 teaspoon salt
sauce	1 chicken bouillon cube, crushed
15 mℓ (1 T) prepared mustard	
2–5 mℓ (½–1 t) salt	
1 chicken bouillon cube, crushed	

METHOD Heat oil in a medium-sized saucepan and fry onions until golden. Add remaining ingredients and simmer for approximately 5 minutes. Cool. Prick steaks well on both sides, pour marinade over and refrigerate for 1–2 days, turning occasionally.

Remove from marinade; grill or barbecue for approximately

7–10 minutes on each side. To serve steak, slice diagonally into thin slices. The remaining marinade may be heated separately and served as a sauce.

Makes sufficent for 2 kg (4 lb) rump (flank) or fillet steak

Oriental Marinade

METRIC	AMERICAN
200 mℓ (¾ C) soy sauce	¾ cup soy sauce
125 mℓ (½ C) oil	½ cup oil
Juice of ½ lemon	Juice of ½ lemon
4 spring onions, diced	4 green onions, diced
2 cloves garlic, crushed or	2 cloves garlic, crushed or
5 mℓ (1 t) garlic powder	1 teaspoon garlic powder
2 mℓ (½ t) grated fresh ginger	½ teaspoon grated ginger-root
or ground ginger	or ground ginger
2 mℓ (½ t) salt	½ teaspoon salt
2 mℓ (½ t) black pepper	½ teaspoon black pepper

METHOD Combine all ingredients. Prick steaks well on both sides and pour marinade over. Refrigerate for 1–2 days, turning occasionally. Remove from marinade, grill or barbecue as above and serve.

Makes sufficient for 2 kg (4 lb) rump (flank) or fillet steak

Pickling Solution for Corned Beef or Tongue

METRIC	AMERICAN
250 mℓ (1 C) coarse salt	1 cup coarse salt
250 mℓ (1 C) water	1 cup water
15 mℓ (1 T) brown sugar	1 tablespoon brown sugar
10 mℓ (2 t) saltpeter	2 teaspoons saltpeter
5 mℓ (1 t) dry mustard	1 teaspoon dry mustard
15 mℓ (1 T) pickling spices	1 tablespoon pickling spices
3–4 cloves garlic, crushed	3–4 cloves garlic, crushed
Few bay leaves & peppercorns	Few bay leaves & peppercorns

METHOD Place meat in an earthenware dish (not metal). Combine all other ingredients and pour mixture over meat.

Cover meat with a plate and weigh down with a brick or any heavy object. Allow to pickle for 7–10 days in the refrigerator, turning every third day.

Makes sufficient to pickle 2–3 kg (4–6 lb) fresh brisket or tongue

Glazed Corned Beef

METRIC	AMERICAN
1,5 kg pickled beef	3 lb corned beef
1 onion	1 onion
1 carrot	1 carrot
1 stick celery	1 stick celery
2 cloves garlic	2 cloves garlic
Whole cloves	Whole cloves

GLAZE	GLAZE
250 ml (1 C) orange juice	1 cup orange juice
30 ml (2 T) Dijon mustard	2 tablespoons Dijon mustard
30 ml (2 T) prepared mustard	2 tablespoons prepared mustard
30 ml (2 T) mustard powder	2 tablespoons mustard powder
45 ml (3 T) brown sugar	3 tablespoons brown sugar
1 x 475 g tin pineapple rings	1 x 20 oz can pineapple rings
Maraschino cherries	Maraschino cherries

METHOD Place beef in a large pot with onion, carrot, celery and garlic. Cover with boiling water. Bring to the boil again, then lower heat. Cover and cook until tender but firm (approximately 2–3 hours). Do not allow to become too soft, as it will fall apart when you slice it.

Place cooked meat in a baking pan, fat side up. Score the fat in squares with the point of a very sharp knife. Stud with whole cloves.

GLAZE Combine orange juice, prepared mustards, mustard powder and sugar. Pour over the meat. Form a design with pineapple rings and cherries, using toothpicks to secure. Bake in 200°C (400°F) oven for 30 minutes, or until nicely browned.

Serves 6 to 8

Beef Goulash

METRIC	AMERICAN
1–1,5 kg cubed topside	2–3 lb cubed top round
Salt & pepper	Salt & pepper
Crushed garlic powder	Garlic powder
Oil or butter for frying	Oil or butter for frying
2 onions, chopped	2 onions, chopped
250 g mushrooms, sliced	½ lb mushrooms, sliced
1 x 250 g tin tomato purée	1 x 8 oz can tomato sauce
½ chicken bouillon cube, crushed	½ chicken bouillon cube, crushed
30–45 ml (2–3 T) Worcestershire sauce	2–3 tablespoons Worcestershire sauce
5 ml (1 t) paprika	1 teaspoon paprika
5 ml (1 t) mixed herbs	1 teaspoon Italian seasoning
125 ml (½ C) sour cream	½ cup sour cream

METHOD Season meat with salt, pepper and garlic powder

and brown in a large pot in hot oil. Remove and set aside. Add onions to pot and sauté for a few minutes, then add mushrooms and cook for a few minutes longer.

Return meat to pot with tomato purée (sauce), bouillon cube, Worcestershire sauce, paprika and mixed herbs (Italian seasoning). Simmer (covered) over gentle heat for 1½–2 hours or until tender.

Stir in cream. Heat thoroughly and serve on noodles.

CHEF'S TIP If the sauce becomes too thick, add a dash of red wine or water.

Serves 8

Braised Beef in Red Wine

METRIC	AMERICAN
1,5–2 kg piece aitchbone	3–4 lb piece top round, blade or rump roast
5 ml (1 t) dry mustard	1 teaspoon dry mustard
5 ml (1 t) paprika	1 teaspoon paprika
5 ml (1 t) salt	1 teaspoon salt
5 ml (1 t) crushed garlic powder	1 teaspoon garlic powder
2 onions, chopped	2 onions, chopped
2 cloves garlic, crushed	2 cloves garlic, crushed
Oil for browning	Oil for browning
1 package minestrone soup mix or vegetable soup mix	1 envelope minestrone soup mix or vegetable soup mix
125 ml (½ C) red wine	½ cup red wine
125 ml (½ C) water	½ cup water
2 sticks celery, diced	2 sticks celery, diced
2 carrots, diced	2 carrots, diced
1 leek, sliced	1 leek, sliced
250 ml (1 C) sour cream or non-dairy cream	1 cup sour cream or non-dairy cream

METHOD Wash and dry meat. Mix together the mustard, paprika, salt and garlic powder; rub well into the meat. Brown the onions and garlic lightly in oil. Remove and brown meat.

Return onions and garlic to the saucepan with the meat. Add remaining ingredients, except cream. Cover and simmer slowly until tender (approximately 3–4 hours). Before serving, stir in the cream.

Serves 8

Beef Stew with Dumplings

METRIC	AMERICAN
1–1,5 kg cubed stewing beef	2–3 lb cubed stewing beef
60 mℓ (¼ C) oil	4 tablespoons oil
2 onions, diced	2 onions, diced
1 stick celery, diced	1 stick celery, diced
2 carrots, peeled & diced	2 carrots, peeled & diced
2 tomatoes, skinned & diced	2 tomatoes, skinned & diced
250 g frozen peas	½ lb frozen peas
1 x 410 g tin butter beans (optional)	1 x 15½ oz can butter beans (optional)
5–10 mℓ (1–2 t) salt	1–2 teaspoons salt
5 mℓ (1 t) black pepper	1 teaspoon black pepper
2 mℓ (½ t) ground ginger	½ teaspoon ground ginger
2 mℓ (½ t) seasoning salt	½ teaspoon seasoned salt
2 mℓ (½ t) crushed garlic powder	½ teaspoon garlic powder
1 beef or chicken bouillon cube, crushed	1 beef or chicken bouillon cube, crushed
500–750 mℓ (2–3 C) water	2–3 cups water

DUMPLINGS	DUMPLINGS
180 g (1½ C) flour	1½ cups all purpose flour
5 mℓ (1 t) sugar	1 teaspoon sugar
2 mℓ (½ t) ground cinnamon	½ teaspoon ground cinnamon
5 mℓ (1 t) salt	1 teaspoon salt
Pinch of pepper	Pinch of pepper
30 mℓ (2 T) chicken or vegetable fat	2 tablespoons chicken or vegetable fat
15 mℓ (1 T) grated onion	1 tablespoon grated onion
1 egg	1 egg
60 mℓ (¼ C) water	¼ cup water

METHOD Heat oil in large saucepan. Add beef (half at a time) and brown. Remove and set aside. Sauté onions. Return meat to the pot with the vegetables, seasonings, spices and water.

Cover and cook over low heat for 1 hour, adding more water if necessary. Add dumplings and continue to cook covered for another 20–30 minutes.

DUMPLINGS Combine dry ingredients and rub in fat. Add grated onion, then add beaten egg with water and mix to form a soft dough. Drop by tablespoonfuls into stew.

CHEF'S TIP The dumplings may also be boiled separately in a pot of boiling, salted water.

Serves 8

Curried Meat Pies

METRIC	AMERICAN
1 kg puff pastry*	2 lb puff pastry*

FILLING	FILLING
125 mℓ (½ C) oil	½ cup oil
1,5 kg cubed stewing beef or left-over beef roast	3 lb cubed stewing beef or left-over beef roast
2 onions, diced	2 onions, diced
2 carrots, diced	2 carrots, diced
2 sticks celery, diced	2 sticks celery, diced
1 large potato, cubed	1 large potato, cubed
250 mℓ (1 C) frozen peas	1 cup frozen peas
375 mℓ (1½ C) water	1½ cups water
1 chicken or beef bouillon cube	1 chicken or beef bouillon cube
5 mℓ (1 t) salt	1 teaspoon salt
2 mℓ (½ t) pepper	½ teaspoon pepper
2 mℓ (½ t) crushed garlic powder	½ teaspoon garlic powder
45 mℓ (3 T) apricot jam	3 tablespoons apricot preserves
15 mℓ (1 T) vinegar	1 tablespoon vinegar
30 mℓ (2 T) curry powder	2 tablespoons curry powder
15 mℓ (1 T) cornflour	1 tablespoon cornstarch

* Use ready-made pastry or see recipe on p 20

METHOD Heat oil in large pot. Brown meat and set aside (if using left-over cooked beef this is not necessary). Adding more oil if required, lightly brown the onion, carrot and celery.

Return meat to pot with potato, peas, water and remaining ingredients, except curry powder and cornflour (cornstarch). Cover and allow to cook over low heat until meat is tender (about 1 hour).

Mix curry powder and cornflour (cornstarch) to a paste with water and stir in. Cook until thickened. Allow to cool completely before using.

Roll out pastry and cut into squares or rounds about 15 cm (6 inches) in diameter. Place a spoonful of filling in the centre of each one. Gather the edges up over the filling, press together and twist into a 'knot'. Brush with beaten egg and bake in a 200°C (400°F) oven until golden brown (about 30–35 minutes).

CHEF'S TIPS If you wish, drain off some of the gravy and heat separately, then spoon over pies before serving.

These pies freeze well (unbaked). Wrap individually, freeze and bake as required.

Makes 16 pies

Fricadelles

METRIC	AMERICAN
1 kg beef mince	2 lb ground beef
1 bread roll or 30 mℓ (2 T) matzo meal	1 bread roll or 2 tablespoons matzo meal
1 ripe tomato	1 ripe tomato
1 medium onion	1 medium onion
1 medium potato	1 medium potato
125 mℓ (½ C) cold water	½ cup cold water
1 chicken bouillon cube, crushed	1 chicken bouillon cube, crushed
2 mℓ (½ t) pepper	½ teaspoon pepper
10 mℓ (2 t) salt	2 teaspoons salt
2 mℓ (½ t) ground ginger	½ teaspoon ground ginger
Dash of crushed garlic powder	Dash of garlic powder
Oil for frying	Oil for frying

TOPPING	TOPPING
2 onions, sliced	2 onions, sliced

METHOD Grate bread roll, tomato, onion and potato and add to meat. Add water, crushed bouillon cube, seasonings and spices and mix well with fork.

Shape into patties and fry in oil until nicely browned and cooked through. Fry onion slices and spoon on top of patties.

Makes 8 patties

Cottage Pie

METRIC	AMERICAN
1 kg beef mince	2 lb ground beef
2 mℓ (½ t) seasoning salt	½ teaspoon seasoned salt
10 mℓ (2 t) salt	2 teaspoons salt
2 mℓ (½ t) pepper	½ teaspoon pepper
200 mℓ (¾ C) fresh bread-crumbs	¾ cup fresh breadcrumbs
1 chicken bouillon cube, crushed	1 chicken bouillon cube, crushed
1 medium potato, peeled & grated	1 medium potato, peeled & grated
1 small onion, peeled & grated	1 small onion, peeled & grated
10 mℓ (2 t) gravy powder	2 teaspoons gravy browner or mix
300 mℓ (1¼ C) cold water	1¼ cups cold water

TOPPING	TOPPING
7–8 medium potatoes	7–8 medium potatoes
1 egg, beaten	1 egg, beaten
15 mℓ (1 T) flour	1 tablespoon flour
15 mℓ (1 T) oil or margarine	1 tablespoon oil or margarine
2 mℓ (½ t) baking powder	½ teaspoon baking powder
Salt & pepper	Salt & pepper

METHOD Combine all ingredients for meat mixture and place in 20 x 30 cm (8 x 12 inch) oblong ovenware dish.

TOPPING Peel and halve potatoes and boil until soft. Drain off excess water, mash and add remaining ingredients. Spread on top of meat mixture, make decorative lines with a fork and bake in 180°C (350°F) oven for 40 minutes.

Serves 6 to 8

Stuffed Cabbage

METRIC	AMERICAN
1 kg beef mince (not too lean)	2 lb ground beef (not too lean)
1 bread roll, grated	1 bread roll, grated
1 medium onion, grated	1 medium onion, grated
1 ripe tomato, skinned & grated	1 ripe tomato, skinned & grated
1 potato, grated	1 potato, grated
10 mℓ (2 t) salt	2 teaspoons salt
5 mℓ (1 t) crushed garlic powder	1 teaspoon garlic powder
2 mℓ (½ t) barbecue spice or seasoning salt	½ teaspooon barbecue spice or seasoned salt
2 mℓ (½ t) ground ginger	½ teaspoon ground ginger
2 mℓ (½ t) pepper	½ teaspoon pepper
½ chicken bouillon cube	½ chicken bouillon cube
1 large cabbage	1 large cabbage
Approximately 250 mℓ (1 C) cold water	Approximately 1 cup cold water

SAUCE	SAUCE
2 tomatoes, skinned & grated	2 tomatoes, skinned & grated
Juice of 1 lemon	Juice of 1 lemon
30 mℓ (2 T) tomato sauce	2 tablespoons tomato ketchup
1 chicken bouillon cube, crushed	1 chicken bouillon cube, crushed
30 mℓ (2 T) golden syrup	2 tablespoons golden syrup
15–30 mℓ (1–2 T) brown sugar	1–2 tablespoons brown sugar
Salt & pepper to taste	Salt & pepper to taste
250 mℓ (1 C) water	1 cup water
6–8 ginger snaps, crushed	6–8 ginger snaps, crushed

METHOD Prepare meat mixture by combining all ingredients, except cabbage and water, very well. Soften the cabbage leaves in boiling water, removing the hard vein from the surface with a sharp knife. Shape the meat mixture into balls; place each one in a cabbage leaf and roll up. Place in a large saucepan.

SAUCE Combine all ingredients except ginger snaps and pour over cabbage parcels. Simmer covered over low heat for about 1½ hours. Thicken sauce with crushed ginger snaps (use more if necessary) and adjust seasonings.

Transfer stuffed cabbage and gravy to a large casserole dish and arrange in a single layer. Place in a 180°C (350°F) oven to brown (approximately ½ hour).

CHEF'S TIP As an alternative to the grated onion, use a package of onion soup mix.

Serves 8

Tostados

METRIC	AMERICAN
TORTILLAS	**TORTILLAS**
See recipe for Mexican Pizza on p 19	See recipe for Mexican Pizza on p 19
FILLING	**FILLING**
2 onions, diced	2 onions, diced
15 ml (1 T) oil	1 tablespoon oil
1 kg beef mince	2 lb ground beef
15 ml (1 T) tomato purée	1 tablespoon tomato purée
2 large tomatoes, diced	2 large tomatoes, diced
½ of 370 g jar green chillis, drained (use less for milder tastes)	1 can green chilis, drained (use less for milder tastes)
2 cloves garlic, crushed	2 cloves garlic, crushed
7 ml (1½ t) salt	1½ teaspoons salt
5 ml (1 t) dried origanum	1 teaspoon dried oregano
1 x 440 g tin kidney beans	1 x 15½ oz can kidney beans
1 chicken or beef bouillon cube	1 chicken or beef bouillon cube
5 ml (1 t) crushed Mexican red pepper or cayenne pepper	1 teaspoon crushed Mexican red pepper
500 ml (2 C) water*	2 cups water*
GUACAMOLE	**GUACAMOLE**
2 avocados, peeled & seeded	2 avocados, peeled & seeded
2 cloves garlic	2 cloves garlic
5 ml (1 t) lemon juice	1 teaspoon lemon juice
10 ml (2 t) vinegar	2 teaspoons vinegar
30 ml (2 T) mayonnaise	2 tablespoons mayonnaise
Salt, pepper & crushed garlic powder	Salt, pepper & garlic powder
GARNISH	**GARNISH**
1 head lettuce, shredded	1 head lettuce, shredded
Diced tomato	Diced tomato
Grated Parmesan or Cheddar cheese	Grated Parmesan or Cheddar cheese
Sour cream	Sour cream

* If necessary, thicken with cornflour (cornstarch) or gravy mix

METHOD First prepare filling. Brown onions in oil; add beef and brown as well. Add remaining ingredients and simmer gently for 2 hours before thickening.

TORTILLAS Fry in oil until crisp. Spoon meat filling on top of each tortilla.

GUACAMOLE Combine all ingredients in food processor. Spoon on top of meat filling and garnish with shredded lettuce, sliced tomato, grated Parmesan or Cheddar cheese and sour cream.

Serves 8

Hot 'n Spicy Texas Chili

METRIC	AMERICAN
1 kg beef mince	2 lb ground beef
1 onion, finely chopped	1 onion, finely chopped
30 ml (2 T) oil	2 tablespoons oil
15 ml (1 T) chilli powder	1 tablespoon chili powder
1 x 250 g tin tomato soup	1 x 8 oz can tomato soup
250 ml (1 C) water	1 cup water
7 ml (1½ t) salt	1½ teaspoons salt
2 ml (½ t) cayenne pepper	½ teaspoon cayenne pepper
5 ml (1 t) mustard powder	1 teaspoon mustard powder
2 cloves garlic, crushed	2 cloves garlic, crushed
1 x 440 g tin red kidney beans	1 x 15½ oz can red kidney beans

METHOD Brown onion in oil, then add meat and brown well. Add remaining ingredients and bring to the boil.

Reduce heat and simmer for about 1 hour. Serve in soup bowls with crackers.

Serves 6

Quick Spaghetti Bolognaise

METRIC	AMERICAN
500 g boerewors or farmer's sausage	1 lb Italian sausage
30–45 ml (2–3T) oil	2–3 tablespoons oil
1 onion, chopped	1 onion, chopped
1 stick celery, sliced	1 stick celery, sliced
1 x 425 g tin tomatoes	1 x 15 oz can tomatoes
Parsley, sweet basil, salt & black pepper to taste	Parsley, sweet basil, salt & black pepper to taste
2 cloves garlic, crushed	2 cloves garlic, crushed
1 x 225 g tin sliced mushrooms, drained	1 x 8 oz can sliced mushrooms, drained
250 g spaghetti	½ lb spaghetti
Butter	Butter
Grated Parmesan cheese	Grated Parmesan cheese

METHOD Remove casing from sausage. Heat oil in pot; add onion and celery and sauté lightly. Add meat and brown. Drain off excess fat. Add remaining ingredients, except spaghetti, butter and cheese. Simmer gently for 20–25 minutes.

Cook spaghetti according to package directions. Drain and toss lightly with butter. Serve with meat sauce on top, sprinkled with Parmesan cheese.

Serves 6

Veal

Veal Myrna

METRIC	AMERICAN
500 g veal escalopes	1 lb veal scallopini
Salt & pepper	Salt & pepper
Oil or butter for frying	Oil or butter for frying

SAUCE	SAUCE
500 g mushrooms, sliced	1 lb mushrooms, sliced
3 spring onions, diced	3 green onions, diced
30 mℓ (2 T) brandy	2 tablespoons cognac
½ chicken bouillon cube, crushed	½ chicken bouillon cube, crushed
250 mℓ (1 C) boiling water	1 cup boiling water
250 mℓ (1 C) cream	1 cup cream
30 mℓ (2 T) sherry	2 tablespoons sherry
10 mℓ (2 t) cornflour, mixed to a paste with cold water	2 teaspoons cornstarch, mixed to a paste with cold water

PASTA ACCOMPANIMENT	PASTA ACCOMPANIMENT
250 g noodles	½ lb fettucini
125 g butter	½ cup butter
Salt & pepper	Salt & pepper
5 mℓ (1 t) dried mixed herbs	1 teaspoon Italian seasoning
30–45 mℓ (2–3 T) grated Parmesan cheese	2–3 tablespoons grated Parmesan cheese

METHOD Season meat with salt and pepper. Fry in butter or oil until golden brown and remove from pan.

SAUCE Sauté mushrooms and onions, adding more butter or oil if necessary. Remove from pan. Pour brandy (cognac) into the pan; stir well, scraping bottom of pan. Return meat to pan. Add chicken bouillon cube, water, cream, sherry and cornflour (cornstarch). Stir over low heat until thickened. Finally stir in mushroom and onion mixture.

PASTA Cook noodles (fettucini) according to package directions. Drain, then toss with butter, salt, pepper, mixed herbs or Italian seasoning and Parmesan cheese.

Serve veal with sauce on noodles.

Serves 4

Quick 'n Easy Veal Chops

METRIC	AMERICAN
8 veal chops	8 veal chops
Salt & pepper	Salt & pepper
Seasoning salt	Seasoned salt
Crushed garlic powder	Garlic powder
Ground ginger	Ground ginger
Flour for coating	Flour for coating
Oil for frying	Oil for frying
2–3 onions, sliced	2–3 onions, sliced

METHOD Season chops with salt, pepper, seasoning salt, garlic and ginger. Dust lightly with flour. Fry in oil until golden brown. Remove and set aside.

Fry sliced onions until golden. Place chops in a casserole dish and cover with onions. Cover with foil and bake for 30–40 minutes in 180°C (350°F) oven. Uncover and bake for another 10–15 minutes, until brown.

Serves 8

Escalopes à la Crème

METRIC	AMERICAN
500 g veal schnitzels or veal escalopes	1 lb veal scallopini
Salt & freshly ground black pepper	Salt & freshly ground black pepper
Crushed garlic powder	Garlic powder
250 mℓ (1 C) sour cream	1 cup sour cream
2 spring onions, diced	2 green onions, diced
1 egg, beaten	1 egg, beaten
90 g (1½ C) fresh breadcrumbs	1½ cups fresh breadcrumbs
Mixture of butter & oil for frying	Mixture of butter & oil for frying
15–30 mℓ (1–2 T) marsala or white wine	1–2 tablespoons marsala or white wine
Finely chopped fresh parsley	Finely chopped fresh parsley

METHOD Beat veal with a mallet, until very thin. Season with salt, pepper and garlic powder.

Combine sour cream and onions. Spread a layer of cream mixture on one half of each escalope. Sandwich by folding over; press edges together well.

Dip in beaten egg, allowing excess to drip off. Coat lightly with breadcrumbs and sauté in butter and oil until golden brown. Add marsala or wine. Sprinkle with parsley and serve immediately.

Serves 4

Veal & Mushroom Casserole

METRIC	AMERICAN
15 mℓ (1 T) oil (for browning)	*1 tablespoon oil (for browning)*
2 large onions, diced	*2 large onions, diced*
1,5–2 kg veal, cubed	*3–4 lb veal, cubed*
15 mℓ (1 T) butter or oil (for sauce)	*1 tablespoon butter or oil (for sauce)*
30 mℓ (2 T) flour	*2 tablespoons flour*
375 mℓ (1½ C) boiling water	*1½ cups boiling water*
5 mℓ (1 t) dried mixed herbs	*1 teaspoon Italian seasoning*
1 x 250 g tin mushrooms, drained	*1 x 8 oz can mushrooms, drained*
Salt to taste	*Salt to taste*
1 mℓ (¼ t) pepper	*¼ teaspoon pepper*
1 chicken bouillon cube, crushed	*1 chicken bouillon cube, crushed*
250 mℓ (1 C) red wine	*1 cup red wine*
1 packet mushroom soup, mixed to a paste with cold water	*1 envelope mushroom soup, mixed to a paste with cold water*

GARNISH	GARNISH
Carrots & peas	*Carrots & peas*

METHOD Brown onions in oil. Remove and brown meat, then remove meat and set aside.

Using the same saucepan, blend 15 mℓ (1 tablespoon) butter or oil with flour. Add remaining ingredients to make a creamy sauce and pour into casserole dish with meat.

Cover and bake at 180°C (350°F) for approximately 2–3 hours (until meat is tender), adding more water if necessary. Garnish with steamed carrots and peas.

Serves 8

Tasty Veal Chops

METRIC	AMERICAN
6–8 veal chops	*6–8 veal chops*
Salt & pepper	*Salt & pepper*
Flour for coating	*Flour for coating*
60 g butter or 60 mℓ (4 T) oil	*4 tablespoons butter or oil*
1 large onion, sliced	*1 large onion, sliced*
30 mℓ (2 T) brandy	*2 tablespoons cognac*
2 cloves garlic, quartered	*2 cloves garlic, quartered*
5 mℓ (1 t) dried parsley	*1 teaspoon dried parsley*
2 mℓ (½ t) dried thyme	*½ teaspoon dried thyme*
1–2 bay leaves	*1–2 bay leaves*
125 mℓ (½ C) white wine	*½ cup white wine*
250 g fresh mushrooms, sliced	*½ lb fresh mushrooms, sliced*

METHOD Season veal with salt and pepper, then dust lightly with flour. Heat butter or oil and brown meat. Remove meat from pan and brown onion in same pan. Return chops to pan and flame brandy (cognac). Add garlic, parsley, thyme and bay leaves; pour wine over chops.

Cover tightly and simmer for approximately 1 hour, or until tender. Add mushrooms 20 minutes before serving and remove garlic.

CHEF'S TIP The chops may also be covered and baked in 180°C (350°F) oven until tender.

Serves 6

Veal Délicieuse

METRIC	AMERICAN
1 kg veal (breast, shoulder or chops)	*2 lb veal (breast, shoulder or chops)*
5 mℓ (1 t) dry mustard	*1 teaspoon dry mustard*
5 mℓ (1 t) salt	*1 teaspoon salt*
5 mℓ (1 t) pepper	*1 teaspoon pepper*
5 mℓ (1 t) crushed garlic powder	*1 teaspoon garlic powder*
2 mℓ (½ t) ground ginger	*½ teaspoon ground ginger*
2 mℓ (½ t) seasoning salt	*½ teaspoon seasoned salt*
2 mℓ (½ t) cayenne pepper	*½ teaspoon cayenne pepper*
2 mℓ (½ t) paprika	*½ teaspoon paprika*
½ chicken bouillon cube, crushed	*½ chicken bouillon cube, crushed*
1 onion, diced	*1 onion, diced*
2 sticks celery, diced	*2 sticks celery, diced*
2 carrots, diced	*2 carrots, diced*
1 green pepper, diced	*1 green pepper, diced*
250 g mushrooms, sliced	*½ lb mushrooms, sliced*
1 clove garlic, crushed	*1 clove garlic, crushed*
250 mℓ (1 C) water	*1 cup water*
1–2 bay leaves	*1–2 bay leaves*
Few peppercorns	*Few peppercorns*
10 mℓ (2 t) cornflour	*2 teaspoons cornstarch*

METHOD Rub meat with mustard and season with salt, pepper, garlic powder, ground ginger, seasoning salt, cayenne pepper and paprika. Combine crushed bouillon cube with diced vegetables and garlic and place half of the mixture in the bottom of a roasting pan. Place meat on top; cover with remaining vegetables. Pour water over, add bay leaves and peppercorns.

Cover with foil and bake in 180°C (350°F) oven until tender (approximately 2 hours). Uncover, increase heat to 230°C (450°F) and allow to brown for 30 minutes. Thicken juices with cornflour (cornstarch) mixed to a paste with water.

Serves 4

Veal Goulash with Spaetzle

METRIC	AMERICAN
2 large onions, finely chopped	2 large onions, finely chopped
2–3 cloves garlic, crushed	2–3 cloves garlic, crushed
Oil for frying	Oil for frying
1 kg cubed veal	2 lb cubed veal
Flour for coating	Flour for coating
250 g mushrooms, sliced	½ lb mushrooms, sliced
1 green pepper, coarsely chopped	1 green pepper, coarsely chopped
1 red pepper, coarsely chopped	1 red pepper, coarsely chopped
1 x 425 g tin tomatoes	1 x 15 oz can tomatoes
1 chicken bouillon cube, crushed	1 chicken bouillon cube, crushed
125 mℓ (½ C) water	½ cup water
15 mℓ (1 T) tomato purée	1 tablespoon tomato purée
7 mℓ (1½ t) dried mixed herbs	1½ teaspoons Italian seasoning
7 mℓ (1½ t) caraway seeds (optional)	1½ teaspoons caraway seeds (optional)
20 mℓ (4 t) paprika	4 teaspoons paprika
5 mℓ (1 t) salt	1 teaspoon salt
Freshly ground black pepper	Freshly ground black pepper
250 mℓ (1 C) sour cream	1 cup sour cream

SPAETZLE	SPAETZLE
1 egg	1 egg
60 g (½ C) flour	½ cup flour
80 mℓ (⅓ C) water	⅓ cup water
1 mℓ (¼ t) salt	¼ teaspoon salt
60 g butter	4 tablespoons butter

METHOD Sauté onions and garlic in oil for 3–5 minutes. Dredge veal with flour and fry briskly until browned on all sides. Add mushrooms, green and red peppers, tomatoes, bouillon cube, water and tomato purée; bring to the boil. Lower heat, stir in herbs, caraway seeds, paprika, salt and pepper.

Transfer to a large casserole dish; cover and place in a slow oven (150°C / 300°F) for approximately 2–2½ hours. Before serving, adjust seasoning and pour sour cream over veal. Serve with buttered spaetzle.

SPAETZLE Beat egg well. Add flour, water and salt, stirring until batter is smooth. Drop batter from the tip of a spoon into a pot of boiling water. Cook until spaetzle come to the surface. Drain with a slotted spoon. Toss with butter and serve with goulash.

Serves 4 to 6

Lamb

Simple Madras Curry

METRIC	AMERICAN
30 mℓ (2 T) oil	2 tablespoons oil
1,5 kg lamb, mutton or beef, cubed	3 lb lamb, mutton or beef, cubed
2 onions, diced	2 onions, diced
1 large apple (preferably Granny Smith), peeled & diced	1 large apple (preferably Granny Smith), peeled & diced
2 sticks celery, diced	2 sticks celery, diced
2 tomatoes, skinned & diced	2 tomatoes, skinned & diced
1 chicken bouillon cube, crushed	1 chicken bouillon cube, crushed
¾–1 ℓ (3–4 C) water	3–4 cups water
1 carrot, sliced	1 carrot, sliced
10 mℓ (2 t) salt	2 teaspoons salt
2 mℓ (½ t) pepper	½ teaspoon pepper
15 mℓ (1 T) vinegar	1 tablespoon vinegar
15 mℓ (1 T) apricot jam or chutney	1 tablespoon apricot preserves or chutney
15 mℓ (1 T) flour	1 tablespoon flour
15 mℓ (1 T) curry powder	1 tablespoon curry powder
2–3 potatoes, halved & parboiled	2–3 potatoes, halved & parboiled

METHOD Heat oil in a large saucepan and brown meat, half at a time. Remove and set aside.

Using the same saucepan, sauté onions lightly. Return meat to saucepan and add remaining ingredients, except flour, curry powder and potatoes. Simmer for 1½ hours.

Mix flour and curry powder to a paste with a little cold water; stir into stew. Add parboiled potatoes and simmer over low heat for an additional 30 minutes.

Serves 6

Roast Rack of Spring Lamb

METRIC	AMERICAN
1 rack of lamb weighing approximately 2–2,5 kg	1 rack of lamb weighing approximately 4–5 lb
Juice of 1 lemon	Juice of 1 lemon
5 ml (1 t) salt	1 teaspoon salt
5 ml (1 t) coarsely ground black pepper	1 teaspoon coarsely ground black pepper
5 ml (1 t) crushed garlic powder	1 teaspoon garlic powder
2 ml (½ t) cayenne pepper	½ teaspoon cayenne pepper
10 ml (2 t) dry mustard	2 teaspoons dry mustard
5 ml (1 t) paprika	1 teaspoon paprika
15 ml (1 T) dried rosemary	1 tablespoon dried rosemary
10 ml (2 t) finely chopped fresh parsley	2 teaspoons finely chopped fresh parsley
1 large onion, sliced	1 large onion, sliced
125 ml (½ C) oil	½ cup oil

MINT SAUCE	MINT SAUCE
Few sprigs mint, finely chopped	Few sprigs mint, finely chopped
125 ml (½ C) oil	½ cup oil
250 ml (1 C) brown vinegar	1 cup brown vinegar
5 ml (1 t) sugar	1 teaspoon sugar
Salt & pepper to taste	Salt & pepper to taste

ALTERNATIVE SAUCE	ALTERNATIVE SAUCE
375 ml (1½ C) currant jelly or red plum jam	1½ cups currant jelly or red plum jam
Juice of ½ lemon	Juice of ½ lemon
15 ml (1 T) port wine	1 tablespoon port wine
20 ml (4 t) prepared horse-radish	4 teaspoons prepared horse-radish
20 ml (4 t) prepared mustard	4 teaspoons prepared mustard

METHOD Wash meat off well. Sprinkle with lemon juice. Combine seasonings, spices and herbs and rub into meat well.

Place some of the onion slices on a large piece of foil. Put meat on top, then place remaining onion slices over and around meat. Enclose completely in foil and refrigerate for at least 12 hours, to allow flavours to permeate the meat.

Place in roasting pan (meat side up), pour oil over and roast in 230°C (450°F) oven for 10 minutes. Reduce temperature to 200°C (400°F) and roast for a further 20–30 minutes.

Allow meat to 'rest' for a few minutes before carving. Serve with Mint Sauce or the alternative sauce.

MINT SAUCE Combine all ingredients thoroughly. Refrigerate for several hours before serving.

ALTERNATIVE SAUCE Combine all ingredients, heat gently and serve.

Serves 6

Braised Lamb Chops with Lima Beans

METRIC	AMERICAN
10 lamb shoulder chops	10 lamb shoulder chops
Oil for browning	Oil for browning
1 large onion, diced	1 large onion, diced
1 stick celery, diced	1 stick celery, diced
1 carrot, sliced	1 carrot, sliced
2 tomatoes, skinned & diced	2 tomatoes, skinned & diced
5 ml (1 t) salt	1 teaspoon salt
2 ml (½ t) pepper	½ teaspoon pepper
2 ml (½ t) crushed garlic powder	½ teaspoon garlic powder
2 ml (½ t) seasoning salt	½ teaspoon seasoned salt
1 beef or chicken bouillon cube	1 beef or chicken bouillon cube
500 ml (2 C) water	2 cups water
5 potatoes, halved	5 potatoes, halved
250 g lima beans*	½ lb lima beans*

* If unavailable, use canned butter beans or great northern beans

METHOD Brown chops in oil and set aside. Sauté onion and celery. Add carrot, tomatoes, meat, seasonings, bouillon cube and water. Cover and simmer slowly for ½ hour, adding a little more water only if necessary.

Add potatoes and lima beans and continue to simmer over low heat for another 45 minutes – 1 hour. If desired, thicken with 5 ml (1 teaspoon) gravy mix or cornflour (cornstarch), mixed to a paste with a small amount of cold water. Serve over rice.

Serves 6 to 8

Overleaf: Rib Roast with Green Peppercorn Sauce and (right) Wild Rice with Water Chestnuts & Mushrooms. At the back (left) Harvard Beets, Green Beans with Almonds & Broccoli and (right) Corn Pudding

Lamb in Mustard Sauce

METRIC	AMERICAN
2 kg leg of lamb or crown roast	4 lb leg of lamb or crown roast
60 mℓ (¼ C) soy sauce	4 tablespoons soy sauce
30 mℓ (2 T) oil	2 tablespoons oil
250 mℓ (1 C) prepared mustard	1 cup Dijon mustard
5 mℓ (1 t) crushed garlic powder	1 teaspoon garlic powder
5 mℓ (1 t) dried rosemary	1 teaspoon dried rosemary
7 mℓ (1½ t) dried thyme	1½ teaspoons dried thyme
4 cloves garlic, crushed	4 cloves garlic, crushed
2 mℓ (½ t) pepper	½ teaspoon pepper

METHOD Combine soy sauce, oil, mustard, seasonings, herbs and spices and rub very well into the lamb. Allow to marinate in the sauce for a few hours, or preferably overnight.

Roast uncovered in 180°C (350°F) oven for 2 hours, basting regularly with the sauce.

Serves 8 to 10

Shashlik

METRIC	AMERICAN
1 kg deboned lamb, cubed	2 lb deboned lamb, cubed
250 mℓ (1 C) oil	1 cup oil
Juice of ½ lemon	Juice of ½ lemon
5 mℓ (1 t) salt	1 teaspoon salt
5 mℓ (1 t) coarsely ground black pepper	1 teaspoon coarsely ground black pepper
1 bay leaf, crushed	1 bay leaf, crushed
2 mℓ (½ t) dried dill	½ teaspoon dillweed
5 mℓ (1 t) dried rosemary	1 teaspoon dried rosemary
2 cloves garlic, crushed	2 cloves garlic, crushed
2 stalks celery with leaves, coarsely chopped	2 stalks celery with leaves, coarsely chopped
Baby onions	Baby onions
2 green peppers, cut into squares	2 green peppers, cut into squares
Button mushrooms	Button mushrooms

METHOD Place lamb in a large bowl. In a screw-top jar combine oil, lemon juice, salt, pepper, bay leaf, dill, rosemary, garlic and celery. Pour over the lamb. Cover and allow to marinate in the refrigerator overnight.

Using 6 skewers, thread lamb cubes, onions, green pepper squares and mushrooms onto each. Grill or barbecue in the oven under the broiler for 10–15 minutes. Serve on a bed of rice.

Serves 6

Barbecue Lamb en Croûte

METRIC	AMERICAN
1,5–2 kg leg of lamb, deboned	3–4 lb leg of lamb, deboned
500 g puff pastry*	1 lb puff pastry*
MARINADE	MARINADE
60 mℓ (¼ C) oil	¼ cup oil
200 mℓ (¾ C) vinegar	¾ cup vinegar
250 mℓ (1 C) water	1 cup water
125 mℓ (½ C) tomato sauce	½ cup tomato ketchup
2 mℓ (½ t) black pepper	½ teaspoon black pepper
2 mℓ (½ t) dried thyme	½ teaspoon dried thyme
2 mℓ (½ t) dried origanum	½ teaspoon dried oregano
2 mℓ (½ t) dried parsley	½ teaspoon dried parsley
5 mℓ (1 t) dried rosemary	1 teaspoon dried rosemary
1 large onion, chopped	1 large onion, chopped
2 cloves garlic, crushed	2 cloves garlic, crushed
15 mℓ (1 T) Worcestershire sauce	1 tablespoon Worcestershire sauce
30 mℓ (2 T) lemon juice	2 tablespoons lemon juice
10 mℓ (2 t) mustard powder	2 teaspoons mustard powder
5 mℓ (1 t) chilli powder	1 teaspoon chili powder
Few bay leaves	Few bay leaves
5 mℓ (1 t) salt	1 teaspoon salt
15 mℓ (1 T) sugar	1 tablespoon sugar

* *Recipe on p 20*

METHOD Mix together all marinade ingredients in a saucepan over medium heat. Stir until boiling, then allow to simmer for 7–10 minutes. Cool thoroughly.

Wash meat well and prick all over. Dry thoroughly and place in a roasting pan or earthenware pot. Pour marinade mixture over meat and leave to marinate overnight.

Place meat in a roasting pan with 250 mℓ (1 cup) of the marinade and roast in a 180°C (350°F) oven for 1½ hours, basting occasionally and adding more of the marinade if required. Remove from oven; allow to cool completely.

Roll out pastry sufficiently to enclose lamb completely. Place seam side down on baking tray and bake on the centre shelf of 180°C (350°F) oven, until pastry is golden brown (approximately 35–40 minutes).

Heat remaining barbecue sauce, thicken with a paste made of cornflour (cornstarch) and water and serve with the lamb.

Serves 8 to 10

Vegetables, Pasta & Side Dishes

Broccoli or Fresh Green Asparagus with
Mushroom Sauce 82
Oriental Peas 82
Asparagus with Seasame Seeds..................... 82
Eggplant Parmesan 82
Baked Bean Casserole 83
Terry's Scalloped Tomaotes 83
Laurie's Carrot & Grape Mélange.................. 83
Stir-fried Cabbage 83
Green Beans with Almonds......................... 83
Sweetcorn Fritters 83
Harvard Beets 84
Fried Courgettes (Zucchini) 84
Israeli Potato Pudding............................ 84
Ukranian Cheese Dumplings 84
Individual Yorkshire Puddings 85
Crispy Potato Muffins............................ 85
Corn Pudding 85
Grits Casserole................................... 85
Wild Rice with Mushrooms & Water Chestnuts 86
Curried Rice with Nuts & Raisins 86
Spicy Rice 86
Chinese Fried Rice 86
Spinach-stuffed Canneloni with
Tomato Cream Sauce 87
Spaghetti Primavera 87
Fettucini Alfredo 87
Fettucini with Pesto............................. 88
Apricot Chutney 88
Spicy Cranberry Chutney......................... 88
Pickled Cucumbers 88

Broccoli or Fresh Green Asparagus with Mushroom Sauce

METRIC	AMERICAN
500 g broccoli or fresh green asparagus	1 lb broccoli or fresh green asparagus
Salt	Salt
Bicarbonate of soda	Baking soda

SAUCE	SAUCE
250 g mushrooms, sliced	½ lb mushrooms, sliced
60 g butter	4 tablespoons butter
30 mℓ (2 T) flour	2 tablespoons flour
500 mℓ (2 C) milk	2 cups milk
30 mℓ (2 T) sherry	2 tablespoons sherry
Salt & black pepper	Salt & black pepper
Crushed garlic powder	Garlic powder
Paprika to taste	Paprika to taste

METHOD Peel off the tough outer skin of the broccoli by pulling from the bottom of the stem upwards. If using asparagus, break off the bottom tips, discard, and scrape off tough outer skin with a carrot scraper.

Boil for 4 minutes in salted water, to which a pinch of bicarbonate of soda (baking soda) has been added. Drain very well. Place in buttered dish and spoon sauce over.

SAUCE Sauté mushrooms in butter for 3 minutes. Stir in flour, then remove from heat and stir in milk until smooth and fairly thick. Return to low heat. Stir constantly until simmering. Stir in sherry, salt, black pepper, garlic powder and paprika to taste.

Serves 4

Oriental Peas

METRIC	AMERICAN
15 mℓ (1 T) chopped onion	1 tablespoon chopped onion
60 g margarine or butter	4 tablespoons margarine or butter
1 x 225 g tin sliced button mushrooms, drained	1 x 8 oz can sliced button mushrooms, drained
1 x 227 g tin water chestnuts, drained & sliced	1 x 8 oz can water chestnuts, drained & sliced
15 mℓ (1 T) soy sauce	1 tablespoon soy sauce
300 g frozen peas	1 x 10 oz package frozen peas

METHOD Sauté onion in margarine or butter. Add mushrooms, water chestnuts and soy sauce. Cook over low heat for 5 minutes. Add peas, heat thoroughly and serve.

Serves 8

Asparagus with Sesame Seeds

METRIC	AMERICAN
500 g green asparagus	1 lb green asparagus
125 g butter	½ cup butter
45 mℓ (3 T) sesame seeds	3 tablespoons sesame seeds
15 mℓ (1 T) lemon juice	1 tablespoon lemon juice
Salt & black pepper	Salt & black pepper
Grated Parmesan cheese	Grated Parmesan cheese

METHOD Break off ends of asparagus and discard; scrape off the tough outer skin with a carrot scraper. Boil in salted water for 3–4 minutes. Drain and set aside.

Melt butter in frying pan and sauté the sesame seeds until golden brown. Add lemon juice, salt and pepper. Pour over asparagus and sprinkle with Parmesan cheese.

CHEF'S TIP A pinch of bicarbonate of soda (baking soda) added to the cooking water will keep all green vegetables bright and retain their colour.

Serves 6

Eggplant Parmesan

METRIC	AMERICAN
2 aubergines or eggplant, peeled & sliced into 2,5 cm thick rounds	2 eggplant, peeled & sliced into 1 inch thick rounds
Salt & pepper	Salt & pepper
Flour for coating	Flour for coating
2 eggs, lightly beaten	2 eggs, lightly beaten
Oil for frying	Oil for frying
1 large onion, diced	1 large onion, diced
2–3 cloves garlic, crushed	2–3 cloves garlic, crushed
1 x 425 g tin tomato purée	2 x 8 oz cans tomato sauce
250 mℓ (1 C) water	1 cup water
5 mℓ (1 t) dried origanum	1 teaspoon dried oregano
2 mℓ (½ t) dried sweet basil	½ teaspoon dried sweet basil
Grated Parmesan cheese	Grated Parmesan cheese

METHOD Season eggplant with salt and pepper. Dip in flour, then in beaten egg and fry in oil until golden brown. Drain on absorbent paper and place in a large, rectangular casserole dish.

Sauté onion in a little oil until tender. Add garlic, tomato purée (sauce), water and herbs. Pour over eggplant. Sprinkle liberally with Parmesan cheese and bake uncovered in a 180°C (350°F) oven for 20–30 minutes.

CHEF'S TIP If desired, top with slices of Mozzarella cheese after baking and place under broiler just until cheese melts.

Serves 8

Baked Bean Casserole

METRIC	AMERICAN
2 x 410 g tins baked beans in tomato sauce	2 x 16 oz cans baked beans in tomato sauce
50 g (¼ C) brown sugar	6 tablespoons brown sugar
60 mℓ (¼ C) tomato sauce	4 tablespoons tomato ketchup
60 mℓ (¼ C) Worcestershire sauce	4 tablespoons Worcestershire sauce
1 large onion, diced	1 large onion, diced
2 mℓ (½ t) salt	½ teaspoon salt

METHOD Mix all ingredients together and pour into casserole dish. Bake at 180°C (350°F) for approximately 40–45 minutes.

CHEF'S TIP This dish makes a tasty accompaniment to hamburgers and fried chicken.

Serves 8

Terry's Scalloped Tomatoes

METRIC	AMERICAN
500 mℓ (2 C) bread cubes	2 cups bread cubes
125 g butter or margarine	½ cup butter or margarine
1 x 1 kg tin tomatoes	1 x 32 oz can tomatoes
250 mℓ (1 C) diced celery	1 cup diced celery
1 large onion, finely diced	1 large onion, finely diced
30 mℓ (2 T) sugar	2 tablespoons sugar
2 mℓ (½ t) salt	½ teaspoon salt
1 mℓ (¼ t) pepper	¼ teaspoon pepper

METHOD Sauté bread cubes in butter, then place under broiler until golden. Combine remaining ingredients and fold in bread cubes. Place mixture in greased casserole dish and bake in a 190°C (375°F) oven for 45 minutes.

Serves 10 to 12

Laurie's Carrot & Grape Mélange

METRIC	AMERICAN
6–8 carrots, sliced into rounds	6–8 carrots, sliced into rounds
30–45 mℓ (2–3 T) butter	2–3 tablespoons butter
Salt & pepper to taste	Salt & pepper to taste
Purple grapes, halved & seeded	Purple grapes, halved & seeded

METHOD Steam carrots until crisp and tender. Add butter and salt and pepper to taste. Remove from heat. Add grapes and serve immediately.

Serves 6

Stir-fried Cabbage

METRIC	AMERICAN
1 head cabbage	1 head cabbage
Oil for frying	Oil for frying
1 onion, diced	1 onion, diced
Crushed garlic powder to taste or 2 cloves garlic, crushed	Garlic powder to taste or 2 cloves garlic, crushed
Salt & pepper	Salt & pepper

METHOD Cut cabbage into quarters and slice thickly. Soak in cold, salted water for 10 minutes, then rinse off thoroughly.

Heat oil in pan or wok. Sauté onions and garlic (if using fresh garlic) until golden. Add cabbage, stir and fry for a few minutes until it is tender but not limp. Season to taste with salt, pepper and garlic powder.

Serves 6 to 8

Green Beans with Almonds

METRIC	AMERICAN
500 g green beans	1 lb green beans
5 mℓ (1 t) sugar	1 teaspoon sugar
Pinch of salt	Pinch of salt
Pinch of bicarbonate of soda	Pinch of baking soda
100 g (1 C) slivered almonds	1 cup flaked almonds
15 mℓ (1 T) butter	1 tablespoon butter

METHOD Wash and prepare beans for cooking. Boil water with sugar and salt. Add beans and bicarbonate of soda (baking soda); cook over medium heat until crisp and tender (5–7 minutes). Drain well.

Sauté almonds in butter until golden. Toss with cooked green beans and serve.

Serves 6 PHOTOGRAPH ON PAGE 78

Sweetcorn Fritters

METRIC	AMERICAN
1 x 420 g tin creamed sweetcorn	1 x 13½ oz can creamed corn
1 egg	1 egg
60 mℓ (¼ C) flour	¼ cup flour
5 mℓ (1 t) baking powder	1 teaspoon baking powder
Salt & pepper to taste	Salt & pepper to taste
Oil for frying	Oil for frying

METHOD Combine all ingredients and mix well. Heat oil in a frying pan (skillet) and drop in spoonfuls of the mixture. Fry until golden brown, then drain on paper towels.

Makes 8

Harvard Beets

METRIC	AMERICAN
1 x 400 g jar beetroot, sliced	1 x 1 lb can beets, sliced
30 mℓ (2 T) sugar	2 tablespoons sugar
60 mℓ (¼ C) vinegar	4 tablespoons vinegar
15 mℓ (1 T) butter or margarine	1 tablespoon butter or margarine
2 mℓ (½ t) salt	½ teaspoon salt
1 mℓ (¼ t) pepper	¼ teaspoon pepper
10 mℓ (2 t) cornflour mixed to a paste with a little water	2 teaspoons cornstarch mixed to a paste with a little water

METHOD Drain liquid from beetroot (beets) into a saucepan. Add sugar, vinegar, butter or margarine, salt and pepper and bring to the boil. Thicken with cornflour (cornstarch) paste, then fold in sliced beetroot (beets) and heat through.

Serves 4   PHOTOGRAPH ON PAGE 78

Fried Courgettes (Zucchini)

METRIC	AMERICAN
500 g courgettes (baby marrows), sliced	1 lb zucchini, sliced
Flour seasoned with salt, pepper & crushed garlic powder	Flour seasoned with salt, pepper & garlic powder
1 egg, lightly beaten	1 egg, lightly beaten
Breadcrumbs	Breadcrumbs
Oil for frying	Oil for frying
Grated Parmesan cheese	Grated Parmesan cheese

METHOD Toss sliced courgettes (zucchini) in seasoned flour; dip into beaten egg, then coat with breadcrumbs. Fry in deep oil until golden brown. Sprinkle with Parmesan cheese before serving.

CHEF'S TIP Cauliflowerets or whole mushrooms may be cooked in the same way.

Serves 4

Israeli Potato Pudding

METRIC	AMERICAN
6 large potatoes, finely grated	6 large potatoes, finely grated
1 large onion, finely grated	1 large onion, finely grated
5 mℓ (1 t) baking powder	1 teaspoon baking powder
2 mℓ (½ t) sugar	½ teaspoon sugar
5 mℓ (1 t) salt	1 teaspoon salt
1 mℓ (¼ t) pepper	¼ teaspoon pepper
3 eggs, separated	3 eggs, separated
45 mℓ (3 T) oil	3 tablespoons oil

METHOD Combine all ingredients, except egg whites and oil. Beat egg whites stiffly and fold in. Pour oil into a 23 cm (9 inch) square ovenware dish and place in oven until very hot. Pour potato mixture into dish and bake at 180°C (350°F) for 1¼ hours.

Serves 6

Ukranian Cheese Dumplings

METRIC	AMERICAN
DOUGH	DOUGH
350 g (3 C) flour	3 cups flour
5 mℓ (1 t) salt	1 teaspoon salt
80 mℓ (⅓ C) oil	⅓ cup oil
250 mℓ (1 C) warm water	1 cup warm water
CHEESE FILLING	CHEESE FILLING
500 g of cottage cheese	2 cups dry curd cottage cheese
1 egg, beaten	1 egg, beaten
Salt & pepper to taste	Salt & pepper to taste
60–125 g butter & 15–30 mℓ (1–2 T) oil for frying	4–8 tablespoons butter & 1–2 tablespoons oil for frying
1 onion, finely diced	1 onion, finely diced

METHOD To prepare dough, sift flour and salt together. Make a well in the centre and add oil and water. Knead dough well, cover and leave to 'rest' for 30 minutes.

FILLING Combine cottage cheese and egg. Season with salt and pepper to taste.

TO COOK Roll out dough very thinly on a floured board. Cut into 15 cm (6 inch) rounds and place a tablespoon of filling on each. Fold over and pinch edges together firmly.

Place dumplings in a large pot of boiling, salted water and boil for 7–10 minutes. Drain.

Melt butter and oil in pan and sauté onion until glassy. Add dumplings and fry over medium to low heat until golden and crispy.

CHEF'S TIP Various other fillings may be used, such as potato (prepare as for Knishes – recipe on p 167), sauerkraut or stewed prunes.

Makes about 35

Individual Yorkshire Puddings

METRIC	AMERICAN
2 onions, halved & sliced	2 onions, halved & sliced
Butter or oil for sautéing	Butter or oil for sautéing
2 mℓ (½ t) seasoning salt	½ teaspoon seasoned salt
120 g (1 C) flour	1 cup flour
2 eggs	2 eggs
200 mℓ (¾ C) milk	¾ cup milk
Pinch of salt	Pinch of salt

METHOD Sauté onion lightly in butter or oil. Add seasoning salt (seasoned salt). Beat together the flour, eggs, milk and salt.

Heat 15 mℓ (1 tablespoon) oil in each section of a muffin tin, until very hot. Spoon a small amount of onion into each. Three-quarter fill with mixture. Bake at 200°C (400°F) for 20–30 minutes, until puffed and golden.

Makes 12

Crispy Potato Muffins

METRIC	AMERICAN
5 potatoes, finely grated	5 potatoes, finely grated
1 onion, grated	1 onion, grated
2 eggs, slightly beaten	2 eggs, slightly beaten
30 mℓ (2 T) flour	2 tablespoons flour
5 mℓ (1 t) salt	1 teaspoon salt
2 mℓ (½ t) pepper	½ teaspoon pepper
5 mℓ (1 t) baking powder	1 teaspoon baking powder
30 mℓ (2 T) oil or melted butter	2 tablespoons oil or melted butter

METHOD Combine all ingredients. Heat an additional 15 mℓ (1 tablespoon) oil in each section of a muffin tin, until very hot. Three-quarter fill each one with potato mixture. Bake at 180°C (350°F) for 40–50 minutes.

Makes 12

Corn Pudding

METRIC	AMERICAN
4 eggs	4 eggs
15 mℓ (1 T) sugar	1 tablespoon sugar
20 mℓ (4 t) flour	4 teaspoons all purpose flour
2 mℓ (½ t) salt	½ teaspoon salt
1 x 410 g tin evaporated milk	1 x 13 oz can evaporated milk
60 g butter	4 tablespoons butter
1 x 420 g tin creamed sweetcorn	1 x 16½ oz can creamed corn
1 x 410 g tin kernel corn, drained	1 x 16½ oz can whole kernel corn, drained

METHOD Beat eggs, sugar, flour, salt and evaporated milk together in a blender or processor. Melt butter in a 23 x 33 cm (9 x 13 inch) casserole dish. Mix both cans of corn into the milk mixture and pour into casserole dish over butter.

Set in a *bain-marie* (a pan half-filled with boiling water). Bake in 180°C (350°F) oven for 40–50 minutes, or until blade of knife inserted comes out clean.

CHEF'S TIP Cover the pudding with foil if you see it is getting too brown and has not yet set.

Serves 8 to 10   PHOTOGRAPH ON PAGE 79

Grits Casserole

METRIC	AMERICAN
1 ℓ (4 C) boiling, salted water	4 cups boiling, salted water
120 g (1 C) mealie meal or corn meal	1 cup grits
125 g butter	½ cup butter
2–3 cloves garlic, crushed	2–3 cloves garlic, crushed
100 g (1 C) grated Cheddar cheese	1 cup grated Cheddar cheese
5 mℓ (1 t) salt	1 teaspoon salt
2 mℓ (½ t) paprika	½ teaspoon paprika
3–4 drops Tabasco	3–4 drops Tabasco
2 eggs	2 eggs
Milk	Milk

METHOD Bring salted water to the boil. Slowly stir in mealie meal or corn meal (grits). Cook until thick, stirring constantly. Remove from heat and stir in butter, garlic, cheese, salt, paprika and Tabasco.

Break eggs into a cup and add milk to measure 250 mℓ (1 cup). Beat well and add to the grits mixture. Bake in a greased casserole dish at 160°C (325°F) for 45–50 minutes.

Serves 8

Wild Rice with Mushrooms & Water Chestnuts

METRIC	AMERICAN
400 g (2 C) wild rice or brown rice	2 cups wild rice
Butter for sautéing	Butter for sautéing
250 g mushrooms, sliced	½ lb mushrooms, sliced
1 x 227 g tin water chestnuts, drained	1 x 8 oz can water chestnuts, drained

METHOD Cook rice according to package directions. Sauté mushrooms in butter; add water chestnuts and brown lightly. Stir into cooked rice.

Press into a lightly greased mould. Cover with foil and heat in oven. To serve, unmould and garnish with sprigs of parsley or watercress.

Serves 12 PHOTOGRAPH ON PAGE 79

Curried Rice with Nuts & Raisins

METRIC	AMERICAN
200 g (1 C) rice	1 cup rice
2 onions, diced	2 onions, diced
60 g butter or margarine	4 tablespoons butter or margarine
15 mℓ (1 T) curry powder	1 tablespoon curry powder
100 g flaked almonds	1 cup flaked almonds
250 mℓ (1 C) plumped raisins	1 cup plumped raisins
Salt to taste	Salt to taste

METHOD Cook rice according to package directions. Sauté onion in butter or margarine. Stir in curry powder. Add nuts and raisins and combine this mixture with cooked rice. Season to taste with salt.

CHEF'S TIP To plump raisins, allow to soak in boiling water for a few minutes, then drain well.

Serves 6

Spicy Rice

METRIC	AMERICAN
200 g (1 C) long-grain & wild rice or brown rice	1 x 6 oz box long-grain & wild rice
125 mℓ (½ C) Italian salad dressing	½ cup Italian salad dressing
15 mℓ (1 T) Worcestershire sauce	1 tablespoon Worcestershire sauce
2 mℓ (½ t) sugar	½ teaspoon sugar
15 mℓ (1 T) diced spring onion	1 tablespoon diced green onion
125 mℓ (½ C) cooked peas	½ cup cooked peas
15 mℓ (1 T) diced pimento	1 tablespoon diced pimento

METHOD Cook rice in salted water according to package directions. While still hot, add remaining ingredients and toss well.

Serves 4

Chinese Fried Rice

METRIC	AMERICAN
400 g (2 C) white long-grain rice	2 cups white long-grain rice
250 g bacon or Kosher beef fry	½ lb bacon or Kosher beef fry
2 eggs, beaten	2 eggs, beaten
30–45 mℓ (2–3 T) peanut oil	2–3 tablespoons peanut oil
60 mℓ (¼ C) spring onions, chopped	4 tablespoons green onions, chopped
30–45 mℓ (2–3 T) soy sauce	2–3 tablespoons soy sauce

METHOD Cook rice according to package directions.

Chop bacon or beef fry and fry in a wok until crispy. Remove and in the same fat cook the eggs, omelet-style. Turn out of wok and cut into narrow strips.

Spoon peanut oil into wok and heat. Add cooked rice and fry for 5 minutes, stirring occasionally. Add bacon, egg, spring onions (green onions) and soy sauce. Heat through and serve.

CHEF'S TIP This dish may be prepared in advance and reheated in the oven.

Serves 6 to 8

Spinach-stuffed Canneloni with Tomato Cream Sauce

METRIC	AMERICAN
1 x 250 g package canneloni	1 x 8 oz package canneloni or manicotti
Grated Parmesan cheese	Grated Parmesan cheese

FILLING

METRIC	AMERICAN
300 g frozen chopped spinach	1 x 10 oz package frozen chopped spinach
½ onion, grated	½ onion, grated
30 mℓ (2 T) butter	2 tablespoons butter
15 mℓ (1 T) flour	1 tablespoon flour
125 mℓ (½ C) milk	½ cup milk
2 eggs, slightly beaten	2 eggs, slightly beaten
125 g Ricotta cheese	1 cup Ricotta cheese
50 g (½ C) grated Mozzarella cheese	½ cup grated Mozzarella cheese
Salt & pepper to taste	Salt & pepper to taste
Dash of nutmeg	Dash of nutmeg

TOMATO SAUCE

METRIC	AMERICAN
125 g butter	½ cup butter
125 mℓ (½ C) cream of tomato soup or tomato sauce	½ cup cream of tomato soup or tomato sauce
250 mℓ (1 C) cream	1 cup cream
Salt & pepper to taste	Salt & pepper to taste
125 mℓ (½ C) grated Parmesan cheese	½ cup grated Parmesan cheese

METHOD Boil canneloni or manicotti according to package directions.

FILLING Defrost spinach and drain well. Sauté onion in butter, stir in flour and add milk slowly, to make a white sauce. Remove from stove, add beaten eggs very slowly, then return to heat and cook until thickened. Add cheeses and spinach and season to taste with salt, pepper and nutmeg. Allow to cool thoroughly.

TOMATO SAUCE Melt butter; stir in tomato soup (or sauce) and cream. Season with salt and pepper and stir in Parmesan cheese.

TO BAKE Stuff boiled canneloni shells with spinach filling. Place in a buttered ovenware dish and spoon over tomato sauce. Sprinkle liberally with additional Parmesan cheese and bake in 180°C (350°F) oven until heated through and sizzling.

CHEF'S TIP As an alternative, use lasagne noodles instead of canneloni. Spread with filling, roll up and place seam side down in a greased ovenware dish.

Makes 12

Spaghetti Primavera

METRIC	AMERICAN
500 g broccoli or green asparagus, cut into bite-size pieces	1 lb broccoli or green asparagus, cut into bite-size pieces
1 courgette (baby marrow) cut in half lengthwise, then sliced	1 zucchini, cut in half lengthwise, then sliced
125 g butter	½ cup butter
250 g mushrooms, sliced	½ lb mushrooms, sliced
15 mℓ (1 T) pimento	1 tablespoon pimento
3–4 cloves garlic, crushed	3–4 cloves garlic, crushed
15 mℓ (1 T) chopped fresh parsley	1 tablespoon chopped fresh parsley
2 mℓ (½ t) salt	½ teaspoon salt
250 g spaghetti	8 oz spaghetti
125 mℓ (½ C) cream	½ cup cream
60 mℓ (¼ C) grated Parmesan cheese	¼ cup grated Parmesan cheese
5 mℓ (1 t) dried basil	1 teaspoon dried basil
2 mℓ (½ t) freshly ground black pepper	½ teaspoon freshly ground black pepper
125–175 g snow peas, blanched in boiling water*	4–6 oz snow peas, blanched in boiling water*

* Use frozen peas if snow peas are not available

METHOD Bring water to boil in a large saucepan and add 5mℓ (1 teaspoon) salt. Add broccoli or asparagus and courgette (zucchini); boil for 3 minutes. Drain and set aside.

In a small pan, heat butter and sauté mushrooms; add pimento, garlic, parsley and salt. Sauté, stirring constantly, for 2–3 minutes.

Cook spaghetti according to package directions. Drain, then stir in cream, Parmesan cheese, basil, black pepper and all vegetables. Toss well and sprinkle with additional Parmesan cheese to serve.

Serves 6

Fettucini Alfredo

METRIC	AMERICAN
125 g butter	½ cup butter
250 mℓ (1 C) cream	1 cup cream
100 g grated Parmesan cheese	1 cup grated Parmesan cheese
Salt & pepper	Salt & pepper
Nutmeg	Nutmeg
Mixed herbs	Italian seasoning
500 g noodles	1 lb noodles

METHOD Melt butter; stir in cream and cheese. Season to taste with salt, pepper, nutmeg and herbs. Cook noodles according to directions and toss with sauce.

Serves 6

Fettucini with Pesto

METRIC	AMERICAN
250 mℓ (1 C) fresh basil	1 cup fresh basil
125 mℓ (½ C) olive oil	½ cup olive oil
60 mℓ (¼ C) grated Parmesan cheese	¼ cup grated Parmesan cheese
30 mℓ (2 T) pine nuts	2 tablespoons pine nuts
2 cloves garlic	2 cloves garlic
2 mℓ (½ t) salt	½ teaspoon salt
2 mℓ (½ t) freshly ground black pepper	½ teaspoon freshly ground black pepper
500 g fettucini (flat noodles)	1 lb fettucini

METHOD Combine all ingredients (except fettucini) in a food processor or blender. Process until smooth. Cook fettucini in boiling, salted water with 15 mℓ (1 tablespoon) oil, stirring occasionally to prevent sticking, until pasta is 'al dente' or firm but tender.

Mix 30 mℓ (2 tablespoons) of the water from the fettucini with the pesto sauce, drain off the rest of the water and toss the hot fettucini with the sauce.

Serves 8

Apricot Chutney

METRIC	AMERICAN
2,5 kg dried apricots	5 lb dried apricots
1 large onion, grated	1 large onion, grated
1 clove garlic, crushed	1 clove garlic, crushed
750 mℓ (3 C) vinegar	3 cups vinegar
1 kg (5 C) sugar	5 cups sugar
5 mℓ (1 t) cayenne pepper	1 teaspoon cayenne pepper
15 mℓ (1 T) salt	1 tablespoon salt
30 mℓ (2 T) ground ginger	2 tablespoons ground ginger
5 mℓ (1 t) dry mustard	1 teaspoon dry mustard
10 green peppers, seeded & diced	10 green peppers, seeded & diced

METHOD Soak apricots overnight in cold water. Boil in the same water with onion, garlic and vinegar for 10 minutes. Add remaining ingredients and simmer gently over a low heat for 1 hour. Bottle immediately.

Makes about 2 kg / 4 lb

Spicy Cranberry Chutney

METRIC	AMERICAN
500 g cranberries*	1 lb cranberries
150 g (1 C) seedless raisins	1 cup seedless raisins
300 g (1½ C) sugar	1½ cups sugar
15 mℓ (1 T) cinnamon	1 tablespoon cinnamon
7 mℓ (1½ t) ground ginger	1½ teaspoons ground ginger
1 mℓ (¼ t) ground cloves	¼ teaspoon ground cloves
500 mℓ (2 C) water	2 cups water
125 mℓ (½ C) chopped celery	½ cup chopped celery
1 apple, chopped	1 apple, chopped

* If fresh cranberries are not available, use the tinned variety

METHOD Combine cranberries, raisins, sugar, cinnamon, ginger and cloves with water. Cook for 15 minutes, until berries pop. Add celery and apple; simmer for another 15 minutes, until mixture is thick. Cool and refrigerate.

CHEF'S TIP Serve as a delicious accompaniment to roast turkey.

Makes about 1 litre / 2 pints

Pickled Cucumbers

METRIC	AMERICAN
18 small cucumbers	18 small cucumbers
750 mℓ (3 C) water	3 cups water
250 mℓ (1 C) vinegar	1 cup vinegar
15 mℓ (1 T) coarse salt	1 tablespoon coarse salt
15 mℓ (1 T) sugar	1 tablespoon sugar
10 mℓ (2 t) pickling spice	2 teaspoons pickling spice
10 peppercorns	10 peppercorns
2–3 bay leaves	2–3 bay leaves
3–4 cloves garlic, cut up	3–4 cloves garlic, cut up

METHOD Wash cucumbers and pack into bottles. Boil together water, vinegar, salt and sugar; add pickling spice, peppercorns and bay leaves. Pour hot mixture over cucumbers; add garlic.

Allow to stand overnight, then refrigerate for 2–3 days, after which the cucumbers will be ready to eat.

Makes about 2 kg / 4 lb

Salads

Avocado & Orange Salad 90
Special Five-Cup Salad 90
Aunt Celie's Artichoke & Mushroom Salad 90
Italian Salad 90
Lettuce, Artichoke & Parmesan Salad 91
Cabbage Pineapple Slaw 91
Caesar Salad 91
Exotic Waldorf Salad 92
Citrus & Avocado Salad 92
Nutty Broccoli Salad 92
Potato Salad 93
Spinach & Water Chesnut Salad 93
Shrimp & Avocado Salad 93
Toasted Pita Chips 93

Avocado & Orange Salad

METRIC	AMERICAN
1 lettuce (preferably Romaine), torn into pieces	1 lettuce (preferably Romaine), torn into pieces
1 purple onion, thinly sliced (or yellow onion, if purple not available)	1 purple onion, thinly sliced (or yellow onion, if purple not available)
6–8 slices crumbled cooked bacon or Kosher beef fry (optional)	6–8 slices crumbled cooked bacon or Kosher beef fry (optional)
2 x 312 g tins mandarin oranges, drained	2 x 11 oz cans mandarin oranges, drained
1 or 2 avocados, peeled & sliced	1 or 2 avocados, peeled & sliced
100 g flaked almonds (toasted if desired)	4 oz flaked almonds (toasted if desired)

DRESSING	DRESSING
60 mℓ (¼ C) oil	¼ cup oil
60 mℓ (¼ C) vinegar	¼ cup vinegar
15 mℓ (1 T) lemon juice	1 tablespoon lemon juice
30 mℓ (2 T) sugar	2 tablespoons sugar
2 mℓ (½ t) salt	½ teaspoon salt
2 mℓ (½ t) dry mustard	½ teaspoon dry mustard
Few drops of Tabasco	Few drops of Tabasco
2 mℓ (½ t) finely grated onion	½ teaspoon finely grated onion

METHOD Combine lettuce leaves, sliced onion, crumbled bacon or beef fry, mandarin oranges, sliced avocado and flaked almonds. Place dressing ingredients in a screw-top jar or food processor. Blend well and pour over salad.

Serves 8

Special Five-Cup Salad

METRIC	AMERICAN
1 x 312 g tin mandarin oranges	1 x 11 oz can mandarin oranges
1 x 475 g tin crushed pineapple	1 x 20 oz can crushed pineapple
80 g (1 C) dessicated coconut	1 cup dessicated coconut
250 mℓ (1 C) miniature marshmallows	1 cup miniature marshmallows
250 mℓ (1 C) cream*	1 cup cream*
250 g cream cheese	8 oz cream cheese
50 g (¼ C) sugar	¼ cup sugar

* I use sour cream, but this is a personal preference

METHOD Drain oranges and reserve 80 mℓ (⅓ cup) juice. Set aside. Mix together oranges, pineapple, coconut, marshmallows and cream. Chill for several hours.

Soften cream cheese with sugar. Combine with reserved mandarin juice, pour over salad and serve.

Serves 8

Aunt Celie's Artichoke & Mushroom Salad

METRIC	AMERICAN
2 x 400 g tins artichoke hearts	2 x 11½ oz cans artichoke hearts
1 x 410 g tin green beans	1 x 11½ oz can green beans
1 x 440 g tin red kidney beans	1 x 15½ oz can red kidney beans
250 g fresh mushrooms	½ lb fresh mushrooms
1 green pepper, finely chopped	1 green pepper, finely chopped

DRESSING	DRESSING
5 mℓ (1 t) salt	1 teaspoon salt
2 mℓ (½ t) coarsely ground black pepper	½ teaspoon coarsely ground black pepper
125 mℓ (½ C) oil	½ cup oil
125 mℓ (½ C) vinegar	½ cup vinegar
2 cloves garlic, crushed	2 cloves garlic, crushed

GARNISH	GARNISH
2 hard-boiled eggs, quartered	2 hard-boiled eggs, quartered

METHOD Drain all tinned (canned) vegetables; combine with fresh vegetables and toss.

Combine all dressing ingredients in a screw-top jar and shake well, or blend in food processor. Pour over salad, garnish with quartered hard-boiled eggs and serve.

CHEF'S TIP If preferred, use a commercial Italian salad dressing, as Aunt Celie does.

Serves 12

Italian Salad

METRIC	AMERICAN
1 small head lettuce or Romaine, split into leaves, washed & dried	1 small head lettuce or Romaine, split into leaves, washed & dried
2 tomatoes, sliced	2 tomatoes, sliced
125 g Mozzarella cheese, sliced	4 oz Mozzarella cheese, sliced
125 g salami, thinly sliced	4 oz salami, thinly sliced
1 onion, cut into rings	1 onion, cut into rings
Lemon juice	Lemon juice
Olive oil	Olive oil
Origanum	Oregano

METHOD Place a few lettuce leaves on each of four salad plates. Arrange sliced tomato on top, then cheese, salami and onion rings. Drizzle with lemon juice and olive oil and sprinkle with origanum (oregano).

Serves 4

Lettuce, Artichoke & Parmesan Salad

METRIC	AMERICAN
1 large avocado pear, peeled & cubed	1 large avocado pear, peeled & cubed
Lemon juice	Lemon juice
1 lettuce, torn into pieces	1 lettuce, torn into pieces
1 x 400 g tin artichoke hearts, drained & quartered	1 x 11½ oz can artichoke hearts, drained & quartered
125 mℓ (½ C) grated Parmesan cheese	½ cup grated Parmesan cheese
Wholewheat croûtons	Wholewheat croûtons

DRESSING	DRESSING
5 mℓ (1 t) salt	1 teaspoon salt
2 mℓ (½ t) sugar	½ teaspoon sugar
2 mℓ (½ t) paprika	½ teaspoon paprika
1 mℓ (¼ t) pepper	¼ teaspoon pepper
200 mℓ (¾ C) oil	¾ cup oil
60 mℓ (¼ C) vinegar	¼ cup vinegar
2 cloves garlic, crushed	2 cloves garlic, crushed

METHOD Sprinkle avocado with lemon juice to prevent discolouring. Mix with lettuce, artichokes and Parmesan cheese.

Combine dressing ingredients in screw-top jar or food processor and pour over. Top with wholewheat croûtons, made by cubing wholewheat bread and frying in oil until crisp and brown, then draining well.

Serves 6 to 8

Cabbage Pineapple Slaw

METRIC	AMERICAN
1 cabbage, finely shredded	1 cabbage, finely shredded
2 carrots, grated	2 carrots, grated
1 pineapple, diced	1 pineapple, diced
150 g (1 C) raisins	1 cup raisins
150 g (1 C) salted peanuts	1 cup salted peanuts

DRESSING	DRESSING
250 mℓ (1 C) mayonnaise	1 cup mayonnaise
30 mℓ (2 T) honey or sugar	2 tablespoons honey or sugar
30 mℓ (2 T) lemon juice	2 tablespoons lemon juice
30 mℓ (2 T) vinegar	2 tablespoons vinegar
5 mℓ (1 t) dry mustard	1 teaspoon dry mustard
Few drops of Tabasco	Few drops of Tabasco
5 mℓ (1 t) salt	1 teaspoon salt
Dash of pepper	Dash of pepper

METHOD Combine cabbage, carrots, pineapple, raisins and nuts. Blend dressing ingredients in a blender or food processor, or with a whisk. Pour over salad.

Serves 8

Caesar Salad

METRIC	AMERICAN
1 Romaine or ordinary lettuce, washed, dried & torn into bite-size pieces	1 Romaine, washed, dried & torn into bite-size pieces

DRESSING	DRESSING
80 mℓ (⅓ C) oil	⅓ cup oil
3 cloves garlic, crushed	3 cloves garlic, crushed
15 mℓ (1 T) lemon juice	1 tablespoon lemon juice
10 mℓ (2 t) Worcestershire sauce	2 teaspoons Worcestershire sauce
2 mℓ (½ t) salt	½ teaspoon salt
1 mℓ (¼ t) pepper	¼ teaspoon pepper
1 mℓ (¼ t) dry mustard	¼ teaspoon dry mustard
Dash of crushed garlic powder	Dash of garlic powder
80 mℓ (⅓ C) grated Parmesan cheese	⅓ cup grated Parmesan cheese
1 egg yolk	1 egg yolk

GARNISH	GARNISH
1 x 50 g tin anchovies	1 x 2 oz can anchovies
Croûtons	Croûtons

METHOD Combine all dressing ingredients in blender or food processor. Toss with lettuce and garnish with anchovy fillets and croûtons.

Serves 6

Exotic Waldorf Salad

METRIC	AMERICAN
4 red apples, diced	4 red apples, diced
2 green apples, diced	2 green apples, diced
4 bananas, sliced	4 bananas, sliced
Juice of 1 lemon	Juice of 1 lemon
½ head cabbage, shredded	½ head cabbage, shredded
1 x 470 g tin pineapple chunks, drained & juice reserved	1 x 20 oz can pineapple chunks, drained & juice reserved
2 sticks celery, diced	2 sticks celery, diced
100 g (1 C) walnuts, coarsely chopped	1 cup walnuts, coarsely chopped
150 g (1 C) sultanas	1 cup golden raisins
250 mℓ (1 C) mayonnaise	1 cup mayonnaise
5 mℓ (1 t) curry powder	1 teaspoon curry powder
30 mℓ (2 T) honey	2 tablespoons honey

METHOD Sprinkle diced apples and bananas with lemon juice to prevent discolouring. Place cabbage, apples, bananas, pineapple, celery, walnuts and sultanas (golden raisins) in layers in a salad bowl.

Mix together the mayonnaise, curry powder, honey and 200 mℓ (¾ cup) of the reserved pineapple juice. Pour over salad and combine well.

Serves 8

Citrus & Avocado Salad

METRIC	AMERICAN
1 head lettuce, split into leaves, washed & dried	4 Bibb lettuce
2 avocados, peeled & sliced	2 avocados, peeled & sliced
Lemon juice	Lemon juice
1 x 410 g tin grapefruit segments, drained	1 x 15 oz can grapefruit segments, drained
1 x 312 g tin mandarin oranges, drained	1 x 11 oz can mandarin oranges, drained

DRESSING	DRESSING
60 mℓ (¼ C) oil	¼ cup oil
30 mℓ (2 T) honey	2 tablespoons honey
30 mℓ (2 T) lemon juice	2 tablespoons lemon juice
15 mℓ (1 T) poppy seeds	1 tablespoon poppy seeds
2 mℓ (½ t) salt	½ teaspoon salt
Dash of pepper	Dash of pepper

METHOD Arrange lettuce leaves (or whole Bibb lettuce) on plates, sprinkle avocado with lemon juice and place on top of lettuce with fruit. Combine dressing ingredients in blender or food processor and pour over.

Serves 4

Nutty Broccoli Salad

METRIC	AMERICAN
500 g fresh broccoli, broken into flowerets	1 lb fresh broccoli, broken into flowerets
1 onion, diced	1 onion, diced
250 g fresh mushrooms, sliced	½ lb fresh mushrooms, sliced
3 hard-boiled eggs, coarsely diced	3 hard-boiled eggs, coarsely diced
1 x 140 g jar stuffed green olives	1 x 5 oz jar stuffed green olives
125 g salted almonds or cashews	¼ lb salted almonds or cashews
Crushed garlic powder	Garlic powder
Seasoning salt	Seasoned salt
250 mℓ (1 C) mayonnaise	1 cup mayonnaise
30 mℓ (2 T) prepared mustard	2 tablespoons prepared mustard

METHOD Combine broccoli, onion, mushroom, eggs, olives and nuts in large salad bowl. Season with garlic powder and seasoning salt (seasoned salt).

Mix mayonnaise and mustard together and combine gently with vegetables. Cover and refrigerate for several hours, or overnight, before serving.

Serves 8

Potato Salad

METRIC

6 medium potatoes
60 mℓ (¼ C) commercial Italian
  salad dressing
250 mℓ (1 C) mayonnaise
5 mℓ (1 t) salt
2 mℓ (½ t) sugar
15 mℓ (1 T) prepared mustard
Pinch of pepper
Few spring onions, chopped
Paprika

AMERICAN

6 medium potatoes
¼ cup commercial Italian salad
  dressing
1 cup mayonnaise
1 teaspoon salt
½ teaspoon sugar
1 tablespoon prepared mustard
Pinch of pepper
Few green onions, chopped
Paprika

METHOD Boil potatoes in their jackets in salted water until tender. Cool, peel and cut into cubes. Combine with Italian dressing.

Mix together the mayonnaise, salt, sugar, mustard, pepper and onions. Spoon lightly over the potatoes. Sprinkle with paprika and serve.

Serves 8 to 10

Spinach & Water Chestnut Salad

METRIC

8–10 spinach leaves, washed,
  dried & torn into pieces
125 g fresh mushrooms, sliced
1 x 227 g tin water chestnuts,
  sliced
1 small onion, sliced into rings
2 hard-boiled eggs, diced
8 slices bacon or macon, cooked
  & diced

AMERICAN

8–10 spinach leaves, washed,
  dried & torn into pieces
¼ lb fresh mushrooms, sliced
1 x 8 oz can water chestnuts,
  sliced
1 small onion, sliced into rings
2 hard-boiled eggs, diced
8 slices bacon or Kosher beef fry,
  cooked & diced

DRESSING

250 mℓ (1 C) red wine vinegar
250 mℓ (1 C) oil
80 mℓ (⅓ C) tomato sauce
100 g (½ C) sugar
15 mℓ (1 T) Worcestershire
  sauce
1 onion, grated

DRESSING

1 cup red wine vinegar
1 cup oil
⅓ cup tomato ketchup
½ cup sugar
1 tablespoon Worcestershire
  sauce
1 onion, grated

METHOD Combine spinach, mushrooms, water chestnuts, onion rings, eggs and bacon, macon or Kosher beef fry.

Combine all dressing ingredients in a screw-top jar and shake well, or blend in food processor. Pour over salad and toss well.

Serves 8   PHOTOGRAPH ON PAGE 34

Shrimp & Avocado Salad

METRIC

4 avocados, peeled & sliced
Lemon juice
1 onion, diced
1 green pepper, diced
1 x 113 g tin black olives, pipped
  & sliced
500 g cooked shrimp
2 spring onions, diced
Pimento (optional)

AMERICAN

4 avocados, peeled & sliced
Lemon juice
1 onion, diced
1 green pepper, diced
1 x 4 oz can sliced black
  olives
1 lb cooked shrimp
2 green onions, diced
Pimento (optional)

DRESSING

125 mℓ (½ C) vinegar
125 mℓ (½ C) oil
30 mℓ (2 T) water
5 mℓ (1 t) salt
2 mℓ (½ t) dry mustard
1 mℓ (¼ t) pepper
2 cloves garlic, crushed
Few drops of Tabasco
2 mℓ (½ t) sugar
5 mℓ (1 t) crushed red pepper
  or cayenne pepper

DRESSING

½ cup vinegar
½ cup oil
2 tablespoons water
1 teaspoon salt
½ teaspoon dry mustard
¼ teaspoon pepper
2 cloves garlic, crushed
Few drops of Tabasco
½ teaspoon sugar
1 teaspoon crushed red pepper

GARNISH

Tomato wedges
Hard-boiled eggs, quartered
Freshly chopped parsley

GARNISH

Tomato wedges
Hard-boiled eggs, quartered
Freshly chopped parsley

METHOD Sprinkle avocado with lemon juice. Combine remaining salad ingredients with avocado.

Place all dressing ingredients in a screw-top jar and shake well, or blend in a food processor. Pour over salad, garnish with tomato wedges and quartered hard-boiled eggs and sprinkle with chopped parsley.

Serves 8

Toasted Pita Chips

METRIC

4 pita bread rounds
Melted butter*
Sesame, caraway or poppy seeds

AMERICAN

4 pita bread rounds
Melted butter*
Sesame, caraway or poppy seeds

* If desired, add crushed garlic to the melted butter

METHOD Cut each pita round into quarters. Split each quarter in two, brush the insides with butter and sprinkle with seeds. Place under grill (broiler) until crisp and golden.

CHEF'S TIP Pita chips make a delicious accompaniment to salads and dips.

Makes 32

Desserts

HOT

Baked Apples with Caramel Sauce *96*
Crunchy Fruit Cobbler *96*
Luscious Peaches & Cream Dessert *96*
Hot Baked Raspberry & Youngberry Pudding *97*
Cherries Jubilee *97*
Rhubarb & Apple Cobbler *97*
Mercia's Banana Fritters *97*
Fried Custard Creams with Lemon Sauce *100*
Chocolate Soufflé *100*
Chocolate Pie Alaska *101*
Cheese Crêpes with Strawberry Sauce *101*
Spoonbread Soufflé with Strawberry Sauce *102*
Crêpes Suzette *102*
Apple Custard Crêpes *102*
Souffléd Crêpes with Custard *103*

COLD

Chocolate Mint Bombe *103*
Gernadilla Ice-cream *103*
Orange Pineapple Nut Ice-cream *104*
Peanut Crisp Ice-cream Slab *104*
Berry Jelly *104*
Curly Dessert Cups *104*
Frozen Fruit Salad *104*
Lemon Florentine *105*
Greek Meringue *105*
Lemon Cream Puff Ring *105*
Mango Mousse *108*
White Chocolate Mousse with Raspberry Sauce *108*
Marshmallow Ring with Cream & Berries *108*
Rich Chocolate Mousse *109*
Coeur à la Crème *109*
Marbled Chocolate Mousse *109*
Chocolate Meringue *110*
Mercia's Foolproof Pavlova *110*
Mercia's Crème Caramel *110*
Chocolate Mousse Fancy Cake *111*
Friandises *112*
Tapioca Custard Flowers *112*
Chocolate Truffles *112*
Chinese Chocolate Lychees *112*

Hot

Baked Apples with Caramel Sauce

METRIC	AMERICAN
6 Granny Smith apples	6 Granny Smith apples
90 mℓ (6 T) raisins	6 tablespoons raisins
Ground cinnamon	Ground cinnamon
30 mℓ (6 t) butter	6 teaspoons butter
250 mℓ (1 C) water	1 cup water

CARAMEL SAUCE	CARAMEL SAUCE
16 caramels	16 caramels
125 mℓ (½ C) milk	½ cup milk

METHOD Core apples and arrange in an ovenware dish. Press 15 mℓ (1 tablespoon) raisins into each centre. Sprinkle liberally with cinnamon and top with 5 mℓ (1 teaspoon) butter. Pour water around base of apples and bake in 180°C (350°F) oven for 45 minutes–1 hour, or until tender.

CARAMEL SAUCE Combine caramels and milk in a saucepan until melted. (Add more milk if necessary to obtain the right consistency.) Pour over baked apples and serve with vanilla ice-cream or cream.

Serves 6   PHOTOGRAPH ON PAGE 99

Crunchy Fruit Cobbler

METRIC	AMERICAN
1 x 410 g tin strawberries (reserve juice)	1 x 13½ oz can strawberries (reserve juice)
2 x 410 g tins different fruits*	2 x 13½ oz cans different fruits*
15–30 mℓ (1–2 T) sugar	1–2 tablespoons sugar
15 mℓ (1 T) cornflour mixed to a paste with water	1 tablespoon cornstarch mixed to a paste with water
500g ginger snaps	1 lb ginger snaps
60 g butter or margarine, melted	4 tablespoons butter or margarine, melted

* *such as pears, peaches, apples etc*

METHOD Drain fruit (reserving strawberry juice) and mix together. Place fruit mixture in a 23 cm (9 inch) ovenware dish.

Bring strawberry juice to a boil. Add sugar to taste and stir in cornflour (cornstarch) paste until thickened. Pour over fruit.

Crush the ginger snaps finely and stir into the melted butter. Spread the biscuit (cookie) mixture over the fruit. Bake at 180°C (350°F) for 20–30 minutes. Serve with cream or hot custard.

CHEF'S TIP As a variation, substitute canned apples only for the fruit mixture, with 80–125 mℓ (⅓–½ cup) applesauce. Sliced banana is also a delicious addition.

Serves 6

Luscious Peaches & Cream Dessert

METRIC	AMERICAN
180 g (1½ C) flour	1½ cups all purpose flour
2 packages regular vanilla pudding mix (4 serving size)	2 packages regular vanilla pudding mix (4 serving size)
7 mℓ (1½ t) baking powder	1½ teaspoons baking powder
2 eggs, beaten	2 eggs, beaten
250 mℓ (1 C) milk	1 cup milk
90 mℓ (6 T) melted butter or margarine	6 tablespoons melted butter or margarine
2 x 440 g tins peaches (reserve 250 mℓ juice)	2 x 16 oz cans peaches (reserve 1 cup juice)
375 g cream cheese*	12 oz cream cheese
150 g (¾ C) sugar	¾ cup sugar

TOPPING	TOPPING
Cinnamon & sugar	Cinnamon & sugar

* *To ensure the success of this recipe, I suggest you use the packaged block cream cheese (imported if necessary)*

METHOD Combine flour, pudding mix and baking powder. Mix together the beaten eggs, milk and melted butter and add to dry ingredients. Blend well.

Spread mixture into a greased rectangular ovenware dish, measuring approximately 36 x 25 cm (14 x 10 inches). Dice peaches and sprinkle on top of batter. Beat cream cheese and sugar together, then beat in the reserved peach juice. Pour this mixture carefully over the peaches.

Sprinkle with cinnamon and sugar and bake in 180°C (350°F) oven for 40–45 minutes.

Serves 12

Hot Baked Raspberry or Youngberry Pudding

METRIC	AMERICAN
1 x 410 g tin youngberries or raspberries, undrained	1 x 13½ oz can youngberries or raspberries, undrained
10 mℓ (2 t) custard powder, mixed to a paste with cold water	2 teaspoons dessert mix or cornstarch, mixed to a paste with cold water
90 g butter or margarine	6 tablespoons butter or margarine
100 g (½ C) sugar	½ cup sugar
15 mℓ (1 T) syrup	1 tablespoon syrup
1 egg	1 egg
90 g (¾ C) flour	¾ cup flour
60 mℓ (¼ C) cornflour	¼ cup cornstarch
10 mℓ (2 t) baking powder	2 teaspoons baking powder

METHOD Bring berries and juice to the boil. Stir in custard powder / dessert mix or cornflour (cornstarch) paste and cook until thickened. Pour into a deep ovenware dish.

Cream butter and sugar together very well. Add syrup, egg and then remaining ingredients. Spoon over the berry mixture. Bake at 190°C (375°F) for 30–40 minutes. Serve hot with cream or ice-cream.

Serves 6

Cherries Jubilee

METRIC	AMERICAN
2 x 425 g tins red cherries	2 x 17 oz cans red cherries
15 mℓ (1 T) cornflour	1 tablespoon cornstarch
30 mℓ (2 T) butter	2 tablespoons butter
100 g (½ C) brown sugar	½ cup brown sugar
Juice & rind of 1 orange	Juice & rind of 1 orange
Juice of ½ lemon	Juice of ½ lemon
2 cinnamon sticks	2 cinnamon sticks
2 liqueur glasses of any fruity liqueurs	2 liqueur glasses of any fruity liqueurs
125 mℓ (½ C) brandy	½ cup cognac
Vanilla ice-cream	Vanilla ice-cream

METHOD Drain cherries. Reserve juice and set aside. Dissolve cornflour (cornstarch) in cherry juice and pour into chafing dish. Add butter, sugar, orange juice and rind, lemon juice, cinnamon sticks and liqueurs.

Simmer over low heat for approximately 10–15 minutes. Add cherries and simmer for another 5 minutes. Heat brandy (cognac) to boiling point. Flame and pour over. Serve spooned over vanilla ice-cream.

Serves 10 to 12

Rhubarb & Apple Cobbler

METRIC	AMERICAN
3–4 Granny Smith apples	3–4 Granny Smith apples
500 g fresh rhubarb, chopped	1 lb fresh rhubarb, chopped
150 g (¾ C) sugar or 200 mℓ (¾ C) syrup	¾ cup sugar or corn syrup
Pinch of salt	Pinch of salt

TOPPING	TOPPING
120 g (1 C) flour	1 cup flour
150 g (¾ C) sugar	¾ cup sugar
2 mℓ (½ t) ground cinammon	½ teaspoon ground cinnamon
125 g butter	½ cup butter
50 g (½ C) chopped nuts	½ cup chopped nuts

METHOD Peel, core and slice apples. Combine with rhubarb, sugar or syrup and salt. Place in a greased 20 cm (8 inch) ovenware dish.

TOPPING Stir together the flour, sugar and cinnamon. Cut in butter until mixture resembles coarse breadcrumbs. Stir in nuts. Sprinkle mixture over fruit.

Bake at 200°C (400°F) for 30–35 minutes. Serve hot with whipped cream or custard.

Serves 6 to 8

Mercia's Banana Fritters

METRIC	AMERICAN
6 bananas	6 bananas
45 mℓ (3 T) flour	3 tablespoons all purpose flour
80 mℓ (⅓ C) cornflour	⅓ cup cornstarch
7 mℓ (1½ t) baking powder	1½ teaspoons baking powder
1 mℓ (¼ t) salt	¼ teaspoon salt
125 mℓ (½ C) milk	½ cup milk
1 egg white	1 egg white
Oil for frying	Oil for frying
100 g (½ C) castor sugar	½ cup superfine granulated sugar
5 mℓ (1 t) cinnamon	1 teaspoon cinnamon

METHOD Sift flour, cornflour (cornstarch), baking powder and salt together. Mix to a smooth batter with milk. Whisk egg white until soft peaks form. Fold into batter. Slice bananas in half lengthwise and dip into batter. Deep fry in hot oil. Roll in sugar and cinnamon and serve hot.

CHEF'S TIP Ice-cream makes a delicious accompaniment to these fritters.

Makes 12

Overleaf (rear left) *Chocolate Mousse Fancy Cake,*
(centre, l to r) Crêpes Suzette, Mercia's Crème Caramel and Baked Apples with Caramel Sauce and (in the foreground)
Fruit Tart and a slice of Marshmallow Ring with Cream & Berries

Fried Custard Creams with Lemon Sauce

METRIC	AMERICAN
CUSTARD	CUSTARD
750 mℓ (3 C) milk	3 cups milk
Few drops almond essence	Few drops almond extract
45 mℓ (3 T) cornflour	3 tablespoons cornstarch
20 mℓ (4 t) flour	4 teaspoons flour
100 g (½ C) sugar	½ cup sugar
Pinch of salt	Pinch of salt
4 egg yolks, beaten well	4 egg yolks, beaten well
COATING	COATING
4 egg whites	4 egg whites
250 mℓ (1 C) crushed Marie biscuits	1 cup crushed Graham crackers
Flour	1 cup finely chopped almonds
250 mℓ (1 C) finely chopped almonds	
LEMON SAUCE	LEMON SAUCE
100 g (½ C) sugar	½ cup sugar
20 mℓ (4 t) cornflour	4 teaspoons cornstarch
250 mℓ (1 C) cold water	1 cup cold water
125 mℓ (½ C) fresh lemon juice	½ cup fresh lemon juice
15 mℓ (1 T) butter	1 tablespoon butter
2 mℓ (½ t) finely grated lemon rind	½ teaspoon finely grated lemon peel
Oil for frying	Oil for frying
Icing sugar	Powdered sugar

METHOD First prepare custard. Lightly grease a 20 cm (8 inch) square baking tin. In top of double boiler, heat 500 mℓ (2 cups) of the milk until boiling, then remove from heat. Add almond essence (extract).

In a separate bowl, combine cornflour (cornstarch), flour, sugar and salt and blend in remaining 250 mℓ (1 cup) milk.

Stir this mixture into hot milk in top of double boiler; cook over medium heat, stirring constantly until mixture thickens. Remove from heat.

Stir small amount of hot mixture into well-beaten egg yolks, then stir egg yolks back into hot mixture. Return to heat and cook, stirring constantly, until very thick.

Pour into greased pan. Allow to cool, then refrigerate for a few hours until firm, or preferably overnight.

COATING Beat egg whites slightly and set aside. Place biscuit (cookie) crumbs in a shallow dish.

Cut chilled custard into squares and remove carefully from pan. Coat with flour, dip in egg whites, then coat with crumbs. Place on a tray covered with wax paper, wrap in plastic and refrigerate for at least 8–10 hours, or refrigerate for a few days, until required.

LEMON SAUCE In a small saucepan, combine sugar and cornflour (cornstarch). Slowly stir in cold water until smooth, then add lemon juice. Heat, stirring constantly, until mixture boils and thickens. Remove from heat and stir in butter and grated lemon rind.

TO SERVE Heat a generous amount of oil in a large pan and deep fry custard squares for about 1 minute over medium heat. (Be careful not to let them burn – they should be golden brown.) Drain on paper towels, sprinkle with sifted icing (powdered) sugar and serve warm with lemon sauce.

CHEF'S TIP The creams may also be served with raspberry sauce (see recipe for White Chocolate Mousse on p 108). If fresh raspberries are not available, use the canned variety.

FRIED ICE-CREAM For a delicious variation of this recipe, substitute Fried Ice-Cream for the Custard Creams. Freeze the ice-cream in a foil-lined square pan, then cut into squares, dip in flour, egg white and crumbs and fry quickly. Serve with lemon, chocolate or raspberry sauce.

Makes 16 squares

Chocolate Soufflé

METRIC	AMERICAN
40 g butter	3 tablespoons butter
45 mℓ (3 T) flour	3 tablespoons flour
250 mℓ (1 C) milk	1 cup milk
60 g dark chocolate, grated	⅓ cup semi-sweet chocolate chips
4 eggs, separated	4 eggs, separated
100 g (½ C) sugar	½ cup sugar
5 mℓ (1 t) vanilla essence	1 teaspoon vanilla extract
Pinch of cream of tartar	Pinch of cream of tartar
Icing sugar	Powdered sugar

METHOD Preheat oven to 180°C (350°F). Melt butter in a saucepan and stir in flour; remove from heat and gradually stir in milk. Return to low heat, stirring constantly until smooth and thick. Stir in chocolate until melted. Remove from heat and cool.

Beat egg yolks and sugar together until light and creamy. Fold into chocolate mixture and add vanilla. Beat whites with cream of tartar until stiff. Fold in gently. Spoon into a buttered and sugared 1,5 litre (6 cup) soufflé dish and bake for 35–45 minutes.

Quickly sprinkle the top of the soufflé with sifted icing sugar (powdered sugar) and serve immediately with lightly whipped cream.

Serves 6

Chocolate Pie Alaska

METRIC	AMERICAN
BISCUIT BASE	COOKIE BASE
1 x 200 g packet Romany Creams, crushed or 500 mℓ (2 C) chocolate biscuit crumbs	*½ lb Oreo cookies, crushed*
60 g butter	*¼ cup butter*
CHOCOLATE FILLING	CHOCOLATE FILLING
125 g dark chocolate	*4 squares unsweetened chocolate*
125 g butter or margarine	*½ cup butter or margarine*
3 eggs	*3 eggs*
*100 g (½ C) sugar**	*¾ cup sugar*
15 mℓ (1 T) syrup (use light corn syrup if available)	*1 tablespoon syrup*
50 g (½ C) finely chopped nuts	*½ cup finely chopped nuts*
Vanilla or chocolate ice-cream	*Vanilla or chocolate ice-cream*
TO FLAMBÉ	TO FLAMBÉ
125 mℓ (½ C) brandy	*½ cup cognac*
MERINGUE	MERINGUE
3 egg whites	*3 egg whites*
90 g (6 T) sugar	*6 tablespoons sugar*

* *This measurement differs from the American*

METHOD Combine biscuit (cookie) crumbs and butter; mix with a fork until thoroughly moistened. Press evenly against bottom and sides of a 23 cm (9 inch) pie dish or loose-bottomed pan.

FILLING Melt chocolate and butter over hot water. Beat eggs and sugar together. Blend chocolate mixture with syrup, add to eggs and sugar and mix thoroughly. Fold in nuts. Pour into pie shell and bake in 180°C (350°F) oven for 30–40 minutes, or until set.

Mould vanilla or chocolate ice-cream into 20 cm (8 inch) cake pan which has been lined with foil or plastic wrap for easy removal. Freeze until required.

MERINGUE Beat egg whites until stiff. Add sugar gradually, beating all the time until very stiff and shiny. Unmould ice-cream and place on top of chocolate pie. Cover pie completely with the meringue.

Bake in preheated 250°C (500°F) oven for 3–5 minutes. Set aflame with boiling brandy (cognac) and serve immediately.

Serves 10 to 12

Cheese Crêpes with Strawberry Sauce

METRIC	AMERICAN
BATTER	BATTER
3 eggs	*3 eggs*
180 g (1½ C) flour	*1½ cups flour*
500 mℓ (2 C) cold water	*2 cups cold water*
2 mℓ (½ t) baking powder	*½ teaspoon baking powder*
Pinch of salt	*Pinch of salt*
FILLING	FILLING
500 g smooth cream cheese	*1 lb cream cheese (smooth & creamy style)*
2 eggs	*2 eggs*
30 mℓ (2 T) cornflour	*2 tablespoons cornstarch*
5 mℓ (1 t) vanilla essence	*1 teaspoon vanilla extract*
125 mℓ (½ C) sour cream	*½ cup sour cream*
TOPPING	TOPPING
125 mℓ (½ C) milk	*½ cup milk*
Butter	*Butter*
Cinnamon & sugar	*Cinnamon & sugar*
125 mℓ (½ C) cream	*½ cup cream*
STRAWBERRY SAUCE	STRAWBERRY SAUCE
*250 g sliced strawberries (frozen or fresh)**	*½ lb sliced strawberries (frozen or fresh)**
60 g butter	*¼ cup butter*
30 mℓ (2 T) brandy	*2 tablespoons brandy*
7 mℓ (1½ t) cornflour mixed to a paste with a little cold water	*1½ teaspoons cornstarch mixed to a paste with a little cold water*

* *If frozen, sprinkle with 30 mℓ (2 tablespoons) icing (powdered) sugar and leave to thaw*

METHOD To prepare batter, beat all ingredients together until smooth. Spray a small pan with non-stick spray, heat and pour in a thin layer of batter. Rotate pan to cover the bottom evenly. Fry quickly on one side only until crisp and golden. Transfer to a clean cloth. Stack crêpes one on top of the other as they cool.

FILLING Mix all ingredients together. Place a spoonful of filling on each crêpe, then fold up envelope fashion. Place in a buttered ovenware dish.

Pour 125 mℓ (½ cup) milk over crêpes and dot with knobs of butter. Sprinkle with cinnamon and sugar and bake for 20–25 minutes in 190°C (375°F) oven until hot and bubbling.

STRAWBERRY SAUCE Place all ingredients in a saucepan, except the cornflour (cornstarch). Bring to the boil and thicken with paste.

TO SERVE Pour 125 mℓ (½ cup) cream over crêpes and serve with the strawberry sauce.

Serves 12

Spoonbread Soufflé with Strawberry Sauce

METRIC	AMERICAN
SPOONBREAD SOUFFLÉ	SPOONBREAD SOUFFLÉ
See recipe on p 24	*See recipe on p 24*
STRAWBERRY SAUCE	STRAWBERRY SAUCE
250 g frozen or tinned straw-berries	*½ lb frozen strawberries*
250 g butter, melted	*1 cup butter, melted*
250 mℓ (1 C) icing sugar	*1 cup powdered sugar*

METHOD Prepare soufflé as directed on p 24. Remove from oven and serve immediately accompanied by Strawberry Sauce.

STRAWBERRY SAUCE Combine all ingredients in blender or food processor until smooth.

Serves 6 to 8

Crêpes Suzette

METRIC	AMERICAN
CRÊPES	CRÊPES
4 eggs	*4 eggs*
120 g (1 C) flour	*1 cup flour*
500 mℓ (2 C) milk	*2 cups milk*
SAUCE	SAUCE
100 g (½ C) sugar	*½ cup sugar*
90 g butter	*6 tablespoons butter*
Juice & rind of 1 orange	*Juice & rind of 1 orange*
Juice of 1 lemon	*Juice of 1 lemon*
125 mℓ (½ C) Grand Marnier	*½ cup Grand Marnier*
TO FLAMBÉ	TO FLAMBÉ
125 mℓ (½ C) brandy	*½ cup cognac*

METHOD To prepare crêpes, beat all ingredients together until smooth. Pour through a strainer to remove lumps. (This is not necessary if using a food processor.) Spray a small non-stick pan with non-stick spray and heat on high, then turn heat down to medium. Spoon in enough batter to cover the bottom of the pan. Fry on one side only until crisp and golden. Turn crêpes out onto a clean cloth and stack one on top of the other until ready to use.

SAUCE Heat sugar in a large pan over a steady flame until it caramelizes. Add butter and blend thoroughly. Add orange juice, rind and lemon juice. Stir in Grand Marnier and reduce flame to low.

Add the pancakes, a few at a time; coat thoroughly and fold into triangles. Arrange pancakes in centre of pan. Turn up the flame, add brandy (cognac) and ignite. Serve hot with vanilla ice-cream.

CHEF'S TIP As a variation, fill crêpes with vanilla ice-cream, roll up and arrange on a serving platter. Prepare the sauce, pour it over the crêpes and flame with brandy (refer to photograph on p 98).

Makes 24 PHOTOGRAPH ON PAGE 98

Apple Custard Crêpes

METRIC	AMERICAN
BATTER	BATTER
120 g (1 C) flour	*1 cup flour*
4 eggs	*4 eggs*
500 mℓ (2 C) milk	*2 cups milk*
Pinch of salt	*Pinch of salt*
Oil for frying	*Oil for frying*
FILLING	FILLING
6–8 Granny Smith apples, peeled & quartered	*6–8 Granny Smith apples, peeled & quartered*
Juice of 1 lemon	*Juice of 1 lemon*
150 g (¾ C) sugar	*¾ cup sugar*
2 egg yolks	*2 egg yolks*
250 mℓ (1 C) cream	*1 cup cream*
TOPPING	TOPPING
Cinnamon & sugar	*Cinnamon & sugar*
15 mℓ (1 T) butter	*1 tablespoon butter*

METHOD To prepare batter, beat all ingredients (except oil) together until smooth. Heat oil in a small pan (or use a non-stick spray) and pour in 15–30 mℓ (1–2 tablespoons) of batter. Rotate to cover pan evenly. Fry quickly on one side only until crisp and golden. Transfer to a clean cloth; when cool, stack crêpes one on top of another.

FILLING Combine apples, lemon juice and sugar in a saucepan over low heat. Cook gently until apples are tender but not mushy. Cool. Beat egg yolks, add cream and mix with apples.

Place a spoonful of filling on each crêpe and roll up. Arrange in a greased ovenware dish. Sprinkle with cinnamon and sugar. Dot with butter and bake until hot in 180°C (350°F) oven.

Makes 25

Soufflèd Crêpes with Custard

METRIC	AMERICAN
CRÊPES	**CRÊPES**
4 eggs	4 eggs
120 g (1 C) flour	1 cup flour
500 mℓ (2 C) milk	2 cups milk
Toasted almonds to sprinkle over crêpes	Toasted almonds to sprinkle over crêpes
FILLING	**FILLING**
4 egg whites	4 egg whites
Pinch of salt	Pinch of salt
200 g (1 C) sugar	1 cup sugar
2 mℓ (½ t) vanilla essence	½ teaspoon vanilla extract (remains as is)
CUSTARD SAUCE	**CUSTARD SAUCE**
250 mℓ (1 C) cream	1 cup cream
375 mℓ (1½ C) milk	1½ cups milk
4 egg yolks	4 egg yolks
30 mℓ (2 T) sugar	2 tablespoons sugar
15 mℓ (1 T) cornflour	1 tablespoon cornstarch
15 mℓ (1 T) Grand Marnier	1 tablespoon Grand Marnier

METHOD Prepare crêpes. Beat together all ingredients (except sugar) until smooth. Strain to remove any lumps. (This is not necessary if using a food processor.)

Spray a small non-stick pan with non-stick spray and heat on high, then turn heat down to medium. Spoon in enough batter to cover the bottom of the pan. Fry on one side only until crisp and golden. Turn out onto a clean cloth and stack one on top of the other until ready to use.

FILLING Beat egg whites with salt until they form soft peaks, then add sugar, 1 tablespoon at a time. Continue beating until stiff and glossy. Add vanilla. Set aside.

CUSTARD SAUCE Scald the cream and milk in the top of a double boiler. Beat the egg yolks and sugar until light and creamy, then add cornflour (cornstarch). Beat until blended. Slowly add the scalded mixture to the egg yolks, beating constantly. Return mixture to double boiler and cook until thickened, stirring constantly with a wooden spoon. Stir in Grand Marnier.

TO ASSEMBLE & BAKE Top each crêpe with a heaped tablespoon of meringue. Fold sides over to cover. Arrange crêpes, seam sides down, in a buttered baking dish. Bake in 180°C (350°F) oven for 5–7 minutes.

TO SERVE Spoon warmed custard sauce over the crêpes and sprinkle with toasted almonds.

CHEF'S TIP If desired, serve a raspberry or strawberry sauce on the side.

Makes 24

Chocolate Mint Bombe

METRIC	AMERICAN
1 ℓ chocolate ice-cream	2 pints chocolate ice-cream
2 egg whites	2 egg whites
30 mℓ (2 T) sugar	2 tablespoons sugar
250 mℓ (1 C) cream	½ pint cream
1 peppermint crisp, crushed	1 cup diced peppermint chocolate
2 mℓ (½ t) peppermint essence	½ teaspoon peppermint extract
Few drops green food colouring	Few drops green food color
Chocolate sauce	Chocolate sauce

METHOD Line a mould with ice-cream, leaving centre hollow. Freeze. Beat egg whites stiffly and add sugar. Fold peppermint flavouring and colouring into whipped cream. Add crushed chocolate, then fold cream mixture into egg whites.

Spoon mixture into centre of mould, cover with foil and return to freezer. Unmould, drizzle with chocolate sauce and serve.

Serves 12

Grenadilla Ice-cream

METRIC	AMERICAN
4 egg yolks	4 egg yolks
1 x 396 g tin sweetened condensed milk	1 x 14 oz can sweetened condensed milk
500 mℓ (2 C) cream, whipped	2 cups cream, whipped
500 mℓ (2 C) grenadilla pulp	2 cups passion fruit pulp

METHOD Beat the egg yolks and condensed milk together well. Fold in the whipped cream, then fold in the grenadilla pulp. Pour into a mould and freeze.

CHEF'S TIP If you do not have a mould, line a bowl or square pan with foil, pour mixture in and freeze. To serve, unmould and peel off foil.

Serves 8

Orange Pineapple Nut Ice-cream

METRIC	AMERICAN
2 ℓ vanilla ice-cream	1 quart vanilla ice-cream
250 mℓ (1 C) cream, whipped	1 cup cream, whipped
2 egg yolks	2 egg yolks
1 x 475 g tin crushed pineapple with juice	1 x 20 oz can crushed pineapple with juice
½ of 400 mℓ tin orange juice concentrate	1 x 6 fl oz can orange juice concentrate
250 mℓ (1 C) diced pecan nuts	1 cup diced pecans

METHOD Soften ice-cream. Mix in remaining ingredients. Spoon into mould, cover with plastic and freeze until firm. Unmould, drizzle with chocolate sauce and garnish with orange slices.

Serves 8 to 10

Peanut Crisp Ice-cream Slab

METRIC	AMERICAN
250 mℓ (1 C) syrup	1 cup syrup
250 mℓ (1 C) peanut butter	1 cup peanut butter
500 mℓ (2 C) rice crispies	2 cups rice crispies
150 g (1 C) salted peanuts	1 cup salted peanuts
1 large slab vanilla ice-cream	1 large slab vanilla ice-cream

METHOD Melt syrup and peanut butter together. Add rice crispies and peanuts. Cool thoroughly.

Using the back of a spoon, press mixture onto and around the ice-cream slab. Wrap in foil and freeze until ready to serve.

Serves 8

Berry Jelly (Jello)

METRIC	AMERICAN
4 x 410 g tins different berries*	4 x 13½ oz cans different berries*
1½ packets red or black jelly	1½ packets red or black jello

* strawberries, cherries, youngberries, blackberries or raspberries

METHOD Boil juice from canned fruit. Add jelly (jello) and stir until dissolved, then stir in fruit. Refrigerate to set. (This makes a very large dessert.)

Serves 12 to 15

Curly Dessert Cups

METRIC	AMERICAN
3 egg whites	3 egg whites
250 mℓ (1 C) cream	1 cup cream
125 mℓ (½ C) icing sugar	½ cup powdered sugar
120 g (1 C) flour	1 cup all purpose flour

METHOD Using a whisk, blend egg whites and cream by hand. Add sifted sugar and flour and beat until smooth.

Allowing 30 mℓ (2 tablespoons) of mixture for each 'cup', spoon two onto a greased, non-stick baking tray. Using the back of the spoon in a circular motion, spread each one into a 20 cm (8 inch) circle. Bake in 160°C (325°F) oven for 5 minutes. (They should still be very pale, or just slightly browned around the edges.)

Remove from oven and place each 'cup' over the base of an inverted glass. Place the inverted glasses over an inverted muffin pan (to prevent them from sliding around and burning you) and return to the oven for another 5 minutes, or until nicely browned. Remove from oven and cool on a rack. Repeat, using remaining mixture. Store in an airtight tin until ready to use.

TO SERVE Fill with ice-cream and top with a purée of sweetened strawberries. Reserve a few whole, choice berries for decoration.

CHEF'S TIP These cups may also be filled with chocolate mousse or a vanilla custard and fruit or berries of your choice. If desired, brush the edges with melted chocolate and sprinkle with chopped pistachio nuts.

Makes 10

Frozen Fruit Salad

METRIC	AMERICAN
250 g cream cheese	1 x 8 oz package cream cheese
250 mℓ (1 C) sour cream	1 cup sour cream
50 g (¼ C) sugar	¼ cup sugar
Pinch of salt	Pinch of salt
875 mℓ (3½ C) drained, mixed tinned fruit (lychees, mangoes & peaches)	3½ cups drained, mixed canned fruit (lychees, mangoes & peaches)
1 x 475 g tin crushed pineapple	1 x 20 oz can crushed pineapple
500 mℓ (2 C) marshmallows, quartered	2 cups miniature marshmallows

METHOD Soften cream cheese and beat until fluffy. Stir in cream, sugar and salt. Fold in fruit and marshmallows.

Pour into a pan or individual foil cups and freeze for 6 hours. Cut into squares and serve.

Serves 8 to 10

Lemon Florentine

By courtesy of Timothy Johnson

METRIC	AMERICAN
250 mℓ (1 C) cream	1 cup heavy or whipping cream
250 mℓ (1 C) milk	1 cup milk
200 g (1 C) sugar	1 cup sugar
Juice of 3 or 4 lemons	Juice of 3 or 4 lemons
15 mℓ (1 T) lemon zest, finely grated	1 tablespoon lemon zest, finely grated

METHOD Heat cream, milk and sugar until sugar has dissolved. Pour into freezer tray and freeze until semi-solid.

Remove, crush and add lemon juice and zest. Taste and if necessary, add more sugar or lemon. Beat until frothy. Return to freezer and freeze until solid.

CHEF'S TIP An attractive serving idea for this dessert is to scoop out large lemons, slice off the ends so that they can stand upright and fill with the lemon cream as you would an ice-cream cone. Garnish with flowers or leaves.

Serves 8

Greek Meringue

METRIC	AMERICAN
6 egg whites	6 egg whites
3,5 mℓ (¾ t) cream of tartar	¾ teaspoon cream of tartar
300 g (1½ C) sugar*	2 cups sugar
500 mℓ (2 C) coarsely crushed cream crackers	2 cups coarsely crushed crackers
100 g (1 C) chopped nuts	1 cup chopped nuts
5 mℓ (1 t) vanilla essence	1 teaspoon vanilla extract

TOPPING	TOPPING
500 mℓ (2 C) cream, whipped	1 pint cream, whipped (or whipped topping)
Strawberries or other fruit of your choice	Strawberries or other fruit of your choice

* *This measurement differs from the American*

METHOD Beat egg whites until frothy. Add cream of tartar and continue to beat until stiff. Gradually add sugar, beating after each addition until stiff and shiny. Fold in crackers, nuts and vanilla.

Line a 23 x 32 cm (9 x 13 inch) pan with foil, or use a buttered ovenware dish. Pour mixture in and bake at 180°C (350°F) for 25 minutes. Remove from pan and cool.

Spread with whipped cream (flavoured with a liqueur of your choice, if desired) and top with strawberries.

Serves 12

Lemon Cream Puff Ring

METRIC	AMERICAN
250 mℓ (1 C) water	1 cup water
125 g butter	½ cup butter
150 g flour	1 heaped cup all purpose flour
4 eggs	4 eggs

FILLING	FILLING
1 package lemon instant pudding	1 package lemon instant pudding
500 mℓ (2 C) cream	2 cups cream
250 mℓ (1 C) milk	1 cup milk
1 x 410 g tin youngberries or raspberries	1 x 15 oz can youngberries or raspberries
15 mℓ (1 T) cornflour mixed to a paste with cold water	1 tablespoon cornstarch mixed to a paste with cold water

TOPPING	TOPPING
400 g (2 C) sugar	2 cups sugar
250 mℓ (1 C) water	1 cup water
Good pinch cream of tartar	Good pinch cream of tartar

METHOD Bring water and butter to the boil. Quickly stir in flour until mixture leaves the sides of the saucepan. Beat in eggs, one at a time, beating well after each addition. Drop in teaspoonfuls (or pipe) onto a greased and floured baking sheet, to form a 20 cm (8 inch) circle.

Bake in 190°C (375°F) oven for 15–20 minutes. Turn oven off and leave for another 10–15 minutes, to dry out. Cool.

FILLING Beat together the lemon instant pudding, 250 mℓ (1 cup) cream and the milk until thick. Set aside. Drain juice from berries and thicken over medium heat with cornflour (cornstarch) paste. Fold in berries, then allow to cool. Whip remaining 250 mℓ (1 cup) cream.

Split cream puff ring through the middle and fill with a layer of lemon filling, followed by a layer of berries, then cream.

TOPPING Boil sugar, water and cream of tartar together over medium heat (without stirring), until syrup turns a light caramel colour. Remove from heat immediately. Allow to cool a little.

Using a spoon, spin the thread in a circular motion until you build up the spun sugar like a layer of straw. As the mixture cools, pull the sugar to form long threads and stack on top of the pastry.

CHEF'S TIP If you do not feel confident enough to spin the sugar, simply dust the top of the cream puff ring with icing sugar (powdered sugar).

Serves 12   PHOTOGRAPH ON PAGE 106

Overleaf: Lemon Cream Puff Ring

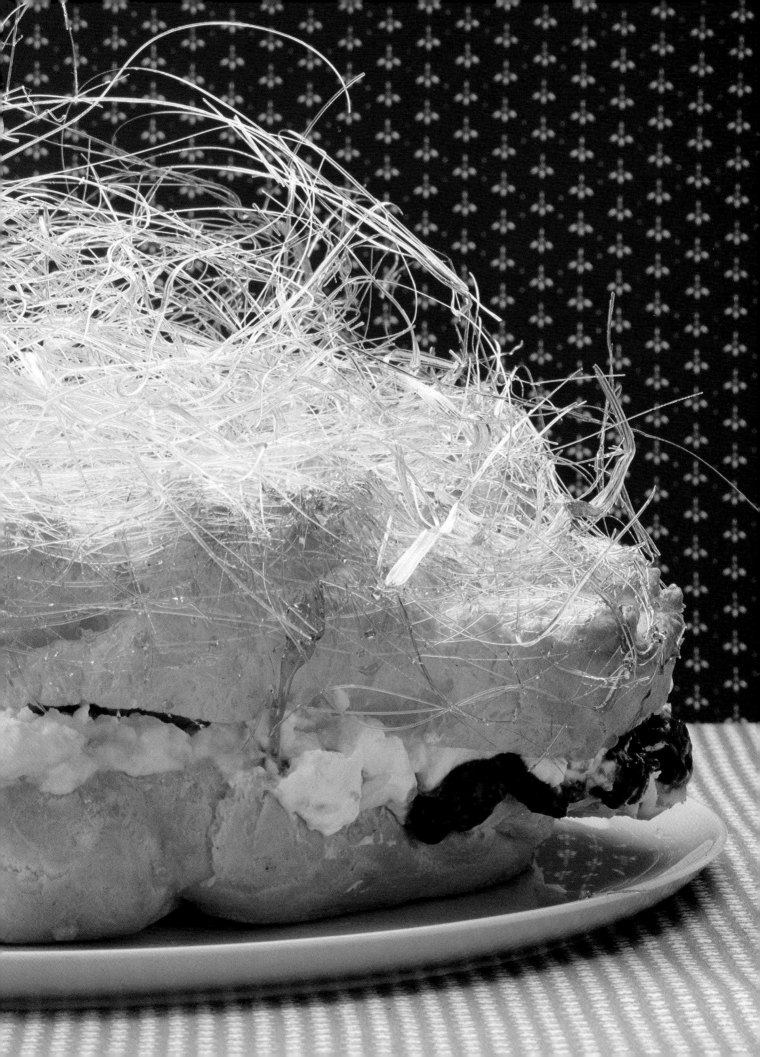

Mango Mousse

METRIC	AMERICAN
200 g (1 C) sugar	1 cup sugar
125 mℓ (½ C) water	½ cup water
Pinch of cream of tartar	Pinch of cream of tartar
4 egg whites, stiffly beaten	4 egg whites, stiffly beaten
Pulp of 4 mangoes, puréed	Pulp of 4 mangoes, puréed
15 mℓ (1 T) lemon juice	1 tablespoon lemon juice
30 mℓ (2 T) orange-flavoured liqueur	2 tablespoons orange-flavored liqueur
250 mℓ (1 C) cream, whipped	1 cup cream, whipped

METHOD Combine sugar, water and cream of tartar in a saucepan. Stir until sugar has dissolved. Allow to boil gently until sugar spins a thread and then pour slowly onto stiffly beaten egg whites. Beat until mixture is thick.

Fold in mango purée, lemon juice and orange liqueur, then fold in stiffly beaten cream. Pour into a glass bowl and refrigerate until ready to serve.

CHEF'S TIP Other fruit purée, such as raspberry or strawberry, may be used instead of the mango.

Serves 8 to 10

White Chocolate Mousse with Raspberry Sauce

METRIC	AMERICAN
500 g high quality white chocolate	1 lb quality white chocolate
6 eggs, separated	6 eggs, separated
30 mℓ (2 T) icing sugar	2 tablespoons powdered sugar
125 g butter, melted & cooled	½ cup butter, melted & cooled
125 mℓ (½ C) Amaretto or Grand Marnier	½ cup Amaretto or Grand Marnier
1 envelope gelatin	1 envelope geltain
250mℓ (1 C) cream, whipped	1 cup cream, whipped

RASPBERRY SAUCE	RASPBERRY SAUCE
300 g frozen or tinned raspberries	10 oz frozen raspberries
Juice of ½ lemon	Juice of ½ lemon
30 mℓ (2 T) sugar	2 tablespoons sugar
5 mℓ (1 t) cornflour	1 teaspoon cornstarch
30 mℓ (2 T) Framboise, Kirsch or Crème de Cassis	2 tablespoons Framboise, Kirsch or Crème de Cassis

METHOD Melt chocolate in microwave on 50% power for 3 minutes, or in top of double boiler. (Do not stir.) Beat egg yolks and sugar together until pale and thick. Beat in melted chocolate, then butter. Dissolve gelatin in liquer over gentle heat. Cool and fold in. Fold in whipped cream and lastly, the stiffly beaten egg whites. Pour into glass bowl and refrigerate.

Alternatively, if you wish to make a large white chocolate 'cabbage' (see photograph on p 118), pour mixture into a dome-shaped glass bowl which has been lined with foil (or use a plastic mould) and place in freezer. Unmould onto serving platter.

Using whipped cream to hold the leaves in place, cover the frozen mousse with moulded chocolate cabbage leaves (see Chocolate Decorations on p 114), so as to resemble a large cabbage.

Serve with raspberry sauce.

RASPBERRY SAUCE Combine raspberries and lemon juice in food processor. Purée until smooth and strain. Pour mixture into a saucepan; add sugar and bring to the boil. Dissolve the cornflour (cornstarch) in the liqueur and stir in over low heat. Cool, cover and refrigerate until ready to use.

Serves 12 PHOTOGRAPH ON PAGE 118

Marshmallow Ring with Cream & Berries

METRIC	AMERICAN
6 egg whites (200 mℓ)	6 egg whites (¾ cup)
1 mℓ (¼ t) cream of tartar	¼ teaspoon cream of tartar
Pinch of salt	Pinch of salt
200 g (1 C) castor sugar	1 cup superfine granulated sugar
5 mℓ (1 t) vanilla essence	1 teaspoon vanilla extract
5 mℓ (1 t) lemon juice	1 teaspoon lemon juice

TO FILL & GARNISH	TO FILL & GARNISH
250 mℓ (1 C) cream	1 cup cream
Strawberries & raspberries	Strawberries & raspberries

METHOD Grease a bundt tin, or a fluted tin with a hole in the middle, with butter. Beat egg whites with cream of tartar and salt until very stiff. Gradually add sugar, beating until very stiff and shiny. Add vanilla and lemon juice.

Spoon mixture into prepared tin, set in a dish of cold water and bake in 160°C (325°F) oven for 1 hour. Remove from oven and allow to cool to room temperature. Loosen edges with a spatula and invert onto a serving platter.

TO SERVE Whip cream until stiff, pipe rosettes around the base of the marshmallow ring and on top. Fill the centre with berries and place a few on top of the cream rosettes. If using strawberries, leave the green stems on a few of the choice ones to garnish.

CHEF'S TIP The berries may also be marinated in a liqueur such as Grand Marnier or Kirsch before using.

Serves 8 PHOTOGRAPH ON PAGE 99

Rich Chocolate Mousse

METRIC	AMERICAN
30 ml (2 T) butter	2 tablespoons butter
500 g dark chocolate*	1 lb semi-sweet chocolate chips*
4 eggs, separated	4 eggs, separated
50 g (¼ C) sugar	¼ cup sugar
5 ml (1 t) vanilla essence	1 teaspoon vanilla extract
30 ml (2 T) Grand Marnier	2 tablespoons Grand Marnier
1 x 170 g tin evaporated milk	1 x 6 oz can evaporated milk
Pinch of salt	Pinch of salt
250 ml (1 C) double cream	1 cup heavy cream

I prefer to use a high-quality chocolate if possible

METHOD Melt butter and chocolate in double boiler or microwave. Allow to cool. Beat egg yolks and sugar together until light and creamy, then beat in vanilla, liqueur, chocolate and evaporated milk.

Whisk egg whites with salt until stiff. In a separate bowl, beat cream until stiff. Combine egg whites and cream and fold into chocolate mixture . Refrigerate until set (at least 2 hours).

Serves 8

Coeur à la Crème

METRIC	AMERICAN
250 g cottage cheese	1 cup cottage cheese
250 g cream cheese	8 oz cream cheese
250 ml (1 C) icing sugar	1 cup powdered sugar
250 ml (1 C) cream, whipped	1 cup cream, whipped
5 ml (1 t) vanilla essence or	1 teaspoon vanilla extract or
5 ml (1 t) finely grated orange rind	1 teaspoon finely grated orange rind

SAUCE	SAUCE
300 g frozen, fresh or tinned raspberries or strawberries	10 oz frozen or fresh raspberries or strawberries
Juice of ½ lemon	Juice of ½ lemon
30 ml (2 T) sugar	2 tablespoons sugar
5 ml (1 t) cornflour	1 teaspoon cornstarch
30 ml (2 T) Framboise, Kirsch or Crème de Cassis	2 tablespoons Framboise, Kirsch or Crème de Cassis

GARNISH	GARNISH
125 ml (½ C) cream	½ cup cream
Strawberries dipped in melted chocolate, or raspberries & mint leaves	Strawberries dipped in melted chocolate, or raspberries & mint leaves

METHOD Combine cheeses and sugar in blender or food processor. Fold in whipped cream and vanilla or orange rind.

Line a heart-shaped mould or baking tin with a double thickness of cheese cloth which has been wrung out with cold water. Drape well over the edges. Pour in mixture; fold over edges and chill overnight.

SAUCE Combine raspberries or strawberries and lemon juice in blender or food processor. Purée until smooth and strain. Pour into a saucepan. Add sugar and bring to the boil. Dissolve cornflour (cornstarch) in the liqueur and stir into sauce over low heat. Cool, cover and refrigerate.

TO SERVE Unmould dessert onto a serving platter, peel off cloth and pour 30–45 ml (2–3 tablespoons) of the unwhipped cream over the mould. Beat the remainder of the cream until thick and pipe rosettes around the edge of the heart.

Garnish with strawberries (dipped in melted chocolate and refrigerated until set), or with raspberries and mint leaves. Pour raspberry or strawberry sauce around mould and serve.

CHEF'S TIP If preferred, freeze dessert in a mould and serve frozen with the sauce.

Serves 8

Marbled Chocolate Mousse

METRIC	AMERICAN
250 ml (1 C) cream	1 cup heavy or whipping cream
6 eggs, separated	6 eggs, separated
125 ml (½ C) icing sugar	½ cup powdered sugar
125 g butter	½ cup butter
350 g white chocolate	12 oz white chocolate
125 ml (½ C) Amaretto or Grand Marnier	½ cup Amaretto or Grand Marnier
50 g dark chocolate	2 oz semi-sweet chocolate

GARNISH	GARNISH
Whipped cream	Whipped cream
Chocolate Curls	Chocolate Curls

METHOD Whip cream until it forms soft peaks. Set aside. Beat egg yolks with sugar until thick and creamy. Melt butter, white chocolate and Amaretto or Grand Marnier in a double boiler or microwave. Beat the chocolate / butter mixture into the beaten egg yolks until smooth.

Whisk egg whites until they form soft peaks, then fold into mixture and lastly, fold in the whipped cream. Divide the mixture in half. Melt the dark chocolate and add to one half. Stir well until blended. Refrigerate both mixtures for 10–15 minutes, until slightly thickened.

Carefully spoon in alternate layers into a glass serving dish, then zig-zag through mixture with a knife. Decorate with whipped cream and / or Chocolate Curls (see Chocolate Decorations on p 114).

Serves 12

Chocolate Meringue

METRIC	AMERICAN
4 egg whites	4 egg whites
300 g (1½ C) castor sugar	1½ cups superfine granulated sugar
20 mℓ (4 t) cocoa	4 teaspoons cocoa

FILLING	FILLING
500 mℓ (2 C) cream	2 cups cream
Sugar to taste	Sugar to taste
30 mℓ (2 T) rum or Kirsch	2 tablespoons rum or Kirsh

GARNISH	GARNISH
Whipped cream	Whipped cream
Grated chocolate	Grated chocolate
Glacé cherries	Glacé cherries
Nuts	Nuts

METHOD Whisk egg whites until stiff. Add 15 mℓ (1 tablespoon) castor sugar (superfine granulated sugar) and whisk again, until very stiff. Mix cocoa with remaining sugar and fold into whites. Spread mixture in two rounds or squares on wax paper or foil, place on baking sheet and bake at 120°C (250°F) for 2–3 hours or longer, if necessary.

FILLING Beat cream until thick. Fold in sugar and liqueur.

TO SERVE Sandwich meringues together with filling and decorate with whipped cream, grated chocolate, cherries and nuts.

Serves 10

Mercia's Foolproof Pavlova

METRIC	AMERICAN
6 egg whites (200 mℓ)	6 egg whites (¾ cup)
1 mℓ (¼ t) cream of tartar	¼ teaspoon cream of tartar
300 g (1½ C) sugar	1½ cups sugar
2 mℓ (½ t) vanilla essence	½ teaspoon vanilla extract
7 mℓ (1½ t) lemon juice	1½ teaspoons lemon juice
7 mℓ (1½ t) cornflour	1½ teaspoons cornstarch

TOPPING	TOPPING
Whipped cream	Whipped cream
Whole strawberries, sliced kiwi fruit, sliced bananas or grenadilla pulp	Whole strawberries, sliced kiwi fruit, sliced bananas or passion fruit pulp

METHOD Beat egg whites with cream of tartar until very stiff. Gradually add sugar and continue beating until very stiff and shiny. Beat in vanilla, lemon juice and cornflour (cornstarch).

Cover a baking sheet with foil. Using a 23 cm (9 inch) square cake tin, trace a square onto the foil with a pencil. Spray with non-stick spray and pile the meringue onto the traced square, building up the sides and centre until they are even.

Preheat oven to 180°C (350°F), then turn down to 120°C (250°F) and bake meringue for 20 minutes. Reduce oven temperature to 100°C (200°F) and bake for a further hour.

The pavlova should slide off the foil very easily but if necessary, loosen with a spatula. Transfer to a serving platter.

When cool, top with whipped cream and your choice of fruit and serve.

Serves 10 to 12

Mercia's Crème Caramel

METRIC	AMERICAN
150 g (¾ C) sugar	¾ cup sugar
4 eggs	4 eggs
30 mℓ (2 T) sugar	2 tablespoons sugar
5 mℓ (1 t) vanilla essence	1 teaspoon vanilla extract
750 mℓ (3 C) milk, scalded	3 cups milk, scalded

METHOD Melt sugar in a heavy saucepan over low heat. Pour into a round ovenware dish, 15 cm (6 inches) in diameter and 9 cm (3½ inches) deep. Swirl around to coat base and halfway up the sides of the dish.

Beat eggs with 30 mℓ (2 tablespoons) sugar and the vanilla, just until blended, then pour the milk very slowly onto the egg mixture, beating constantly as you do so. Pour over cooled caramelized sugar and place the dish in a *bain-marie* (a large baking dish which has been half-filled with boiling water).

Cover top with foil and keep covered throughout the baking period. Bake in 180°C (350°F) oven for 20 minutes, then turn oven down to 150°C (300°F) and bake for another 40 minutes or until set. (The centre becomes firm after standing for a while.)

Cool and refrigerate overnight. To unmould, loosen around edges with a knife and invert onto serving platter.

CHEF'S TIP For a larger crème caramel, add 1 egg and 15 mℓ (1 tablespoon) sugar for each additional cup of milk.

Serves 6 to 8   PHOTOGRAPH ON PAGE 98

Chocolate Mousse Fancy Cake

METRIC	AMERICAN
CAKE	**CAKE**
60 g (½ C) flour	*½ cup cake flour*
60 mℓ (¼ C) cocoa powder	*¼ cup cocoa powder*
5 mℓ (1 t) baking powder	*1 teaspoon baking powder*
2 eggs	*2 eggs*
100 g (½ C) castor sugar	*½ cup superfine granulated sugar*
2 mℓ (½ t) vanilla essence	*½ teaspoon vanilla extract*
30 mℓ (2 T) butter	*2 tablespoons butter*
60 mℓ (¼ C) milk	*¼ cup milk*
CHOCOLATE BASE	**CHOCOLATE BASE**
250 g dark chocolate	*8 oz semi-sweet chocolate chips*
MOUSSE	**MOUSSE**
30 mℓ (2 T) butter	*2 tablespoons butter*
500 g dark chocolate	*16 oz semi-sweet chocolate chips*
1 x 170 g tin evaporated milk	*1 x 6 oz can evaporated milk*
4 eggs, separated	*4 eggs, separated*
50 g (¼ C) sugar	*¼ cup sugar*
5 mℓ (1 t) vanilla essence	*1 teaspoon vanilla extract*
30 mℓ (2 T) Grand Marnier	*2 tablespoons Grand Marnier*
1 envelope gelatine	*1 envelope gelatin*
Pinch of salt	*Pinch of salt*
250 mℓ (1 C) cream	*1 cup heavy cream*
CHOCOLATE STRIPS	**CHOCOLATE STRIPS**
1 large slab dark chocolate	*1 cup semi-sweet chocolate chips*
1 large slab white chocolate	*6 oz white chocolate*
GARNISH	**GARNISH**
Chocolate Leaves	*Chocolate Leaves*

METHOD First prepare cake. Sift together flour, cocoa and baking powder and set aside. Beat eggs and sugar until thick and creamy. Add vanilla.

Combine butter and milk in a saucepan and bring gently to the boil, then add slowly to the egg mixture alternately with the sifted dry ingredients.

Pour into a greased and floured 23 cm (9 inch) cake pan and bake in 190°C (375°F) oven for 10–15 minutes. Turn out onto a cooling rack.

CHOCOLATE BASE Melt chocolate in double boiler or microwave oven. Line a 23 cm (9 inch) springform or loose-bottomed pan with foil. Spoon in and spread enough chocolate to cover the bottom evenly. Allow to set in refrigerator for a few minutes; using a sharp knife, cut the chocolate first in half, then into quarters and finally into eighths, so that you have eight wedges. Return to refrigerator until thoroughly hardened.

MOUSSE Melt butter, chocolate and evaporated milk in double boiler or microwave. Allow to cool. Beat egg yolks and sugar until light and creamy. Beat in vanilla, liqueur and chocolate mixture. Dissolve gelatine in 15 mℓ (1 tablespoon) cold water, then add 60 mℓ (¼ cup) boiling water and stir until thoroughly dissolved. Add to mixture.

Beat egg whites with salt until stiff, then beat cream until stiff. Combine and fold into chocolate mixture.

TO ASSEMBLE Spoon mousse over the chocolate base and press cake on top of mousse. Cover and allow to set in refrigerator overnight. Unmould by inverting onto a serving platter. Remove first the ring, then the base of the cake pan.

CHOCOLATE STRIPS Make the chocolate strips that surround the cake (see photograph on p 98) by melting white and dark chocolate separately. Measure two double thicknesses of foil to the same width as the cake pan. Lay flat on a board, spread one with melted dark chocolate and the other with melted white chocolate. Refrigerate for a few minutes until slightly set, then using a ruler as a guide, cut into 5 cm (2 inch) strips. Return to refrigerator to set. When solid, peel foil off the back and store in refrigerator until required. Press alternate strips of dark and white chocolate around the sides of the cake.

GARNISH Using additional chocolate, make Chocolate Leaves to decorate (see Chocolate Decorations on p 114). Arrange in the centre on top of the cake, as in the photograph.

Serves 10 to 12   PHOTOGRAPH ON PAGE 98

Friandises

METRIC	AMERICAN
500 mℓ (2 C) syrup	2 cups syrup
250 mℓ (1 C) water	1 cup water
Good pinch cream of tartar	Good pinch cream of tartar
Assorted fruits*	Assorted fruits*

* Naartjie (mandarin) segments, pith removed & left to dry
Pitted prunes, with a whole almond inserted in the middle
Brazil nuts or peanuts, stuck on toothpicks with glacé cherries
Grapes (leave a small stalk)
Strawberries (do not remove leaves)
Marzipan balls, with a blanched almond pressed into the middle

METHOD Combine syrup, water and cream of tartar in a saucepan. Allow to boil over medium heat until it turns a light caramel colour. (Do not stir while boiling.)

Remove from stove, place saucepan on wooden board and, working quickly before it hardens, dip the fruits into the syrup, using a spoon and fork and being careful not to burn yourself. Allow excess to drip off, then place on an oiled baking (cookie) sheet to set.

Serve in paper cups with coffee.

Makes approximately 70

Tapioca Custard Flowers

METRIC	AMERICAN
6 sheets phyllo pastry	6 sheets phyllo pastry
Melted butter for brushing pastry	Melted butter for brushing pastry
FILLING	FILLING
90 g (½ C) sago	½ cup tapioca
750 mℓ (3 C) milk	3 cups milk
1 mℓ (¼ t) salt	¼ teaspoon salt
3 eggs	3 eggs
30 mℓ (2 T) sugar	2 tablespoons sugar
2 mℓ (½ t) vanilla or finely grated lemon rind	½ teaspoon vanilla or finely grated lemon rind
Raspberry or strawberry jam	Raspberry or strawberry preserves

METHOD Place a sheet of phyllo pastry on a wooden board, brush lightly with melted butter, cover with another sheet of phyllo and continue the process until you have 6 layers.

Using a sharp knife, cut pastry into 13 cm (5 inch) squares and press into lightly greased muffin pans so as to resemble flowers. (They should have an overlap.)

Bake in 180°C (350°F) oven for 8–10 minutes, or until golden brown. Remove pan from oven and allow 'flowers' to cool before removing.

FILLING Combine sago (tapioca), milk and salt in a saucepan. Stir until boiling. Simmer for 2 minutes over lowest heat.

Beat eggs with sugar; equalize the temperature by slowly adding a small amount of warm sago (tapioca) mixture to beaten eggs (to avoid curdling).

Add egg mixture to saucepan and continue to cook on lowest heat for 3 minutes, stirring constantly. Remove from heat and add vanilla or lemon rind. Allow to cool.

TO SERVE Spoon a generous amount of filling into each pastry shell and drop a teaspoon of raspberry or strawberry jam (preserves) into the centre of each 'flower'.

Serves 12

Chocolate Truffles

METRIC	AMERICAN
175 g dark chocolate	1 cup semi-sweet chocolate chips
60 g butter	4 tablespoons butter
30 mℓ (2 T) icing sugar	2 tablespoons powdered sugar
3 egg yolks	3 egg yolks
15 mℓ (1 T) Grand Marnier	1 tablespoon Grand Marnier
Chocolate vermicelli	Chocolate sprinkles

METHOD Melt chocolate in double boiler. Stir in butter and sugar. Beat in egg yolks and lastly stir in Grand Marnier. Allow to cool, but do not refrigerate.

Roll mixture into balls with greased hands, then roll in chocolate vermicelli (chocolate sprinkles). Alternatively, freeze, then insert a toothpick into each ball and dip into melted and cooled white or dark chocolate.

Makes 24 PHOTOGRAPH ON PAGE 154

Chinese Chocolate Lychees

METRIC	AMERICAN
2 x 280 g tins lychees, drained	2 x 10 oz cans lychees, drained
Preserved ginger	Stem ginger
100 g dark chocolate	4 oz semi-sweet chocolate chips
Cream	Cream

METHOD Stuff lychees with pieces of ginger. Melt chocolate and add enough cream to form a medium consistency. Coat lychees with melted chocolate and drop onto a foil-lined cookie sheet. Allow to set in refrigerator. Serve in paper cups.

Serves 12

Cakes

Banana Loaf 115
Best Carrot Cake. 115
Pumpkin Loaf 115
Zucchini Nut Cake. 116
Caramel Crunch Cake 116
Orange Sponge Layer Cake 116
Quick Orange-glazed Cake 117
Butter Grenadilla Cake 117
Gooseberry or Blueberry Sour Cream Cake 117
Macadamia Pineapple & Ginger Delight 120
Pineapple Ginger Cake 120
Lemon Upside-down Cake 120
Boiled Fruitcake 121
Poppy Seed Cake. 121
Orange Pineapple Cake 121
Plum Kuchen 122
Coconut Cake Supreme 122
Coconut Chocolate Cake. 122
Israeli Cheese Cake. 123
Cheese Cake with Sour Cream Topping. 123
Custard Cheese Cake 123
Butter Cheese Cake 124
Marble Cheese Cake 124
Jam Cake. 124
Lemon Cheese Gâteau 125
Cape Brandy Cake 125
Chocolate Gâteau 128
Hazlenut Gâteau 128
Brandy Alexander Gâteau 129
Chocolate Raspberry or Strawberry Roulade. 129
Black Forest Cherry Cake. 130
White Chocolate Cake. 130
Mocha Chocolate Cream Cake 131
Delicious Chocolate Cake 131
Viennese Chocolate Cream Torte 132
Dark Chocolate Mocha Cake 132
Triple Chocolate Torte. 133
Devonshire Cream Cake. 133

Baking Tips & Cake Decorations

Baking Do's & Don'ts

When measuring in cups, use well-rounded measurements of flour and level sugar measurements. Too much sugar is the main cause of cakes failing.

Always grease cake pans very generously with butter, not margarine, as the latter causes cakes to stick. If using a non-stick cooking spray, use it very generously.

When baking with yeast, ensure that liquids are lukewarm or blood heat, never hot. Yeast doughs must be kept out of a draught. If you observe these two rules, you need not be nervous of working with yeast, as it is not at all finicky.

Egg whites should always be at room temperature when used, in order to produce more volume. They freeze very successfully, but must be thawed to room temperature before using.

BAKING BLIND
To bake blind, roll out dough and press into a greased ovenware dish, then place a piece of waxpaper or foil over the dough and fill the shell with dried butter beans. This prevents the sides from collapsing. The pastry shell is then partially baked before being filled. Using this method will ensure that your tarts and pies never have soggy bottom crusts.

Chocolate Decorations

CHOCOLATE CURLS
Melt chocolate in double boiler or microwave. Do not stir. Spread over back of biscuit tray (cookie sheet) placed over marble slab. Allow to set, but do not refrigerate. Using a cheese slicer, draw the blade lengthwise over the chocolate using long, fairly firm strokes. Store the chocolate curls in a plastic container in the refrigerator.

CHOCOLATE ROSE LEAVES
Melt chocolate as for Chocolate Curls. Using a knife, coat the back of rose leaves very thickly with the melted chocolate. Place in refrigerator to set, then peel leaves off.

CHOCOLATE CABBAGE LEAVES
Melt chocolate as for Chocolate Curls. Coat cabbage leaves thickly, covering some leaves on the inside and others on the outside. Allow to set in refrigerator. Peel off the cabbage leaves carefully and use as required.

CHOCOLATE SPIRALS
Melt chocolate as for Chocolate Curls. Cover a biscuit tray (cookie sheet) with foil. Using a pencil, trace concentric circles lightly on foil. Pour melted chocolate into a pastry bag with a very small tip. Pipe onto the outlined shapes. Allow to set in refrigerator, then peel foil off gently.

CHOCOLATE CUPS
Melt chocolate as for Chocolate Curls. Place paper cookie cups in cookie tin (muffin pan). Using the back of a spoon, coat the inside of the paper cups thickly. Allow to set in refrigerator. Peel off paper gently when set.

Other Decorations

BUTTER ROSES
Allow a solid 500 g (1 lb) slab of butter to reach room temperature, or a stage at which it is pliable. Use a cheese slicer to make butter curls for as many petals as you require. Beginning with the centre of the rose, use your fingers to mould individual petals, then press the bases together to form a flower. Place on foil and allow to set in freezer. Arrange on a plate and surround with rose leaves. (Refer to photograph on p 35.)

PRALINE
A very useful, attractive cake decoration which is made as follows:
Melt 200 g (1 cup) sugar in a heavy saucepan over gentle heat. Stir in 100 g (1 cup) sliced almonds. Pour into an oiled Swiss roll tin (jelly roll pan) and allow to set. Pulverise in a food processor or blender. Store in an airtight container until required.

Banana Loaf

METRIC	AMERICAN
125 g butter	*½ cup butter*
150 g (¾ C) sugar	*¾ cup sugar*
2 eggs	*2 eggs*
250 g (2 C) flour	*2 cups all purpose flour*
5 mℓ (1 t) bicarbonate of soda	*1 teaspoon baking soda*
125 mℓ (½ C) buttermilk	*½ cup buttermilk*
250 mℓ (1 C) mashed bananas	*1 cup mashed bananas*

METHOD Cream butter and sugar very well. Add eggs; beat well again. Sift dry ingredients together and add to creamed mixture alternately with the liquid. Stir in bananas.

Pour into a greased and floured 23 x 13 x 7 cm (9 x 5 x 3 inch) loaf pan. Bake in 180°C (350°F) oven for 1 hour. (This loaf may also be baked in a bundt tin.)

Serves 12

Best Carrot Cake

METRIC	AMERICAN
300 g (2½ C) flour	*2½ cups all purpose flour*
10 mℓ (2 t) baking powder	*2 teaspoons baking powder*
7 mℓ (1½ t) bicarbonate of soda	*1½ teaspoons baking soda*
15 mℓ (3 t) ground cinnamon	*3 teaspoons ground cinnamon*
5 mℓ (1 t) salt	*1 teaspoon salt*
300 g (1½ C) sugar*	*2 cups sugar*
375 mℓ (1½ C) oil	*1½ cups oil*
4 eggs	*4 eggs*
500 mℓ (2 C) grated carrots	*2 cups grated carrots*
250 g tinned crushed pineapple, drained	*1 x 8½ oz can crushed pineapple, drained*
50 g (½ C) chopped pecan nuts	*½ cup chopped pecans*
75 g (½ C) sultanas	*½ cup golden raisins*
CREAM CHEESE ICING	CREAM CHEESE ICING
125 g butter	*½ cup butter*
500 g icing sugar	*1 lb powdered sugar*
5 mℓ (1 t) vanilla essence	*1 teaspoon vanilla extract*
250 g cream cheese	*8 oz cream cheese*
GARNISH	GARNISH
Chopped pecan nuts	*Chopped pecans*
Red & green glacé cherries	*Red & green glacé cherries*

* This measurement differs from the American

METHOD Preheat oven to 180°C (350°F). Butter and flour one bundt pan. Sift flour with baking powder, bicarbonate of soda (baking soda), cinnamon and salt.

In a mixing bowl beat together sugar, oil and eggs until well blended. Add carrots, pineapple, nuts and sultanas (golden raisins). Mix well.

Gradually add flour mixture, beating just enough to combine well. (The batter will be thin.) Pour into prepared pan and bake for 45 minutes. Turn out and cool.

CREAM CHEESE ICING Beat together butter, icing sugar (powdered sugar) and vanilla. (The mixture will be crumbly.) Stir in the cream cheese by hand. Mix lightly but do not beat too much, as the mixture tends to become watery if beaten for too long after adding cream cheese (this does not happen when using the packaged cream cheese).

Ice top and sides of cake and decorate with additional chopped pecans and red and green cherries.

CHEF'S TIP If preferred, substitute 3 x 125 mℓ (4½ oz) jars strained carrot baby food for grated carrots and reduce oil to 250 mℓ (1 cup).

Serves 12

Pumpkin Loaf

METRIC	AMERICAN
300 g (1½ C) sugar*	*2 cups sugar*
4 eggs, beaten	*4 eggs, beaten*
500 mℓ (2 C) cooked & mashed pumpkin	*2 cups cooked & mashed pumpkin*
420 g (3½ C) flour	*3½ cups all purpose flour*
5 mℓ (1 t) baking powder	*1 teaspoon baking powder*
5 mℓ (1 t) salt	*1 teaspoon salt*
7 mℓ (1½ t) bicarbonate of soda	*1½ teaspoons baking soda*
5 mℓ (1 t) ground cinnamon	*1 teaspoon ground cinnamon*
5 mℓ (1 t) ground nutmeg	*1 teaspoon ground nutmeg*
200 mℓ (¾ C) water	*¾ cup water*
250 mℓ (1 C) oil	*1 cup oil*
100 g (1 C) chopped nuts	*1 cup chopped nuts*
CREAM CHEESE ICING	CREAM CHEESE ICING
See recipe opposite	*See recipe opposite*

* This measurement differs from the American

METHOD Combine sugar and eggs; beat until light and fluffy. Add pumpkin to egg mixture, then add sifted dry ingredients alternately with water and oil. Beat well. Fold in nuts.

Pour into two greased loaf pans and bake in 180°C (350°F) oven for 1 hour. Cool and serve plain or ice with cream cheese icing.

ICING Cream butter. Add softened cream cheese; stir in sugar and vanilla. Mix together well to form a smooth consistency.

Makes 2 loaves

Zucchini Nut Cake

METRIC	AMERICAN
250 g (2 C) flour	2 cups all purpose flour
5 mℓ (1 t) mixed spice	1 teaspoon allspice
5 mℓ (1 t) ground cloves	1 teaspoon ground cloves
15 mℓ (3 t) ground cinnamon	3 teaspoons ground cinnamon
5 mℓ (1 t) salt	1 teaspoon salt
7 mℓ (1½ t) baking powder	1½ teaspoons baking powder
3 eggs	3 eggs
250 g (1¼ C) sugar	1¼ cups sugar
300 mℓ (1 ¼ C) oil	1 ¼ cups oil
5 mℓ (1 t) vanilla essence	1 teaspoon vanilla extract
500 mℓ (2 C) grated courgettes or baby marrows	2 cups grated zucchini
50 g (½ C) chopped nuts, mixed with 5 mℓ (1 t) flour	½ cup chopped nuts, mixed with 1 teaspoon flour
5 mℓ (1 t) bicarbonate of soda	1 teaspoon baking soda

METHOD Sift together first six ingredients and set aside. Beat eggs well. Gradually add sugar and oil to eggs, mixing thoroughly. Add vanilla and sifted dry ingredients. Stir in courgettes (zucchini), then stir in nut and flour mixture.

Pour into a greased and floured bundt pan and bake in 180°C (350°F) oven for 1 hour.

Serves 12

Caramel Crunch Cake

METRIC	AMERICAN
270 g (2¼ C) flour	2¼ cups cake flour
5 mℓ (1 t) salt	1 teaspoon salt
300 g (1½ C) sugar	1½ cups sugar
6 egg yolks	6 egg yolks
125 mℓ (½ C) oil	½ cup oil
200 mℓ (¾ C) cold water	¾ cup cold water
5 mℓ (1 t) vanilla essence	1 teaspoon vanilla extract
8 egg whites (250 mℓ)	8 egg whites (1 cup)
2 mℓ (½ t) cream of tartar	½ teaspoon cream of tartar
15 mℓ (3 t) baking powder	3 teaspoons baking powder

FILLING	FILLING
500 mℓ (2 C) cream	2 cups cream
30 mℓ (2 T) icing sugar	2 tablespoons powdered sugar
15 mℓ (1 T) Amaretto (or any nutty-flavoured liqueur)	1 tablespoon Amaretto (or any nutty-flavored liqueur)

CARAMEL CRUNCH TOPPING	CARAMEL CRUNCH TOPPING
300 g (1½ C) sugar	1½ cups sugar
100 g flaked almonds	1 cup flaked almonds

METHOD Sift together flour, salt and sugar. Make a well in the centre and add the egg yolks, oil, water and vanilla. Beat for 5–7 minutes. Meanwhile beat the egg whites until frothy.

Add the cream of tartar to the egg whites and continue to beat until very stiff. Fold the baking powder into the egg yolk mixture and then fold this mixture gently over the well-beaten egg whites.

Pour into an ungreased chiffon cake (angel cake) pan and bake in 180°C (350°F) oven for 1 hour. Invert cake and leave upside down until thoroughly cooled. Remove from pan with a metal spatula or a long, sharp knife. Split cooled cake crosswise into four layers, using cotton and a sawing motion to cut.

FILLING Whip cream and sugar until stiff. Fold in Amaretto. Spread between layers of cake and frost top and sides.

TOPPING Heat sugar in saucepan until thoroughly dissolved. Stir in nuts. Pour onto a lightly oiled baking tray. Allow to cool thoroughly. Crush coarsely with a rolling pin or use a food processor. Sprinkle over top and sides of frosted cake.

Serves 12

Orange Sponge Layer Cake

METRIC	AMERICAN
250 g (2 C) flour	2 cups all purpose flour
300 g (1½ C) sugar	1½ cups sugar
5 mℓ (1 t) salt	1 teaspoon salt
15 mℓ (3 t) baking powder	3 teaspoons baking powder
125 mℓ (½ C) oil	½ cup oil
4 egg yolks	4 egg yolks
200 mℓ (¾ C) orange juice	¾ cup orange juice
Grated rind of 2 oranges	Grated rind of 2 oranges
6 egg whites (200 mℓ)	6 egg whites (¾ cup)
2 mℓ (½ t) cream of tartar	½ teaspoon cream of tartar

METHOD Sift flour, sugar, salt and baking powder into large bowl of electric mixer. Make a well in the centre and add (in the following order) the oil, egg yolks, orange juice and rind. Beat on medium speed until smooth, about 3–5 minutes.

Meanwhile, beat egg whites with cream of tartar until very stiff peaks form. Using a rubber spatula and a gentle under-and-over motion, gradually fold flour mixture into egg whites, just until blended. Do not over-mix.

Pour into two ungreased 23 x 4 cm (9 x 1½ inch) round layer pans and bake in a 180°C (350°F) oven for 30–35 minutes. Alternatively, bake in one cake pan for 55 minutes.

Invert cakes, suspending them between three level cooling trays, and allow to cool completely. Using a metal spatula or knife, loosen around edges of cooled cake, pushing cake gently towards centre, then shake vigorously to loosen bottom. Tap on table and remove cake.

Sandwich together with Pineapple Cheese Icing (recipe on p 121), an orange frosting, or whipped cream and mandarin oranges.

Serves 12

116

Quick Orange-glazed Cake

METRIC	AMERICAN
250 g margarine	1 cup margarine
300 g (1½ C) sugar	1½ cups sugar
Grated rind of 1 orange	Grated rind of 1 orange
30 mℓ (2 T) oil	2 tablespoons oil
4 eggs	4 eggs
350 g (3 C) flour	3 cups less 3 tablespoons all
15 mℓ (3 t) baking powder	purpose flour
Pinch of salt	3 teaspoons baking powder
125 mℓ (½ C) milk	Pinch of salt
250 mℓ (1 C) orange juice	½ cup milk
	1 cup orange juice

GLAZE	GLAZE
375 mℓ (1½ C) icing sugar	1½ cups powdered sugar
30–45 mℓ (2–3 T) orange juice	2–3 tablespoons orange juice

METHOD Cream margarine and sugar. Add orange rind and oil. Add eggs, sifted dry ingredients, milk and orange juice; beat until smooth.

Grease and flour a bundt or large loaf pan (use butter not margarine, or the cake will stick). Spoon mixture into pan and bake in 180°C (350°F) oven for 50–60 minutes.

GLAZE Mix together sugar and enough orange juice to make a pouring consistency. Remove cake from oven and pour glaze over whilst still hot.

Serves 12   PHOTOGRAPH ON PAGE 155

Butter Grenadilla Cake

METRIC	AMERICAN
250 g butter	1 cup butter
300 g (1½ C) sugar	1½ cups sugar
4 eggs	4 eggs
350 g (3 C) flour, sifted	3 cups cake flour, sifted
Pinch of salt	Pinch of salt
15 mℓ (3 t) baking powder	3 teaspoons baking powder
250 mℓ (1 C) milk	1 cup milk
5 mℓ (1 t) vanilla or almond essence	1 teaspoon vanilla or almond extract

ICING	ICING
60 g butter	4 tablespoons butter
375 mℓ (1½ C) icing sugar	1½ cups powdered sugar
Pulp of 2–3 grenadillas	Pulp of 2–3 passion fruit

METHOD Cream butter and sugar well. Add eggs one at a time, beating well after each addition. Add sifted dry ingredients alternately with milk, then add vanilla. Beat until smooth. Pour into two greased and floured 23 cm

(9 inch) layer pans. Bake in 180°C (350°F) oven for 30–35 mintues.

ICING Cream butter and sugar, adding sugar gradually. Slowly add the fruit pulp to form a creamy consistency.

Sandwich cooled layers together with icing, then ice top and sides of cake.

Serves 12

Gooseberry or Blueberry Sour Cream Cake

METRIC	AMERICAN
DOUGH	DOUGH
125 g butter	½ cup butter
45 mℓ (3 T) sugar	3 tablespoons sugar
1 egg	1 egg
5 mℓ (1 t) vanilla essence	1 teaspoon vanilla extract
180 g (1½ C) flour	1½ cups all purpose flour
7 mℓ (1½ t) baking powder	1½ teaspoons baking powder
FILLING	FILLING
750 g fresh gooseberries or blueberries	1½ lb fresh blueberries
2 egg yolks	2 egg yolks
500 mℓ (2 C) sour cream	2 cups sour cream
150 g (¾ C) sugar	¾ cup sugar
5 mℓ (1 t) vanilla essence	1 teaspoon vanilla extract
GARNISH	GARNISH
Whipped cream	Whipped cream
Whole gooseberries or blueberries	Whole blueberries

METHOD Cream butter and sugar. Add egg and vanilla, then add sifted flour and baking powder. Pat into a greased 25 cm (10 inch) springform pan, pressing dough three-quarter way up the sides. Place berries on top, reserving a few choice ones for garnish.

Combine all filling ingredients and pour over berries. Bake in 180°C (350°F) oven for 1 hour. Cool, loosen around edges with knife and remove outer ring of pan.

Decorate with whipped cream and garnish with whole berries.

Serves 8 to 10

Overleaf: White Chocolate Mousse (frozen), surrounded by Chocolate Cabbage Leaves and served with Raspberry Sauce

Macadamia Pineapple & Ginger Delight

METRIC	AMERICAN
180 g (1½ C) flour	1½ cups all purpose flour
150 g (¾ C) sugar	¾ cup sugar
Pinch of salt	Pinch of salt
5 mℓ (1 t) baking powder	1 teaspoon baking powder
500 g macadamia nuts	1 lb macadamia nuts
250 g glacé pineapple	8 oz glacé pineapple
250 g preserved ginger	½ lb stem ginger
160 g (1 C) maraschino cherries	1 cup maraschino cherries
3 eggs	3 eggs
5 mℓ (1 t) vanilla essence	1 teaspoon vanilla extract

METHOD Sift dry ingredients into a bowl and combine with nuts, pineapple, ginger and cherries. Mix thoroughly. Beat eggs until foamy. Add vanilla and stir into mixture.

Grease a 23 x 13 x 7 cm (9 x 5 x 3 inch) loaf pan and line with a double thickness of wax paper. Pour cake mixture into pan and spread evenly. Bake in 150°C (300°F) oven for 1¾ hours.

CHEF'S TIP This loaf cake is at its best after being stored for a few weeks. To serve, slice very thinly with an electric knife.

Makes 1 loaf

Pineapple Ginger Cake

METRIC	AMERICAN
250 g butter	1 cup butter
200 g (1 C) sugar	1 cup sugar
3 eggs, separated	3 eggs, separated
45 mℓ (3 T) syrup*	¾ cup light syrup
250 g (2 C) flour*	1¾ cups all purpose flour
15 mℓ (1 T) ground ginger	1 tablespoon ground ginger
5 mℓ (1 t) ground cinnamon	1 teaspoon ground cinnamon
2 mℓ (½ t) ground nutmeg	½ teaspoon ground nutmeg
2 mℓ (½ t) ground cloves	½ teaspoon ground cloves
Pinch of salt	Pinch of salt
5 mℓ (1 t) bicarbonate of soda	1 teaspoon baking soda
125 mℓ (½ C) milk	½ cup milk
125 mℓ (½ C) water	½ cup water

TOPPING	TOPPING
30 mℓ (2 T) butter	2 tablespoons butter
130 g (⅔ cup) brown sugar	⅔ cup brown sugar
250 mℓ (1 C) crushed pineapple	1 cup crushed pineapple

* *These measurements differ from the American*

METHOD First prepare topping. Melt butter in a non-stick bundt pan. Sprinkle with brown sugar, then top with crushed pineapple. Set aside.

CAKE Cream butter and sugar together very well. Add egg yolks and syrup. Sift together flour, spices, salt and bicarbonate of soda (baking soda). Add to butter mixture alternately with milk and water.

Beat egg whites stiffly and fold in. Pour mixture over topping in pan and bake in 180°C (350°F) oven for 45–50 minutes.

Remove from oven, invert immediately onto a cooling tray and leave pan over cake for a couple of minutes before removing.

Serves 10 to 12

Lemon Upside-down Cake

METRIC	AMERICAN
90 g butter	6 tablespoons butter
130 g (⅔ C) sugar	⅔ cup sugar
2 eggs, separated	2 eggs, separated
5 mℓ (1 t) finely grated lemon rind	1 teaspoon finely grated lemon rind
180 g (1½ C) flour	1½ cups cake flour
10 mℓ (2 t) baking powder	2 teaspoons baking powder
Pinch of salt	Pinch of salt
160 mℓ (⅔ C) milk or water	⅔ cup milk or water
1 whole lemon	1 whole lemon

GLAZE	GLAZE
150 g (¾ C) sugar*	1 cup sugar
30 mℓ (2 T) cornflour	2 tablespoons cornstarch
Pinch of salt	Pinch of salt
200 mℓ (¾ C) hot water	¾ cup hot water
45 mℓ (3 T) fresh lemon juice	3 tablespoons fresh lemon juice
60 g butter	4 tablespoons butter
2 mℓ (½ t) finely grated lemon rind	½ teaspoon finely grated lemon rind

* *This measurement differs from the American*

METHOD Cream butter and sugar. Add egg yolks and lemon rind; beat well. Sift together flour, baking powder and salt and add to mixture alternately with milk. Fold in stiffly beaten egg whites. Set aside.

Peel one lemon and slice thinly. Place lemon slices in a greased 23 cm (9 inch) square baking pan. (For the photograph on p 154, a bundt tin was used.)

GLAZE Combine sugar, cornflour (cornstarch) and salt. Stir in hot water and lemon juice. Cook until boiling, stirring constantly. Boil for 1 minute. Remove from heat and stir in butter and rind.

Spoon glaze over lemon slices; carefully pour in cake mixture and bake in 180°C (350°F) oven for 40–45 minutes. Cool for 5 minutes before inverting onto a serving platter.

Serves 12

PHOTOGRAPH ON PAGE 154

Boiled Fruitcake

METRIC	AMERICAN
500 g mixed fruit	1 lb mixed fruit
200 g (1 C) sugar	1 cup sugar
500 ml (2 C) water	2 cups water
10 ml (2 t) bicarbonate of soda	2 teaspoons baking soda
125 g butter or margarine	½ cup butter or margarine
250 g (2 C) flour	2 cups less 2 tablespoons all purpose flour
10 ml (2 t) baking powder	2 teaspoons baking powder
Pinch of salt	Pinch of salt
2 eggs, beaten well	2 eggs, beaten well
125–250 g whole cherries	¼–½ lb whole cherries
125–250 g pecan nuts	¼–½ lb pecans
125 ml (½ C) brandy	½ cup brandy

METHOD Combine mixed fruit, sugar and water in a saucepan. Boil for 12 minutes. Remove from stove and add bicarbonate of soda (baking soda) and butter; mix well. Add flour sifted with baking powder and salt. Finally, add well-beaten eggs and stir in whole cherries and pecans.

Pour into a cake pan lined with wax paper and sprayed with cooking spray. Bake in 180°C (350°F) oven for 1 hour.

While still hot, pour brandy over the entire cake. Allow to cool before turning out of pan.

Serves 8

Poppy Seed Cake

METRIC	AMERICAN
125 ml (½ C) poppy seeds	½ cup poppy seeds
175 g butter	¾ cup butter
200 g (1 C) sugar	1 cup sugar
3 eggs	3 eggs
5 ml (1 t) lemon rind	1 teaspoon lemon rind
200 ml (¾ C) milk	¾ cup milk
5 ml (1 t) vanilla essence	1 teaspoon vanilla extract
260 g (2 C & 2 T) flour	2 cups all purpose flour
10 ml (2 t) baking powder	2 teaspoons baking powder
Pinch of salt	Pinch of salt

TOPPING	TOPPING
Icing sugar	Powdered sugar

METHOD Cover poppy seeds with hot water and soak for 3–4 hours, or overnight. Boil the seeds in the water for about 30 minutes, adding more water as required. Strain. The poppy seeds are now ready for use.

Cream butter and sugar. Add eggs, lemon rind, milk, vanilla, poppy seeds and sifted dry ingredients; beat together for approximately 1 minute, or until smooth.

Pour into a greased and floured bundt or loaf pan and bake in 180°C (350°F) oven for 1 hour. Cool and dust with icing sugar (powdered sugar).

CHEF'S TIP This cake may also be baked in two 20 cm (8 inch) layer pans and sandwiched together with a package of lemon instant pudding whipped with 250 ml (1 cup) milk and 125 ml (½ cup) cream.

Serves 10

Orange Pineapple Cake

METRIC	AMERICAN
250 g margarine	1 cup margarine
300 g (1½ C) sugar	1½ cups sugar
270 g (2¼ C) flour	2¼ cups all purpose flour
15 ml (3 t) baking powder	3 teaspoons baking powder
4 eggs	4 eggs
1 x 312 g tin mandarin oranges, undrained	1 x 11 oz can mandarin oranges, undrained

PINEAPPLE CHEESE FILLING & ICING	PINEAPPLE CHEESE FILLING & ICING
1 x 475 g tin crushed pineapple, drained	1 x 20 oz can crushed pineapple, drained
15 ml (1 T) sugar	1 tablespoon sugar
1 x 283 g instant cheese cake (no-bake cheese filling cake mix)	1 x 10 oz instant cheese cake (no-bake cheese filling cake mix)
250 ml (1 C) sour cream	1 cup sour cream
250 g Orley Whip, beaten until thick	9 oz Cool Whip

ALTERNATIVE FILLING & ICING	ALTERNATIVE FILLING & ICING
1 package vanilla instant pudding	1 package vanilla instant pudding
250 g cream cheese	½ lb cream cheese
250 ml (1 C) cream	1 cup cream
1 x 475 g tin crushed pineapple (with juice)	1 x 20 oz can crushed pineapple (with juice)
250 g Orley Whip	9 oz Cool Whip

METHOD Cream margarine and sugar. Sift together dry ingredients and set aside. Add eggs one at a time to creamed mixture, beating well after each addition. Add sifted dry ingredients and mandarin segments.

Pour into three 20 cm (8 inch) greased and floured sandwich tins (baking pans) and bake in 180°C (350°F) oven for 25–30 minutes. Cool. Fill and ice with pineapple cheese filling or alternative filling.

PINEAPPLE CHEESE FILLING Stir together all ingredients, except Orley Whip / Cool Whip, until blended. Fold in Whip.

ALTERNATIVE FILLING Beat together vanilla pudding mix, cream cheese and cream. Add crushed pineapple and juice. Fold in Orley Whip / Cool Whip. Refrigerate until thick before using.

Serves 12

Plum Kuchen

METRIC	AMERICAN
250 g (2 C) flour	2 cups all purpose flour
100 g (½ C) sugar	½ cup sugar
Pinch of salt	Pinch of salt
1 mℓ (¼ t) baking powder	¼ teaspoon baking powder
125 g butter	½ cup butter
5 mℓ (1 t) ground cinnamon	1 teaspoon ground cinnamon
1 x 825 g tin plums, drained	1 x 1 lb 12 oz can plums, drained

TOPPING	TOPPING
250 mℓ (1 C) cream	1 cup cream
2 egg yolks, beaten	2 egg yolks, beaten
15 mℓ (1 T) sugar	1 tablespoon sugar
Pinch of ground cinnamon	Pinch of ground cinnamon

METHOD Sift together flour, sugar, salt and baking powder. Work in butter until mixture is fine and crumbly. Grease a 23 cm (9 inch) springform pan and press dough onto bottom and sides, reserving about 125 mℓ (½ cup). Bake in 180°C (350°F) oven for 15 minutes.

Mix remaining crumbly dough mixture with 5 mℓ (1 teaspoon) cinnamon. Arrange the drained fruit in the half-baked pastry shell and sprinkle dough / cinnamon mixture over the plums. Bake for 20 minutes in 180°C (350°F) oven.

TOPPING Combine cream with beaten egg yolks and mix well. Remove kuchen from oven and pour topping over fruit. Sprinkle with a mixture of sugar and cinnamon and bake for a further 10 minutes, or until custard has set.

CHEF'S TIP For a pleasant variation, use canned peaches instead of plums.

Serves 12

Coconut Cake Supreme

METRIC	AMERICAN
175 g butter	¾ cup butter
300 g (1½ C) sugar	1½ cups sugar
300 g (2½ C) flour	2½ cups all purpose flour, sifted
15 mℓ (3 t) baking powder	3 teaspoons baking powder
Pinch of salt	Pinch of salt
250 mℓ (1 C) milk	1 cup milk
5 mℓ (1 t) coconut essence	1 teaspooon coconut extract
4 egg whites, stiffly beaten	4 egg whites, stiffly beaten

FILLING	FILLING
Coconut cream or liqueur	Coconut cream or liqueur
250 mℓ (1 C) cream, whipped	1 cup cream, whipped
250 mℓ (1 C) dessicated coconut or grated fresh coconut	1 cup fresh or dried coconut

METHOD Cream butter and sugar until light and creamy. Sift together dry ingredients and add to creamed mixture alternately with milk. Add coconut essence (extract), then fold in stiffly beaten egg whites.

Pour into two greased and floured 23 cm (9 inch) cake pans. Bake in 180°C (350°F) oven for 30 minutes. Cool. Sprinkle both layers with coconut cream or liqueur, then sandwich together with some of the whipped cream and coconut and top with the remainder.

CHEF'S TIP If using fresh coconut (which makes the filling especially nice), grate it in a food processor.

Serves 12

Coconut Chocolate Cake

METRIC	AMERICAN
5 eggs, separated	5 eggs, separated
200 g (1 C) sugar	1 cup sugar
30 mℓ (2 T) sweet wine	2 tablespoons sweet wine
15 mℓ (1 T) oil	1 tablespoon oil
60 g dark chocolate, grated	2 oz semi-sweet chocolate, grated
80 g (1 C) dessicated coconut	1 cup dessicated coconut (obtainable at specialty or gourmet stores)
70 g (½ C) self-raising flour	½ cup self-rising flour
5 mℓ (1 t) baking powder	1 teaspoon baking powder

TOPPING*	TOPPING*
250 mℓ (1 C) whipping cream	1 cup whipping cream
60 g dark chocolate	⅓ cup semi-sweet chocolate chips

GARNISH	GARNISH
Grated chocolate	Grated chocolate

* The day before making this cake, prepare topping by combining the cream and chocolate and bringing mixture to the boil. Cool and refrigerate overnight

METHOD Beat egg yolks, sugar, wine and oil until light and creamy. Add grated chocolate, coconut, flour and baking powder to egg mixture and mix together. Beat egg whites until stiff; fold into mixture.

Bake in a greased and floured springform tin (loose-bottomed pan) in 180°C (350°F) oven, for 30 minutes.

Whip cream and chocolate mixture (prepared on previous day) until stiff and use to decorate the cake. Garnish with additional grated chocolate.

Serves 8 to 10

Israeli Cheese Cake

METRIC	AMERICAN
BASE	BASE
375 mℓ (1½ C) biscuit crumbs	1½ cups cookie crumbs
60 mℓ (¼ C) melted butter	¼ cup melted butter
FILLING	FILLING
6 eggs, separated	6 eggs, separated
1 kg smooth cream cheese	2 lb smooth & creamy style cottage cheese, sieved
175 g butter, melted	¾ cup butter, melted
Finely grated rind of 1 lemon	Finely grated rind of 1 lemon
45 mℓ (3 T) cornflour	3 tablespoons cornstarch
200 g (1 C) sugar	1–1½ cups sugar
80 mℓ (⅓ C) sour cream	⅓ cup sour cream

METHOD Combine crumbs with butter; mix well and press onto base and sides of a 23 cm (9 inch) loose-bottomed pan.

FILLING Beat egg whites until stiff. Combine cheese with remaining ingredients, then fold in egg whites.

Pour filling over biscuit crust and bake in 180°C (350°F) oven for 30 minutes. Turn oven off completely and leave for another hour, or until set.

Serves 10 to 12

Cheese Cake with Sour Cream Topping

METRIC	AMERICAN
1 x 23 cm tart shell, unbaked*	1 x 9 inch pie crust, unbaked*
FILLING	FILLING
2 x 250 g packages cream cheese	2 x 8 oz packages cream cheese
100 g (½ C) sugar	½ cup sugar
2 eggs	2 eggs
5 mℓ (1 t) vanilla essence	1 teaspoon vanilla extract
1 x 475 g tin crushed pineapple, drained	1 x 20 oz can crushed pineapple, drained
TOPPING	
250 mℓ (1 C) sour cream	TOPPING
30 mℓ (2 T) sugar	1 cup sour cream
2 mℓ (½ t) vanilla essence	2 tablespoons sugar
	½ teaspoon vanilla extract

* *Use Basic Tart Dough recipe on p 136 or see Chef's Tips below*

METHOD Soften cheese. Add sugar, eggs and vanilla; mix well. Fold in drained pineapple. Pour into unbaked shell and bake in 180°C (350°F) oven for 25–30 minutes.

Combine topping ingredients. Spoon over cheese cake and return to 190°C (375°F) oven for 5 minutes. Refrigerate for 24 hours before serving.

CHEF'S TIPS If you wish to omit the pineapple, use an additional 125 g (4 oz) cream cheese instead.

As an alternative to a pastry base, make a biscuit crust using 250 mℓ (1 C) Marie biscuit / Graham cracker crumbs, mixed with 30 mℓ (2 tablespoons) sugar and 80 mℓ (⅓ cup) melted butter. Press onto bottom and sides of a loose-bottomed cake pan.

Serves 8 to 10

Custard Cheese Cake

METRIC	AMERICAN
125 g butter	½ cup butter
70 g (⅓ C) sugar	⅓ cup sugar
1 egg	1 egg
120 g (1 C) flour	1 cup all purpose flour
2 mℓ (½ t) baking powder	½ teaspoon baking powder
Pinch of salt	Pinch of salt
FILLING	FILLING
100 g (½ C) sugar	½ cup sugar
15 mℓ (1 T) flour	1 tablespoon flour
250 g cream cheese	8 oz cream cheese, softened
4 eggs	4 eggs
500 mℓ (2 C) milk	2 cups milk
Juice of ½ lemon	Juice of ½ lemon
5 mℓ (1 t) vanilla essence	1 teaspoon vanilla extract
5 mℓ (1 t) ground cinnamon	1 teaspoon ground cinnamon

METHOD Cream butter and sugar. Add egg and beat well. Beat in flour, baking powder and salt. Spread dough in a springform tin (loose-bottomed pan), using a spatula. Chill for 1 hour.

FILLING Stir sugar and flour into cream cheese. Beat eggs; gradually add milk, lemon juice and vanilla to beaten eggs. Combine cream cheese mixture with egg mixture.

Pour filling into pastry and sprinkle with cinnamon. Bake in 180°C (350°F) oven for 45–55 minutes.

Serves 8 to 10

Butter Cheese Cake

METRIC	AMERICAN
125 g butter	½ cup butter
200 g (1 C) sugar	1 cup sugar
250 g cream cheese	8 oz cream cheese
5 ml (1 t) vanilla essence	1 teaspoon vanilla extract
2 eggs	2 eggs
Pinch of salt	Pinch of salt
250 g (2 C) flour	2 cups cake flour
10 ml (2 t) baking powder	2 teaspoons baking powder
2 ml (½ t) bicarbonate of soda	½ teaspoon baking soda
60 ml (¼ C) milk	¼ cup milk

TOPPING	TOPPING
30 ml (2 T) flour	2 tablespoons flour
5 ml (1 t) ground cinnamon	1 teaspoon ground cinnamon
30 ml (2 T) butter	2 tablespoons butter
30 ml (2 T) sugar	2 tablespoons sugar
30 ml (2 T) chopped nuts	2 tablespoons chopped nuts

METHOD Cream butter and sugar until light and fluffy. Add cream cheese and vanilla, then eggs (one at a time). Sift together dry ingredients and add to mixture alternately with milk. Pour into a greased and floured bundt pan.

Combine all topping ingredients and mix together until crumbly. Sprinkle over cake batter. Bake in 180°C (350°F) oven for 40–50 minutes.

Serves 10

Marble Cheese Cake

METRIC	AMERICAN
250 g (2 C) flour	2 cups flour
5 ml (1 t) baking powder	1 teaspoon baking powder
Pinch of salt	Pinch of salt
30 ml (2 T) sugar	2 tablespoons sugar
125 g butter	½ cup butter
60 g margarine	4 tablespoons margarine
1 egg	1 egg
15 ml (1 T) flour mixed with 15 ml (1 T) sugar	1 tablespoon flour mixed with 1 tablespoon sugar

FILLING	FILLING
750 g smooth cream cheese	1½ lb smooth & creamy style cottage cheese
150 g (¾ C) sugar	¾ cup sugar
3 eggs	3 eggs
45 ml (3 T) cornflour	3 tablespoons cornstarch
200 ml (¾ C) cream	¾ cup cream
5 ml (1 t) vanilla essence	1 teaspoon vanilla extract
50 g dark chocolate, melted & cooled	2 oz semi-sweet chocolate chips, melted & cooled

METHOD Sift together dry ingredients, except the combined tablespoons of flour and sugar. Rub in butter and margarine and mix to a dough with the slightly beaten egg. (If necessary add a little cold water to the dough.) Roll out dough and use to line a greased rectangular ovenware dish. Mix together the tablespoon of flour and the tablespoon of sugar; sprinkle over the unbaked pastry.

FILLING Place all ingredients (except the melted chocolate) in a bowl and mix by hand just until smooth, or use a food processor. Do not beat the mixture – it must remain thick.

Measure off 250 ml (1 cup) of the cheese mixture and stir into the cooled, melted chocolate. Pour half of the remaining mixture into the pastry shell. Spoon chocolate gently over this and top with the rest of the cheese mixture. Zig-zag through with a knife, being careful not to cut into the pastry.

Bake in 190°C (375°F) oven for 20 minutes, then turn off oven completely and leave the cake to set for 45–60 minutes. Remove from oven and cool.

Serves 8 to 10   PHOTOGRAPH ON PAGE 147

Jam Cake

METRIC	AMERICAN
250 g butter	1 cup butter
300 g (1½ C) sugar	1½ cups sugar
3 eggs	3 eggs
250 ml (1 C) buttermilk	1 cup buttermilk
250 ml (1 C) blackberry jam or youngberry jam	1 cup blackberry jam with seeds or youngberry preserves
350 g (3 C) flour	3 cups all purpose flour
5 ml (1 t) bicarbonate of soda	1 teaspoon baking soda
100 g (1 C) chopped nuts (optional)	1 cup chopped nuts (optional)
150 g (1 C) raisins	1 cup raisins
1 apple, peeled & grated	1 apple, peeled & grated

METHOD Cream butter and sugar. Add eggs and beat well. Combine buttermilk and jam (preserves). Add to the creamed mixture alternately with combined sifted dry ingredients. Stir in nuts, raisins and grated apple. Mix well.

Pour into a 25 cm (10 inch) greased and floured tube tin (pan). Bake in 180°C (350°F) oven for 1 hour.

Serves 12

Lemon Cheese Gâteau

METRIC	AMERICAN
4 eggs at room temperature	4 eggs at room temperature
100 g (½ C) castor sugar	½ cup superfine granulated sugar
2 mℓ (½ t) finely grated lemon rind	½ teaspoon finely grated lemon rind
30 mℓ (2 T) milk	2 tablespoons milk
20 mℓ (4 t) butter	1½ tablespoons butter
90 g (¾ C) flour, sifted	¾ cup cake flour, sifted
5 mℓ (1 t) baking powder	1 teaspoon baking powder

CHEESE FILLING	CHEESE FILLING
250 mℓ (1 C) cream, stiffly whipped	1 cup cream, stiffly whipped
500 g creamed cottage cheese	1 lb creamed cottage cheese
130 g (⅔ C) sugar	⅔ cup sugar
15 mℓ (1 T) lemon juice	1 tablespoon lemon juice
5 mℓ (1 t) finely grated lemon rind	1 teaspoon finely grated lemon rind
200 mℓ (¾ C) plain yoghurt	¾ cup plain yoghurt
1 package vanilla instant pudding	1 package vanilla instant pudding

APRICOT GLAZE	APRICOT GLAZE
250 mℓ (1 C) smooth apricot jam	1 cup smooth apricot preserves
Juice of ½ lemon	Juice of ½ lemon
45 mℓ (3 T) water	3 tablespoons water

GARNISH	GARNISH
Toasted almonds	Toasted almonds

METHOD Beat eggs and sugar very well, until thick and creamy. Add lemon rind and beat well. Scald milk and butter and fold in gently but thoroughly with the sifted flour and baking powder.

Bake in a greased and floured 23 cm (9 inch) springform tin (loose-bottomed pan) in 180°C (350°F) oven for 20–25 minutes, or until springy to the touch. Turn out onto a wire rack and cool. Cut into two layers.

CHEESE FILLING Whip cream until stiff. Mix cream cheese with sugar. Add to cream with remaining ingredients.

TO ASSEMBLE Place one sponge layer in springform tin (loose-bottomed pan) in which it was baked. Pour cheese mixture on top, then cover with the second layer. Refrigerate overnight to set.

APRICOT GLAZE Combine all ingredients in saucepan. Bring to the boil, stirring until smooth.

TO SERVE Remove chilled cake from pan. Pour the hot glaze over the cake and decorate with toasted almonds.

Serves 12   PHOTOGRAPH ON PAGE 155

Cape Brandy Cake

METRIC	AMERICAN
150 g (1 C) chopped, stoned dates	1 cup chopped, pitted dates
5 mℓ (1 t) bicarbonate of soda	1 teaspoon baking soda
250 mℓ (1 C) boiling water	1 cup boiling water
180 g (1½ C) flour	1½ cups all purpose flour
2 mℓ (½ t) baking powder	½ teaspoon baking powder
2 mℓ (½ t) salt	½ teaspoon salt
5 mℓ (1 t) mixed spice	1 teaspoon apple pie spice
125 g butter	½ cup butter
200 g (1 C) sugar	1 cup sugar
2 eggs, beaten	2 eggs, beaten

GLAZE	GLAZE
200 g (1 C) sugar	1 cup sugar
200 mℓ (¾ C) water	¾ cup water
50 g butter	3 tablespoons butter
200 mℓ (¾ C) brandy	¾ cup brandy
5 mℓ (1 t) vanilla essence	1 teaspoon vanilla extract

GARNISH	GARNISH
Whipped cream	Whipped cream
Maraschino cherries	Maraschino cherries
Chocolate Curls	Chocolate Curls

METHOD Mix together dates, bicarbonate of soda (baking soda) and boiling water. Set aside. Sift together flour, baking powder, salt and mixed spice (apple pie spice). In another bowl cream the butter and sugar together. Add beaten eggs.

Add sifted dry ingredients to the egg mixture, then stir in date mixture. Pour into a well-greased bundt baking pan and bake in 180°C (350°F) oven for 50–60 minutes.

GLAZE Boil together all ingredients. Pour while still boiling over cake, immediately after it has been taken out of the oven.

TO SERVE Allow cake to cool. Before removing from pan, garnish with swirls of whipped cream, topped with maraschino cherries and Chocolate Curls (see Chocolate Decorations on p 114).

Serves 8 to 10

Overleaf: Black Forest Cherry Cake

Chocolate Gâteau

METRIC	AMERICAN
CAKE	CAKE
4 eggs, separated	4 eggs, separated
200 g (1 C) castor sugar	1 cup superfine granulated sugar
15 mℓ (1 T) butter or oil	1 tablespoon butter or oil
125 mℓ (½ C) boiling water	½ cup boiling water
5 mℓ (1 t) vanilla essence	1 teaspoon vanilla extract
120 g (1 C) flour	1 cup cake flour
125 mℓ (½ C) cocoa powder	½ cup cocoa powder
7 mℓ (1½ t) baking powder	1½ teaspoons baking powder
CHOCOLATE MOUSSE	CHOCOLATE MOUSSE
6 eggs, separated	6 eggs, separated
80 mℓ (⅓ C) sugar	5 tablespoons sugar
250 g dark chocolate	8 oz semi-sweet chocolate
125 mℓ (½ C) boiling water	½ cup boiling water
45 mℓ (3 T) butter	3 tablespoons butter
15 mℓ (1 T) gelatine, dissolved in 45 mℓ (3 T) cold water	1 envelope gelatin, dissolved in 3 tablespoons cold water
500 mℓ (2 C) cream, whipped	2 cups cream, whipped
GLAZE	GLAZE
175 g dark chocolate	6 oz semi-sweet chocolate
60 g butter	4 tablespoons butter
GARNISH	GARNISH
Whipped cream or Chocolate Leaves & cherries	Whipped cream or Chocolate Leaves & cherries

METHOD To prepare cake, cream egg yolks and sugar together very well. Add butter or oil to boiling water, combine with egg mixture and stir in vanilla. Add sifted flour, cocoa and baking powder. Lastly, fold in stiffly beaten egg whites.

Pour into a greased and floured 40 x 27 cm (16 x 11 inch) Swiss roll tin (jelly roll pan). Bake in 190°C (375°F) oven for 8–10 minutes. Turn out onto a clean cloth and allow to cool.

CHOCOLATE MOUSSE Beat egg yolks and sugar together until light and fluffy; set aside. Combine chocolate, boiling water and butter in double boiler. Cook until melted and smooth.

Add an additional 15 mℓ (1 tablespoon) of boiling water to the gelatine; mix well, then stir into chocolate mixture in the double boiler and cook until gelatine has dissolved.

Gradually add hot chocolate mixture to the egg yolks, beating constantly while you do so. Allow to cool to room temperature, then fold in whipped cream. Lastly, fold in stiffly beaten egg whites.

TO ASSEMBLE Line a 30 cm (12 inch) loaf pan with wax paper. Cut the cake into strips and arrange strips next to one another along the bottom and sides of the pan, so that they rest against the wax paper.

Sprinkle cake with 15 mℓ (1 tablespoon) Grand Marnier. Fill with the mousse and cover the top of the mousse with a layer of cake strips. Cover with foil and refrigerate overnight.

TO SERVE Invert cake onto a serving platter. Melt together chocolate and butter for glaze and smooth over top of cake, allowing it to drip down the sides. Decorate with swirls of whipped cream or Chocolate Leaves and cherries (see Chocolate Decorations on p 114).

Serves 10 to 12

Hazelnut Gâteau

METRIC	AMERICAN
MERINGUE	MERINGUE
4 egg whites	4 egg whites
200 g (1 C) sugar	1 cup sugar
15 mℓ (1 T) cornflour	1 tablespoon cornstarch
15 mℓ (1 T) flour	1 tablespoon flour
Few drops almond essence	Few drops almond extract
100 g (1 C) hazelnuts, toasted, skinned & finely chopped	1 cup hazelnuts, toasted, skinned & finely chopped
FILLING	FILLING
250 g butter	1 cup butter
4 egg yolks	4 egg yolks
100 g (½ C) sugar	½ cup sugar
45 mℓ (3 T) water	3 tablespoons water
15 mℓ (3 t) instant coffee powder	3 teaspoons coffee powder
15 mℓ (1 T) brandy or Amaretto	1 tablespoon brandy or Amaretto
75 g (¾ C) hazelnuts, toasted, skinned & ground	¾ cup hazelnuts, toasted, skinned & ground
GARNISH	GARNISH
250 mℓ (1 C) cream	1 cup cream
Icing sugar	Powdered sugar
15 mℓ (1 T) Amaretto	1 tablespoon Amaretto
25 g (¼ C) toasted hazelnuts	¼ cup toasted hazelnuts

MERINGUE Beat egg whites until stiff; gradually add sugar and continue beating until very stiff. Sift cornflour (cornstarch) and flour together; fold into the meringue mixture with almond essence (extract) and hazelnuts. Divide into two portions, spread in foil-lined and greased 25 cm (10 inch) diameter cake pans and bake in 125 °C (250°F) oven for 2 hours.

FILLING Cream butter; set aside. Beat egg yolks until thick and lemon-coloured. Place sugar, water and coffee in a saucepan. Boil until sugar spins a thread, then pour in a slow stream onto the egg yolks, beating all the time, until mixture thickens and cools to room temperature. Add butter, beating in 1–2 tablespoons at a time. Stir in brandy and hazelnuts. Spread in between cooled cake layers.

GARNISH Whip cream with sugar. Stir in Amaretto. Pipe rosettes on top of gâteau and top each swirl with a hazelnut.

Serves 12

Brandy Alexander Gâteau

METRIC	AMERICAN
CAKE	**CAKE**
6 eggs	6 eggs
200 g (1 C) sugar	1 cup sugar
125 mℓ (½ C) cocoa powder	½ cup cocoa powder or squares
60 g (½ C) flour	of unsweetened chocolate,
125 g butter, melted or 125 mℓ	melted
(½ C) oil	½ cup all purpose flour
	½ cup butter, melted or ½ cup
	oil
FILLING	**FILLING**
1 envelope gelatine	1 envelope gelatin
60 mℓ (¼ C) cold water	¼ cup cold water
60 mℓ (¼ C) hot water	¼ cup hot water
60 mℓ (¼ C) brandy	4 tablespoons brandy
60 mℓ (¼ C) Crème de Caçao	4 tablespoons Crème de Caçao
3 eggs, separated	3 eggs, separated
100 g (½ C) sugar	½ cup sugar
250 mℓ (1 C) cream	1 cup cream
CHOCOLATE GLAZE	**CHOCOLATE GLAZE**
60 g butter	4 tablespoons butter
125 mℓ (½ C) syrup	½ cup syrup
60 mℓ (¼ C) hot water	¼ cup hot water
350 g dark chocolate, coarsely	2 cups semi-sweet chocolate
chopped	chips
GARNISH	**GARNISH**
Chocolate Curls	Chocolate Curls
Whipped cream	Whipped cream

METHOD To prepare cake, beat eggs and sugar together until light and creamy. Sift cocoa and flour together and fold in. Add melted butter or oil. If using melted chocolate, add with the melted butter. Pour into 2 greased and floured 25 cm (10 inch) springform cake pans. Bake in 200°C (400°F) oven for 10–15 minutes. Allow to cool.

FILLING Mix gelatine with cold water, then pour into a double boiler with hot water, brandy and Crème de Caçao and heat until gelatine has dissolved completely. Beat egg yolks with sugar; pour hot mixture onto yolks, beating constantly while doing so. Whip cream and fold in. Whip egg whites stiffly and fold in.

TO ASSEMBLE Spoon filling over one of the cooled cake layers while still in the pan. Remove the second layer and press on top of filling. Refrigerate for at least 1 hour.

CHOCOLATE GLAZE Combine butter, syrup and hot water. Cook until boiling, remove from heat and stir in chocolate.

TO SERVE Remove outer ring of springform pan. Pour glaze over cake. Decorate with swirls of whipped cream and Chocolate Curls (see Chocolate Decorations on p 114).

Serves 12

Chocolate Raspberry or Strawberry Roulade

METRIC	AMERICAN
4 eggs, separated	4 eggs, separated
150 g (¾ C) sugar*	1 cup sugar
60 mℓ (¼ C) water	¼ cup water
5 mℓ (1 t) vanilla essence	1 teaspoon vanilla extract
60 mℓ (½ C) flour	½ cup all purpose flour
60 mℓ (¼ C) cocoa powder	¼ cup cocoa powder
Pinch of salt	Pinch of salt
2 mℓ (½ t) bicarbonate of soda	½ teaspoon baking soda
2 mℓ (½ t) baking powder	½ teaspoon baking powder
FILLING	**FILLING**
500 mℓ (2 C) cream	2 cups cream
30 mℓ (2 T) icing sugar	2 tablespoons powdered sugar
1 x 283 g package frozen rasp-	1 x 10 oz package frozen rasp-
berries or strawberries,	berries or strawberries,
thawed**	thawed
GARNISH	**GARNISH**
Whipped cream	Whipped cream
Grated chocolate	Grated chocolate

* This measurement differs from the American
** If unobtainable, substitute tinned and drained raspberries or strawberries

METHOD Line a 39 x 26 x 2 cm (15½ x 10½ x 1 inch) Swiss roll tin (jelly roll pan) with wax paper and spray the paper with non-stick cooking spray.

Beat egg yolks with half the sugar until thick and lemon-coloured. Add water and vanilla. Sift together the flour, cocoa, salt, bicarbonate of soda (baking soda) and baking powder; add this mixture to egg yolks.

Beat egg whites until soft peaks form. Gradually add remaining sugar and continue to beat until stiff. Fold into the chocolate mixture.

Spread evenly in prepared pan and bake in 180°C (350°F) oven for 15–20 minutes. Turn out onto a damp cloth which has been sprinkled with sugar. Roll up quickly and allow to cool while preparing filling.

FILLING Whip cream and sugar together until stiff. Fold in thawed raspberries or strawberries.

TO SERVE Unroll cooled cake, spread filling over it and roll up carefully. Decorate with whipped cream and grated chocolate.

Serves 8

Black Forest Cherry Cake

METRIC	AMERICAN
MERINGUE	MERINGUE
4 egg whites	*4 egg whites*
200 g (1 C) sugar	*1 cup sugar*
15 ml (1 T) cornflour	*1 tablespoon cornstarch*
15 ml (1 T) flour	*1 tablespoon flour*
Few drops almond essence	*Few drops almond extract*
100 g (1 C) flaked almonds	*1 cup flaked almonds*
CHOCOLATE CAKE	CHOCOLATE CAKE
90 g (¾ C) flour	*¾ cup cake flour*
125 ml (½ C) cocoa powder	*½ cup cocoa powder*
10 ml (2 t) baking powder	*2 teaspoons baking powder*
3 eggs	*3 eggs*
150 g (¾ C) castor sugar	*¾ cup superfine granulated sugar*
5 ml (1 t) vanilla essence	*1 teaspoon vanilla extract*
60 g butter or 30 ml (2 T) oil	*2 oz butter or 2 tablespoons oil*
125 ml (½ C) milk	*½ cup milk*
FILLING	FILLING
750 ml (3 C) cream	*3 cups cream*
125 ml (½ C) icing sugar	*½ cup powdered sugar*
5 ml (1 t) vanilla essence	*1 teaspoon vanilla extract*
30–45 ml (2–3 T) Kirsch	*2–3 tablespoons Kirsch*
90 g (¾ C) ground almonds	*¾ cup almond meal*
1 x 575 g cherry pie filling	*1 x 20 oz cherry pie filling*
TOPPING	TOPPING
175 g dark chocolate	*1 cup semi-sweet chocolate chips*
GARNISH	GARNISH
Sifted cocoa powder	*Sifted cocoa powder*
Maraschino cherries	*Maraschino cherries*

METHOD First prepare meringue. Beat egg whites until very stiff; gradually add sugar and continue beating until very stiff again. Sift cornflour (cornstarch) and flour together; fold into the meringue with almond essence and flaked almonds.

Divide into 2 portions and spread in two 25 cm (10 inch) diameter cake pans which have been greased, lined with wax paper and then greased again. Bake in a slow (150°C / 300°F) oven for 2 hours. The layers will harden when cooled.

CHOCOLATE CAKE Sift together flour, cocoa and baking powder. Beat eggs and sugar together until thick and creamy and add vanilla. Place butter and milk in a saucepan and bring gently to the boil, then slowly add the egg mixture alternately with the flour mixture and fold in.

Pour into a greased and floured 25 cm (10 inch) diameter cake pan and bake in 190°C (375°F) oven for 15–20 minutes. Cool and split in half.

FILLING Whip cream with icing sugar (powdered sugar). Add vanilla, Kirsch and ground almonds.

TOPPING Melt chocolate in the top of a double boiler, spread evenly in a foil-lined 25 cm (10 inch) pan and place in refrigerator to set.

TO ASSEMBLE & SERVE Using the meringue as a base, alternate the layers of meringue with the chocolate cake layers, spreading the almond cream and the cherry pie filling in between.

Peel foil off refrigerated chocolate and break into large pieces. Wedge these into the top of the cake. Dust with sifted cocoa and garnish with maraschino cherries (with stems if possible).

CHEF'S TIP If preferred, substitute a cake mix such as Devil's Food Cake or Dark Chocolate Cake, instead of making your own.

Serves 12 PHOTOGRAPH ON PAGE 126

White Chocolate Cake

METRIC	AMERICAN
250 g butter	*1 cup butter*
300 g (1½ C) sugar*	*2 cups sugar*
4 eggs, separated	*4 eggs, separated*
5 ml (1 t) vanilla essence	*1 teaspoon vanilla extract*
100 g white chocolate, melted	*4 oz white chocolate, melted*
300 g (2½ C) flour	*2½ cups cake flour*
5 ml (1 t) baking powder	*1 teaspoon baking powder*
250 ml (1 C) buttermilk	*1 cup buttermilk*
100 g (1 C) chopped pecan nuts	*1 cup chopped pecans*
80 g (1 C) dessicated coconut	*1 cup dessicated coconut*
FROSTING	FROSTING
1 x 396 g tin condensed milk	*1 x 14 oz can condensed milk*
100 g (1 C) chopped nuts	*1 cup chopped nuts*
250 ml (1 C) dessicated coconut	*1 cup dessicated coconut*

* This measurement differs from the American

METHOD Cream butter and sugar. Beat in egg yolks. Add vanilla and melted chocolate. Sift together flour and baking powder and add to mixture alternately with buttermilk. Fold in stiffly beaten egg whites, nuts and coconut.

Pour into a 25 cm (10 inch) greased and floured tube tin (pan) and bake in 180°C (350°F) oven for 45–60 minutes.

FROSTING Caramelize the condensed milk by boiling it in the unopened can in a saucepan of water for 3 hours. After cooking, stir in chopped nuts and coconut. Pour over cake.

Serves 12

Mocha Chocolate Cream Cake

METRIC	AMERICAN
250 g (2 C) flour	2 cups cake flour
15 mℓ (3 t) baking powder	3 teaspoons baking powder
Pinch of salt	Pinch of salt
200 g (1 C) sugar	1 cup sugar
60 mℓ (¼ C) cocoa powder	¼ cup cocoa powder
30 mℓ (2 T) instant coffee powder	2 tablespoons instant coffee powder
125 mℓ (½ C) oil	½ cup oil
5 egg yolks	5 egg yolks
200 mℓ (¾ C) water	¾ cup water
5 mℓ (1 t) vanilla essence	1 teaspoon vanilla extract
8 egg whites	8 egg whites
2 mℓ (½ t) cream of tartar	½ teaspoon cream of tartar

CHOCOLATE CREAM FILLING*	CHOCOLATE CREAM FILLING*
500 mℓ (2 C) cream	2 cups cream
350 g dark chocolate	2 cups semi-sweet chocolate chips
15 mℓ (1 T) coffee liqueur	1 tablespoon coffee liqueur

TOPPING	TOPPING
Icing sugar	Powdered sugar

* Must be prepared in advance and refrigerated for 8 hours or overnight

METHOD To prepare cake, sift flour, baking powder, salt, sugar, cocoa and coffee powder into a large bowl. Make a well in the centre and add, in the following order, the oil, egg yolks, water and vanilla. Blend together by hand and then beat in mixer for 5 minutes, until smooth. Meanwhile using a large bowl, beat the egg whites with the cream of tartar until very stiff.

Add batter to egg whites, folding over and under lightly with a spatula. Pour into an ungreased 25 cm (10 inch) loose-bottomed tube tin (chiffon or angel cake pan) and bake at 180°C (350°F) for 1 hour and 10 minutes.

Remove from oven; immediately invert the cake (while still in the pan) and allow to hang suspended over the neck of a bottle, until completely cooled. Loosen sides and centre tube with spatula or knife. Take off outer ring, loosen bottom and remove cake.

Split cake into 3 layers, using cotton and a sawing motion to cut through. Fill with Chocolate Cream Filling and sprinkle the top with icing (powdered) sugar.

FILLING Place cream and chocolate in a saucepan over medium heat and stir until chocolate has melted. Allow mixture to come to the boil. Remove from stove, cool and refrigerate for 8 hours or overnight. Beat until thick and fold in liqueur.

Serves 12

Delicious Chocolate Cake

METRIC	AMERICAN
175 g butter	¾ cup butter
250 g (1¼ C) sugar*	1½ cups sugar
30 mℓ (2 T) cocoa powder	2 tablespoons cocoa powder
270 g (2¼ C) flour*	2 cups all purpose flour
10 mℓ (2 t) baking powder	2 teaspoons baking powder
5 mℓ (1 t) bicarbonate of soda	1 teaspoon baking soda
4 eggs	4 eggs
375 mℓ (1½ C) milk	1½ cups milk
5 mℓ (1 t) vanilla essence	1 teaspoon vanilla extract
	1 envelope liquid unsweetened chocolate

FROSTING	FROSTING
15 mℓ (1 T) butter	1 tablespoon butter
250 mℓ (1 C) sifted icing sugar	1 cup sifted powdered sugar
60 mℓ (¼ C) milk	¼ cup milk
100 g dark chocolate, diced	1 cup semi-sweet chocolate chips
2 mℓ (½ t) vanilla essence	½ teaspoon vanilla extract
1 egg or 2 yolks	1 egg or 2 yolks

* These measurements differ from the American

METHOD Cream butter and sugar. Sift dry ingredients together. Add eggs, milk, vanilla and sifted dry ingredients to creamed butter. Beat in food mixer for 2–3 minutes, scraping the bottom and sides constantly.

Divide mixture evenly between two greased and floured 23 cm (9 inch) layer pans and bake in a 180°C (350°F) oven for 30 minutes. Turn out onto cooling racks and cool thoroughly before icing.

FROSTING Melt butter in top of double boiler, then add sugar and milk, mixing thoroughly. Add chocolate and stir until completely melted. Allow to stand over hot water for several minutes. Remove from heat; add vanilla and egg.

Set in a pan of ice cubes and water and beat with a rotary beater until frosting has a light, spreading consistency. (This will make sufficient for the middle and the top of the cake; if you wish to frost the sides as well, double the frosting recipe.)

Serves 12

Viennese Chocolate Cream Torte

METRIC	AMERICAN
150 g dark chocolate	¾ cup semi-sweet chocolate chips
30 mℓ (2 T) strong coffee	2 tablespoons strong coffee
125 g butter	½ cup butter
100 g (½ C) & 15 mℓ (1 T) castor sugar	½ cup & 1 tablespoon superfine granulated sugar
3 eggs, separated	3 eggs, separated
Pinch of salt	Pinch of salt
2 mℓ (½ t) vanilla essence	½ teaspoon vanilla extract
60 g (½ C) flour	½ cup cake flour
80 g (⅔ C) ground almonds	⅔ cup almond meal

APRICOT OR RASPBERRY GLAZE	APRICOT OR RASPBERRY GLAZE
125 mℓ (½ C) apricot or raspberry jam	½ cup apricot or raspberry preserves
15 mℓ (1 T) brandy	1 tablespoon cognac

CHOCOLATE GLAZE	CHOCOLATE GLAZE
60 mℓ (4 T) butter	4 tablespoons butter
20 mℓ (4 t) cocoa powder	1 heaped tablespoon cocoa powder
500 mℓ (2 C) icing sugar	2 cups powdered sugar
1 egg white, unbeaten	1 egg white, unbeaten

GARNISH	GARNISH
Flaked almonds	Flaked almonds

METHOD Combine chocolate and coffee and melt in microwave at 50% power for 2–3 minutes, or cook in top of double boiler until smooth. Set aside to cool.

Cream butter and 100 g (½ cup) sugar until light and fluffy. Add egg yolks one at a time, beating well after each addition. Beat egg whites and salt until stiff, add the remaining tablespoon of sugar and continue beating until stiff and shiny. Add cooled chocolate mixture to creamed butter; stir in vanilla.

Sift a third of the flour over the chocolate batter, sprinkle with a third of the ground almonds and fold in with a third of the beaten egg whites, using a spatula and a gentle over-and-under motion. Repeat twice, using remaining two thirds of chocolate batter, almonds and egg whites.

Pour mixture into a greased and floured 20 cm (8 inch) loose-bottomed pan. Make a slight hollow in the middle of the batter. Bake in 180°C (350°F) oven for 30 minutes, or until the centre has risen and is firm to the touch.

APRICOT OR RASPBERRY GLAZE Heat jam (preserves) and brandy until boiling.

CHOCOLATE GLAZE Using a small saucepan, melt butter and stir in cocoa. Remove from heat. Combine icing (powdered) sugar with egg white. Blend with cocoa / butter mixture over low heat, until smooth.

TO SERVE Remove cake from oven and place on cooling rack; run a knife around the sides and remove the outer ring. Spread hot apricot or raspberry glaze evenly over the top of the cake. Allow to set, then pour over chocolate glaze and decorate around the edge with toasted flaked almonds.

Serves 8

Dark Chocolate Mocha Cake

METRIC	AMERICAN
250 g (2 C) flour	2 cups cake flour or 2 cups less 2 tablespoons all purpose flour
5 mℓ (1 t) bicarbonate of soda	1 teaspoon baking soda
2 mℓ (½ t) salt	½ teaspoon salt
5 mℓ (1 t) baking powder	1 teaspoon baking powder
175 g butter	¾ cup butter
150 g (¾ C) castor sugar	¾ cup superfine granulated sugar
3 eggs	3 eggs
200 mℓ (¾ C) syrup	¾ cup light syrup
45 mℓ (3 T) cocoa, mixed to a smooth paste with boiling water	3 tablespoons cocoa, mixed to a smooth paste with boiling water
10 mℓ (2 t) vanilla essence	2 teaspoons vanilla extract
375 mℓ (1½ C) buttermilk	1½ cups buttermilk

MOCHA FROSTING	MOCHA FROSTING
500 g icing sugar	1 lb powdered sugar
10 mℓ (2 t) cocoa powder	2 teaspoons cocoa powder
175 g butter	¾ cup butter
30 mℓ (2 T) instant coffee powder	2 tablespoons instant coffee powder
30–45 mℓ (2–3 T) milk or cream	2–3 tablespoons milk or cream
10 mℓ (2 t) vanilla essence	2 teaspoons vanilla extract
1 egg white	1 egg white

METHOD Sift together flour, bicarbonate of soda (baking soda), salt and baking powder. Set aside. Cream butter and sugar together. Add eggs, one at a time, to creamed mixture, beating after each addition. Add syrup, cocoa paste and vanilla, then add sifted dry ingredients alternately with buttermilk.

Divide batter evenly between three greased and floured 23 cm (9 inch) layer pans. Bake in 190°C (375°F) oven for 25–30 minutes. Fill and top with Mocha Frosting.

MOCHA FROSTING Mix all ingredients together. Beat until light and fluffy.

Serves 12

Triple Chocolate Torte

METRIC	AMERICAN
CAKE	**CAKE**
175 g dark chocolate, diced	1 cup semi-sweet chocolate chips
90 g butter	1 oz unsweetened chocolate
4 eggs, separated	6 tablespoons butter
70 g (⅓ C) sugar	4 eggs, separated
5 mℓ (1 t) vanilla essence	⅓ cup sugar
15 mℓ (1 T) cocoa powder	1 teaspoon vanilla extract
Pinch of salt	Pinch of salt
FILLING*	**FILLING***
500 mℓ (2 C) cream	2 cups cream
30 mℓ (2 T) butter	2 tablespoons butter
350 g dark chocolate, coarsely chopped (or use half milk chocolate)	2 cups semi-sweet chocolate chips (or use half milk chocolate chips)
2 egg yolks	2 egg yolks
15 mℓ (1 T) or 1 envelope gelatine	1 tablespoon or 1 envelope unflavored gelatin
15 mℓ (1 T) Van Der Hum or Grand Marnier	1 tablespoon Grand Marnier or Triple Sec
GLAZE	**GLAZE**
60 g butter	4 tablespoons butter
20 mℓ (4 t) cocoa powder	4 teaspoons cocoa powder
1 egg white, unbeaten	1 egg white, unbeaten
500 mℓ (2 C) icing sugar	2 cups powdered sugar
GARNISH	**GARNISH**
Toasted flaked almonds	Toasted flaked almonds

* Must be partially prepared in advance and refrigerated overnight (see Method)

METHOD Butter the bases and sides of two 23 cm (9 inch) cake pans and line each base with wax paper. Butter the paper again, then sprinkle the paper and the sides of the pans with flour.

CAKE Melt chocolate and butter in microwave at 50% power for 2–3 minutes, or in the top of a double boiler, stirring until smooth. Set aside and allow to cool.

Beat egg yolks and sugar together until light and creamy. Add vanilla, then sifted cocoa (only if using metric ingredients) and beat in. Fold the cooled chocolate mixture into the egg yolks. Beat egg whites with salt until stiff and fold in.

Divide batter between the two pans and bake in 180°C (350°F) oven for 20–25 minutes. Remove from oven and run a knife around edges of cakes. Invert onto wire racks, remove paper and cool.

FILLING Place cream, butter and chocolate in saucepan and bring to the boil, stirring constantly. Cool and refrigerate overnight.

Remove from refrigerator and beat until thick. Fold in beaten egg yolks. Dissolve gelatine with 15 mℓ (1 tablespoon) cold water, then add 15–30 mℓ (1–2 tablespoons) boiling water and stir until dissolved. Add liqueur to gelatine and fold into chocolate mixture.

GLAZE Melt butter and cocoa in a saucepan and stir over medium heat until smooth. Blend unbeaten egg white and sugar and pour into saucepan. Stir together until smooth. Cool before using.

TO ASSEMBLE & SERVE Line one of the 23 cm (9 inch) cake pans with plastic wrap, leaving a generous overlap all round. Place one cake layer in the pan and press down. Spoon filling on top and cover with remaining cake layer. Wrap plastic over and refrigerate for 2 hours, until firm.

Invert cake onto foil, pour glaze over and slide onto serving platter. Sprinkle toasted flaked almonds around the edges to decorate.

Serves 12

Devonshire Cream Cake

METRIC	AMERICAN
BUTTER SPONGE	**BUTTER SPONGE**
5 eggs	5 eggs
200 g (1 C) sugar	1 cup sugar
5 mℓ (1 t) vanilla essence	1 teaspoon vanilla extract
125 mℓ (½ C) milk	½ cup milk
90 g butter	6 tablespoons butter
30 mℓ (2 T) margarine	2 tablespoons margarine
150 g (1¼ C) flour	1¼ cups cake flour
10 mℓ (2 t) baking powder	2 teaspoons baking powder
250 mℓ (1 C) cream, whipped	1 cup cream, whipped
CHOCOLATE GLAZE	**CHOCOLATE GLAZE**
30 mℓ (2 T) butter	2 tablespoons butter
15 mℓ (1 T) cocoa powder	1 tablespoon cocoa powder
375 mℓ (1½ C) icing sugar	1½ cups powdered sugar
1 egg white	1 egg white
5 mℓ (1 t) vanilla essence	1 teaspoon vanilla extract

METHOD Beat eggs with sugar until creamy. Add vanilla. Boil milk with butter and margarine. Add to egg mixture alternately with sifted flour and baking powder, beating as you do so. Bake in two greased and floured layer pans in 190°C (375°F) oven, for 20 minutes. Allow to cool. Sandwich together with whipped cream and pour chocolate glaze over the top.

CHOCOLATE GLAZE Melt butter in a saucepan and stir in cocoa. Combine icing (powdered) sugar with unbeaten egg white. Add to butter and cocoa mixture. Add vanilla; stir until smooth.

CHEF'S TIP This cake may also be sandwiched together and topped with whipped cream and strawberries.

Serves 12

Tarts & Pies

Basic Tart Dough 136
Dutch Apple Pie 136
Brandy Apple Cream Tart 136
Apple, Cheese & Mon (Poppy Seed) Tart 137
Apple Strudel 137
Lemon Sponge Pie 140
Almond Peach Pie 140
Banana Cream Pie 140
Walnut Flan 141
Peaches 'n Cream Pie 141
French Silk Tart 141
Caramelized Pear Tart 142
Melktert 142
Fruit Tart 142
Kentucky Derby Pie 143
Mississippi Mud Pie 143
Pumpkin Chiffon Pie 143

Basic Tart Dough

METRIC	AMERICAN
125 g butter	½ cup butter
30 mℓ (2 T) sugar	2 tablespoons sugar
1 egg	1 egg
150 g (1¼ C) flour	1¼ cups all purpose flour
5 mℓ (1 t) baking powder	1 teaspoon baking powder
2 mℓ (½ t) vanilla essence or grated lemon rind	½ teaspoon vanilla extract or grated lemon rind

METHOD Cream butter and sugar. Add egg, flour, baking powder and vanilla or lemon rind and mix into a dough. Refrigerate for 1 hour before using.

TO BAKE Bake blind (see Baking Tips, p 114) in 180°C (350°F) oven for 10–15 minutes. Remove beans and wax paper or foil and bake for a further 15 minutes, until golden brown.

Makes 1 x 23 cm (9 inch) tart or pie shell

Dutch Apple Pie

METRIC	AMERICAN
180 g (1½ C) flour	1½ cups flour
100 g sugar	½ cup sugar
5 mℓ (1 t) baking powder	1 teaspoon baking powder
Pinch of salt	Pinch of salt
125 g margarine or butter	½ cup butter or margarine
2 egg yolks	2 egg yolks

FILLING	FILLING
6–8 apples, peeled, quartered & thinly sliced	6–8 apples, peeled, quartered & thinly sliced
Juice of 1 lemon	Juice of 1 lemon
70 g (⅓ C) sugar	⅓ cup sugar
30 mℓ (2 T) brown sugar	2 tablespoons brown sugar
45 mℓ (3 T) flour	3 tablespoons flour
5 mℓ (1 t) ground cinnamon	1 teaspoon ground cinnamon
2 mℓ (½ t) ground cardamom	½ teaspoon ground cardamom
125 mℓ (½ C) sultanas	½ cup golden raisins
125 mℓ (½ C) chopped walnuts	½ cup chopped walnuts

METHOD Combine flour, sugar, baking powder and salt. Reserve 15 mℓ (1 tablespoon) margarine and rub remaining margarine into dry ingredients. Blend into a dough with lightly beaten egg yolks.

Reserve one quarter of the dough. Line a greased 23 cm (9 inch) springform pan with the remaining dough, pressing it halfway up the sides.

Combine all filling ingredients and spoon into pastry shell. Crumble remaining dough over the top and dot with reserved margarine. Sprinkle with 15 mℓ (1 tablespoon) sugar.

Bake in 180°C (350°F) oven for 50 minutes–1 hour.

Serves 10 to 12

Brandy Apple Cream Tart

METRIC	AMERICAN
CRUST	CRUST
125 g butter	½ cup butter
45 mℓ (3 T) sugar	3 tablespoons sugar
80 mℓ (⅓ C) flour	6 tablespoons flour
2 mℓ (½ t) finely grated lemon rind	½ teaspoon finely grated lemon rind

FILLING	FILLING
250 g (1¼ C) sugar	1¼ cups sugar
250 mℓ (1 C) water	1 cup water
Juice of 1 lemon	Juice of 1 lemon
8 Granny Smith apples, peeled, cored & sliced	8 Granny Smith apples, peeled, cored & sliced
45 mℓ (3 T) cornflour mixed to a paste with water	3 tablespoons cornstarch mixed to a paste with water
250 mℓ (1 C) cream	1 cup cream
125 mℓ (½ C) raisins, plumped	½ cup raisins, plumped
15 mℓ (1 T) brandy	1 tablespoon brandy

GLAZE	GLAZE
250 mℓ (1 C) apricot jam	1 cup apricot preserves
15 mℓ (1 T) brandy	1 tablespoon brandy

METHOD Place all crust ingredients in food processor and blend well until mixture is crumbly. (Alternatively, rub butter into dry ingredients with fingertips, then add rind.)

Press mixture onto bottom and sides of a 23 cm (9 inch) loose-bottomed tin. Bake in 180°C (350°F) oven for 15 minutes. Cool thoroughly before filling.

FILLING Combine sugar, water and lemon juice in a saucepan. Bring to the boil, add sliced apples and poach just until tender. Drain and reserve 250 mℓ (1 cup) of the syrup.

Pour reserved syrup into a saucepan, bring to the boil and thicken with cornflour (cornstarch) paste. Stir in cream and cook until thickened. Remove from heat; stir in brandy and raisins. Cool.

TO ASSEMBLE & SERVE Pour cream mixture into cooled shell; arrange apple slices on top of mixture. Heat jam and brandy for glaze and brush over the top. Chill and serve with whipped cream, if desired.

Serves 8 to 10

Apple, Cheese & Mon (Poppy Seed) Tart

Bake in a 200°C (400°F) oven for 20 minutes, then turn oven down to 150°C (300°F) and bake for a further 10–15 minutes. Serve at room temperature.

CHEF'S TIP The poppy seed mixture may be prepared well in advance and frozen.

Serves 10

METRIC	AMERICAN
DOUGH	DOUGH
125 g butter	*½ cup butter*
30 mℓ (2 T) sugar	*2 tablespoons sugar*
1 egg	*1 egg*
5 mℓ (1 t) vanilla essence	*1 teaspoon vanilla extract*
180 g (1½ C) flour	*1½ cups all purpose flour*
5 mℓ (1 t) baking powder	*1 teaspoon baking powder*
Pinch of salt	*Pinch of salt*
APPLE FILLING	APPLE FILLING
1 x 765 g tin pie apples	*1 x 1 lb 11 oz can pie apples*
100 g (½ C) sugar	*½ cup sugar*
15 mℓ (1 T) lemon juice	*1 tablespoon lemon juice*
MON (POPPY SEED) MIXTURE	MON (POPPY SEED) MIXTURE
375 mℓ (1½ C) poppy seeds*	*1 x 12 oz can prepared poppy*
45–60 mℓ (3–4 T) syrup	*seed filling*
30 g butter	
2 mℓ (½ t) cinnamon	
CREAM CHEESE FILLING	CREAM CHEESE FILLING
250 g creamed cottage cheese	*8 oz smooth & creamy style*
15 mℓ (1 T) cornflour	*cottage cheese (blend in*
70–100 g (⅓–½ C) sugar	*processor until very smooth*
30 mℓ (2 T) sour cream	*and creamy)*
1 egg, beaten	*1 level tablespoon cornflour*
	⅓–½ cup sugar
	2 tablespoons sour cream
	1 egg, beaten

* Must be prepared in advance. Soak overnight in cold water. Drain, add boiling water to cover and cook over low heat for approximately 2 hours, changing the water once or twice. Drain again, using a strainer and put through mincer

METHOD First prepare dough. Cream butter and sugar very well. Add egg and vanilla and beat well. Sift flour, baking powder and salt together and add to mixture to form dough. Use to line a 23 cm (9 inch) pie plate or loose-bottomed baking pan.

APPLE FILLING Cut pie apples into slightly smaller pieces, then mix all ingredients together. Arrange on top of dough.

MON (POPPY SEED) MIXTURE Add syrup, butter and cinnamon to the minced poppy seeds (unless using the prepared poppy seed filling). Place spoonfuls of the mixture or the prepared filling around the edge of the tart, on top of the apples, at intervals of about 2 cm or 1 inch.

CHEESE FILLING Mix together all ingredients. Cover apples with mixture, being careful to spoon around poppy seeds without covering them.

Apple Strudel

METRIC	AMERICAN
300 g (2½ C) flour*	*2 cups all purpose flour*
250 g butter	*1 cup butter*
250 mℓ (1 C) thick or sour	*1 cup thick or sour cream*
cream	*1 tablespoon sugar & 1 table-*
15 mℓ (1 T) sugar & 15 mℓ (1 T)	*spoon flour, mixed together*
flour, mixed together	
APPLE FILLING	APPLE FILLING
10–12 Granny Smith apples	*10–12 Granny Smith apples*
Juice of 1 lemon	*Juice of 1 lemon*
Sugar to taste (approximately	*Sugar to taste (approximately*
100 g)	*½ cup)*
2 mℓ (½ t) cinnamon	*½ teaspoon cinnamon*
125 mℓ (½ C) chopped pecan	*½ cup chopped pecans or*
nuts or walnuts	*walnuts*
125 mℓ (½ C) sultanas	*½ cup golden raisins*

* This measurement differs from the American

METHOD Measure flour into bowl; rub or grate in butter and mix into a dough with the cream. Leave in refrigerator overnight.

FILLING Peel apples and cut into quarters. Place in a saucepan with the lemon juice; cover and cook over gentle heat until tender but not completely pulped. Add sugar and cinnamon and allow to simmer without the lid until the juice has almost cooked away. Add nuts and sultanas (golden raisins). Cool thoroughly before using.

TO ASSEMBLE & BAKE Roll dough out on floured board into a rectangle ½ cm (¼ inch) thick. Cut in half lengthwise to make 2 strudels. Sprinkle with flour and sugar mixture.

Spoon cooled apple filling lengthwise along edge of dough and roll up. Seal edges. Brush with egg white and sprinkle with sugar. Cut small, horizontal slits into top of pastry. Bake on greased baking tray (without sides) in 200°C (400°F) oven for 30 minutes.

CHEF'S TIP If preferred, use 300 mℓ (1¼ cups) softened vanilla ice-cream for the dough instead of the cream.

Makes 2 strudels

Overleaf: French Silk Tart

Lemon Sponge Pie

METRIC	AMERICAN
1 x 23 cm tart crust, baked blind*	1 x 9 inch pie shell, baked blind*
FILLING	FILLING
30 mℓ (2 T) butter	2 tablespoons butter
200 g (1 C) sugar	1 cup sugar
4 eggs, separated	4 eggs, separated
30 mℓ (2 T) flour	2 tablespoons flour
250 mℓ (1 C) milk	1 cup milk
5 mℓ (1 t) grated lemon rind	1 teaspoon grated lemon rind
80 mℓ (⅓ C) lemon juice	⅓ cup lemon juice
1 mℓ (¼ t) salt	¼ teaspoon salt

* Basic Tart Dough recipe on p 136

METHOD Cream together butter and sugar for filling. Add egg yolks, then flour, milk, lemon rind and juice. Beat egg whites and salt until stiff and fold in.

Bake crust blind for 10-15 minutes. Pour in filling. Bake in 200°C (400°F) oven for a further 30 minutes.

Serves 8

Almond Peach Pie

METRIC	AMERICAN
CRUST	CRUST
250 mℓ (1 C) ground almonds	1 cup almond meal
50 g (¼ C) castor sugar	¼ cup superfine granulated sugar
150 g (1¼ C) flour	1¼ cups all purpose flour
Pinch of salt	Pinch of salt
125 g butter	½ cup butter
Few drops almond essence	Few drops almond extract
FILLING	FILLING
250 mℓ (1 C) sour cream	1 cup sour cream
1 package vanilla instant pudding	1 package vanilla instant pudding
Few drops almond essence	Few drops almond extract
125 mℓ (½ C) milk	½ cup milk
1 x 825 g tin sliced peaches, drained	1 x 1 lb 12 oz can sliced peaches, drained
GLAZE	GLAZE
250 mℓ (1 C) apricot jam	1 cup apricot preserves
15 mℓ (1 T) lemon juice	1 tablespoon lemon juice
30 mℓ (2 T) water	2 tablespoons water

METHOD To prepare crust, sift together ground almonds, sugar, flour and salt. Rub in butter and add almond essence (extract). Press dough into a greased 23 cm (9 inch) pie dish or loose-bottomed pan. Bake in a 180°C (350°F) oven until golden brown (about 15 minutes). Cool and fill.

FILLING Beat together all ingredients, except peaches, until thick. Pour into cooled crust. Arrange sliced peaches in a circular pattern on top of custard and brush with glaze.

GLAZE Place all ingredients in a saucepan and bring to the boil. Allow to cool before using.

Serves 8

Banana Cream Pie

METRIC	AMERICAN
1 baked 23 cm pie crust*	1 baked 9 inch pie crust*
FILLING	FILLING
4 medium bananas	4 medium bananas
Lemon juice	Lemon juice
100 g (½ C) sugar	½ cup sugar
40 g (⅓ C) cornflour	⅓ cup cornstarch
Pinch of salt	Pinch of salt
500 mℓ (2 C) milk	2 cups milk
3 eggs, separated	3 eggs, separated
5 mℓ (1 t) vanilla essence	1 teaspoon vanilla extract

* Basic Tart Dough recipe on p 136

METHOD Slice bananas and dip in lemon juice. Blend half the sugar with the cornflour (cornstarch) and salt in the top of a double boiler. Add 125 mℓ (½ cup) milk and stir until smooth. Add remaining milk and cook in double boiler until thick.

Beat egg yolks; add hot custard to yolks very slowly, beating all the time. Return to double boiler and cook for 2 minutes. Remove from heat and add vanilla. Pour half of the custard into pie shell; cover with sliced bananas and top with remaining custard.

Beat egg whites until stiff. Add remaining sugar gradually. Spread meringue over custard. Bake for 10–15 minutes in 200°C (400°F) oven. Serve hot or cold.

CHEF'S TIP If preferred, top with whipped cream instead of meringue.

Serves 8
PHOTOGRAPH ON PAGE 146

Walnut Flan

METRIC	AMERICAN
CRUST	CRUST
250 g butter	1 cup butter
150 g (¾ C) sugar	¾ cup sugar
350 g (3 C) flour	3 cups all purpose flour
375 ml (1½ C) ground walnuts	1½ cups ground walnuts
2 egg yolks, slightly beaten	2 egg yolks, slightly beaten
Raspberry or red currant jam	Raspberry or red currant preserves
FILLING	FILLING
3 eggs	3 eggs
350 g (1¾ C) brown sugar	1¾ cups brown sugar
60 g (¾ C) dessicated coconut	¾ cup coconut
75 g (¾ C) walnuts, diced	¾ cup walnuts, diced
20 ml (4 t) flour	1½ tablespoons flour
5 ml (1 t) baking powder	1 teaspoon baking powder
Pinch of salt	Pinch of salt

METHOD Cut butter into small pieces and rub into flour and sugar. Add ground walnuts, then add slightly beaten egg yolks. Blend into a dough. Line bottom and sides of a 23 cm (9 inch) springform pan. Spread a layer of jam (preserves) onto dough.

FILLING Beat eggs and sugar until light and creamy. Add remaining ingredients and mix well. Pour filling into shell and bake in 180°C (350°F) oven for 50 minutes–1 hour, or until a tester comes out clean.

Serves 8 to 10

Peaches 'n Cream Pie

METRIC	AMERICAN
125 g butter	½ cup butter
30 ml (2 T) sugar	2 tablespoons sugar
2 ml (½ t) finely grated lemon rind	½ teaspoon finely grated lemon rind
180 g (1½ C) flour	1½ cups all purpose flour
FILLING	FILLING
1 x 825 g tin peach halves, drained	1 x 1 lb 12 oz can peach halves, drained
50 g (¼ C) sugar	¼ cup sugar
30 ml (2 T) flour	2 tablespoons flour
1 ml (¼ t) salt	¼ teaspoon salt
250 ml (1 C) double cream	1 cup heavy cream
2 ml (½ t) ground cinnamon	½ teaspoon ground cinnamon

METHOD Cream butter and sugar. Add lemon rind and flour. (The mixture will be crumbly.) Press into a well-greased 23 cm (9 inch) loose-bottomed pan. Bake in 180°C (350°F) oven for 10–15 minutes, or until slightly golden.

FILLING Arrange peaches in the partially baked pie shell. Combine sugar, flour, salt and cream. Mix together well, then put through a strainer. Pour over peaches and sprinkle with cinnamon.

Return to oven and bake for a further 35–45 minutes.

Serves 8 to 10

French Silk Tart

METRIC	AMERICAN
CHOCOLATE PASTRY	CHOCOLATE PASTRY
120 g (1 C) flour	1 cup flour
100 g (½ C) sugar	½ cup sugar
60 ml (¼ C) cocoa powder	¼ cup cocoa powder
Pinch of salt	Pinch of salt
125 g butter	½ cup butter
FILLING	FILLING
175 g butter	¾ cup butter
130 g (⅔ C) castor sugar*	1 cup superfine granulated sugar
3 eggs	3 eggs
75 g bitter chocolate, melted & cooled	3 oz unsweetened chocolate, melted & cooled
5 ml (1 t) vanilla essence	1 teaspoon vanilla extract
15 ml (1 T) brandy	1 tablespoon brandy
GARNISH	GARNISH
Whipped cream	Whipped cream
Chocolate Curls	Chocolate Curls

* *This measurement differs from the American*

METHOD Sift dry ingredients together. Cut butter into pieces and rub in well with fingers to form dough. Press into a lightly greased 23 cm (9 inch) loose-bottomed pan. Bake in 180°C (350°F) oven for 10–15 minutes. Cool and fill.

FILLING Using an electric mixer, cream butter well. Beat in the sugar, a little at a time, until the mixture is light and fluffy. Add eggs one at a time, beating well after each addition. Beat in cooled chocolate. Continue to beat mixture for several minutes. Add vanilla and brandy.

Spoon filling into crust and refrigerate for 2 hours. To decorate, pipe whipped cream rosettes around edge of tart and sprinkle centre with Chocolate Curls (see Chocolate Decorations on p 114).

CHEF'S TIP The pastry for this tart can be made very easily by placing all ingredients in a food processor and blending into a dough.

Serves 8 to 10   PHOTOGRAPH ON PAGE 138

Caramelized Pear Tart

METRIC	AMERICAN
125 g butter	½ cup butter
30 mℓ (2 T) sugar	2 tablespoons sugar
180 g (1½ C) flour	1½ cups flour
2 mℓ (½ t) finely grated lemon rind	½ teaspoon finely grated lemon rind
1 x 825 g tin pear halves, drained	1 x 1 lb 12 oz can pear halves, drained

GLAZE	GLAZE
250 mℓ (1 C) cream	1 cup cream
150 g (¾ C) sugar	¾ cup sugar
5 mℓ (1 t) caramel or vanilla essence	1 teaspoon caramel or vanilla extract

GARNISH	GARNISH
Toasted almonds	Toasted almonds

METHOD Cream butter and sugar. Add flour and lemon rind. (The mixture will be very crumbly.) Press into a lightly greased, loose-bottomed tart pan or ovenware dish. Bake at 180°C (350°F) for approximately 15 minutes, or until lightly browned. Remove from oven.

Arrange pear halves (rounded sides up) in a circle on the pastry base, with narrow ends pointing towards the centre.

Boil together all glaze ingredients for 5 minutes. Pour over tart. Return tart to oven for an additional 15–20 minutes. Remove and sprinkle toasted almonds around the edge to decorate.

Serves 10

Melktert

METRIC	AMERICAN
CRUST	CRUST
1 x 23 cm tart crust	1 x 9 inch pie shell

FILLING	FILLING
500 mℓ (2 C) milk	2 cups milk
30 mℓ (2 T) sugar	2 tablespoons sugar
75 g butter	5 tablespoons butter
Pinch of salt	Pinch of salt
5 mℓ (1 t) vanilla essence	1 teaspoon vanilla extract
Dash of grated nutmeg	Dash of grated nutmeg
45 mℓ (3 T) cornflour	3 tablespoons cornstarch
125 mℓ (½ C) cream	½ cup cream
3 egg yolks	3 egg yolks
Cinnamon & sugar	Cinnamon & sugar

METHOD Use Basic Tart Dough (recipe on p 136) to make a 23 cm (9 inch) pie shell. Bake blind in 180°C (350°F) oven for 15 minutes; remove beans and foil or wax paper and bake for an additional 5–10 minutes, or until golden brown. Cool.

FILLING Bring milk, sugar, butter, salt, vanilla and nutmeg to the boil. Blend cornflour (cornstarch) smoothly with cream. Pour boiling milk over cream mixture, stirring well.

Beat egg yolks and while beating, slowly pour some of the hot mixture into the egg yolks; return the whole mixture to the saucepan, blend well and cook, beating constantly with a whisk, until thickened. Remove and cool. (If too thick, add more milk.)

Pour cooled custard filling into shell. Sprinkle with cinnamon and sugar and bake in 180°C (350°F) oven for 15–20 minutes.

Serves 8

Fruit Tart

METRIC	AMERICAN
1 x 23 cm tart crust*	1 x 9 inch pie crust*

FILLING	FILLING
200 mℓ (¾ C) milk	¾ cup milk
200 mℓ (¾ C) cream	¾ cup cream
1 package vanilla instant pudding	1 package vanilla instant pudding
15 mℓ (1 T) brandy	1 tablespoon brandy
Fresh or canned fruit**	Fresh or canned fruit**

GLAZE	GLAZE
250 mℓ (1 C) orange juice	1 cup orange juice
30 mℓ (2 T) sugar	2 tablespoons sugar
30 mℓ (2 T) red jelly powder	2 tablespoons red jello powder
15 mℓ (1 T) cornflour	1 tablespoon cornstarch

GARNISH	GARNISH
Whipped cream (optional)	Whipped cream (optional)

* Basic Tart Dough recipe on p 136
** such as strawberries, grapes, kiwi fruit, sliced peaches, pears, canned pineapple or mandarin oranges

METHOD Prepare tart dough and bake blind in 180°C (350°F) oven for 15 minutes. Remove beans and paper and bake for another 10–15 minutes, or until golden brown. Remove from oven and cool.

FILLING Pour milk and cream into a bowl; sprinkle instant pudding over and beat until thick. Stir in brandy. Prepare fruit and set aside.

GLAZE Bring orange juice and sugar to the boil. Add jelly (jello) and thicken with cornflour (cornstarch) mixed to a paste with cold water. Cool.

TO ASSEMBLE Spoon filling into cooled pastry shell and arrange your choice of fruit on top. Spoon cooled glaze over fruit and decorate with whipped cream, if desired.

Serves 8 to 10   PHOTOGRAPH ON PAGE 99

Kentucky Derby Pie

METRIC	AMERICAN
CRUST	CRUST
1 x 23 cm tart crust*	1 x 9 inch pie crust*
FILLING	FILLING
150 g (¾ C) sugar	¾ cup sugar
90 g (¾ C) flour	¾ cup all purpose flour
2 eggs, lightly beaten	2 eggs, lightly beaten
125 g butter, melted	½ cup butter, melted
175 g chocolate, chopped	1 cup chocolate chips
5 mℓ (1 t) vanilla essence	1 teaspoon vanilla extract
30 mℓ (2 T) Bourbon or whisky	2 tablespoons Bourbon
50 g (½ C) chopped pecan nuts	½ cup chopped pecans

* Basic Tart Dough recipe on p 136

METHOD Prepare tart dough and bake blind for 10 minutes in 180°C (350°F) oven.

FILLING Mix sugar and flour together. Add beaten eggs and butter. Stir in remaining ingredients and mix well.

Pour filling into partially baked pie shell. Bake in 160°C (325°F) oven for 50–60 minutes.

Serves 8 to 10

Mississippi Mud Pie

METRIC	AMERICAN
CRUST	CRUST
150 g (1¼ C) flour	1¼ cups all purpose flour
Pinch of salt	Pinch of salt
125 g butter	½ cup butter
30 mℓ (2 T) iced water	2 tablespoons iced water
FILLING	FILLING
125 g butter	½ cup butter
90 g dark chocolate	3 squares unsweetened chocolate
4 eggs	4 eggs
200 g (1 C) sugar	1 cup sugar
30 mℓ (2 T) syrup*	3 tablespoons light syrup
5 mℓ (1 t) vanilla essence	1 teaspoon vanilla extract
15 mℓ (1 T) flour	1 tablespoon all purpose flour

* This measurement differs from the American

METHOD To prepare crust, sift flour and salt together. Cut butter into flour until it resembles fine breadcrumbs. Add water and knead lightly into dough with fingertips.

Roll out to fit a 23 cm (9 inch) greased pie dish or loose-bottomed pan. Bake in a 180°C (350°F) oven for 15 minutes.

FILLING Melt butter and chocolate together. Meanwhile, beat eggs, add sugar, syrup and vanilla and beat again. Add butter / chocolate mixture and sifted flour; beat well.

Pour into partially baked crust and bake in 180°C (350°F) oven for 35–45 minutes. Serve warm with vanilla ice-cream.

Serves 8

Pumpkin Chiffon Pie

METRIC	AMERICAN
CRUST	CRUST
250 mℓ (1 C) crushed Marie biscuits	1 cup crushed Graham crackers
125 mℓ (½ C) melted butter	½ cup melted butter
30 mℓ (2 T) sugar	2 tablespoons sugar
125 mℓ (½ C) dessicated coconut	½ cup coconut
30 mℓ (2 T) finely chopped walnuts or pecan nuts	2 tablespoons finely chopped walnuts or pecans
FILLING	FILLING
30 mℓ (2 T) gelatine	1 envelope unflavored gelatin
30 mℓ (2 T) cold water	2 tablespoons cold water
125 mℓ (½ C) hot milk	½ cup hot milk
3 eggs, separated	3 eggs, separated
Pinch of salt	Pinch of salt
2 mℓ (½ t) freshly grated nutmeg	½ teaspoon freshly grated nutmeg
1 mℓ (¼ t) ground ginger	¼ teaspoon ground ginger
375 mℓ (1½ C) cooked, mashed pumpkin	1 x 16 oz can pumpkin
GARNISH	GARNISH
125 mℓ (½ C) cream	½ cup whipping cream
Freshly grated nutmeg	Freshly grated nutmeg

METHOD Prepare crust. Combine all ingredients and press onto bottom and sides of a 23 cm (9 inch) loose-bottomed pan or pie dish. Bake in 180°C (350°F) oven for 10–15 minutes.

FILLING Combine gelatine with cold water. Add hot milk and stir in top of double boiler until gelatine has dissolved completely. Beat egg yolks very well. Slowly add gelatine mixture to the yolks, beating constantly while you do so. Stir in salt, nutmeg and ginger.

Return mixture to double boiler and cook, stirring constantly with a whisk until mixture thickens. Remove from heat. Whisk in pumpkin. Refrigerate mixture until partially set (about ½ hour).

Beat egg whites until very stiff. Fold into pumpkin mixture. Pour into crust and refrigerate until ready to serve.

Whip cream and pipe rosettes around edge and centre of pie. Sprinkle lightly with freshly grated nutmeg.

Serves 8 to 10

Small Cakes & Biscuits

SMALL CAKES

Petits Fours Made Easy *148*
Butterflies *148*
Galato Boureka *149*
Mille Feuilles *149*
Grasshopper Squares *150*
Koeksusters *150*
Nut Squares *151*
Brownies *151*
Meringues with Coffee Cream & Walnuts *151*
Lemon Squares *152*
Cream Cheese Squares *152*
Greek Doughnuts *152*
Lammington Squares *152*

BISCUITS

Chunky Raisin & Walnut Cookies *153*
Linzer Cookies *153*
Marshmallow Nut Delights *153*
Chocolate Chip Cookies *156*
Double Chocolate Chip Cookies *156*
Nutty Meringue Fingers *156*
Walnut Chocolate Shortbread *156*
Caramel Chocolate Squares *157*
Seven Layer Squares *157*
Lemon Meringue Bars *157*
Thumbprints *157*
Raspberry Almond Slices *158*
Ohio Buckeyes *158*
Date & Nut Spirals *158*
Crunchy Cookies *158*
Florentine Squares *159*
Aunt Hilda's Crispy Butter Biscuits *159*
Mandelbrodt *159*
Viennese Cookies *159*

Small Cakes

Petits Fours Made Easy

METRIC	AMERICAN
SPONGE	SPONGE
4 eggs at room temperature	4 eggs at room temperature
100 g (½ C) castor sugar	½ cup superfine granulated sugar
5 mℓ (1 t) vanilla essence	1 teaspoon vanilla extract
30 mℓ (2 T) milk	2 tablespoons milk
30 g butter	2 tablespoons butter
90 g (¾ C) flour	¾ cup cake flour
5 mℓ (1t) baking powder	1 teaspoon baking powder
BUTTER-CREAM FILLING*	BUTTER-CREAM FILLING*
125 g butter	½ cup butter
500 g icing sugar	1 lb powdered sugar
5 mℓ (1 t) vanilla essence	1 teaspoon vanilla extract
Boiling water	Boiling water
APRICOT GLAZE	APRICOT GLAZE
375 mℓ (1½ C) smooth apricot jam	1½ cups apricot preserves, strained
Juice of ½ lemon	Juice of ½ lemon
45–60 mℓ (3–4 T) water	3–4 tablespoons water
QUICK FONDANT GLAZE	QUICK FONDANT GLAZE
2 egg whites, unbeaten	2 egg whites, unbeaten
400 g (3 C) icing sugar	3 cups powdered sugar
Few drops almond essence	Few drops almond extract
Pink food colouring	Pink food color
Green food colouring	Green food color
GARNISH	GARNISH
Melted chocolate	Melted chocolate
Nuts & cherries	Nuts & cherries
or	or
Candied violets & flowers	Candied violets & flowers

* Optional

METHOD Prepare sponge. Beat eggs and sugar together very well, until thick and creamy. Add vanilla and beat well. Scald milk and butter; fold in gently but thoroughly,

Previous pages (centre) *Banana Cream Pie,* (right) *Koeksusters* and (at the back) *Butterflies and Marble Cheese Cake*

together with the sifted flour and baking powder. Bake in a greased and floured 23 cm (9 inch) springform tin (loose-bottomed pan) in 180°C (350°F) oven for 20–25 minutes, or until springy to the touch.

Turn out onto a wire rack and cool thoroughly. Wrap in wax paper or foil and place in freezer overnight, before cutting into shapes. (This makes the cake easier to handle and prevents it from crumbling when cutting out the shapes.)

Cut into rounds, ovals, squares, diamonds etc; cut through the middle of each shape and spread with a butter-cream filling, if desired. (This last step is optional, not essential.)

BUTTER-CREAM FILLING Cream butter and beat in sugar. Add vanilla and enough boiling water to make a smooth consistency.

APRICOT GLAZE Boil all ingredients together until smooth. Pour over petits fours and allow to set.

QUICK FONDANT GLAZE Mix together the unbeaten egg whites, sugar and almond essence or extract, until smooth. Divide mixture into three parts. Colour one portion pale pink, another pale green and leave the remaining portion white. Pour over apricot-glazed petits fours and decorate with melted chocolate, nuts and cherries or candied violets and flowers.

Makes 24   PHOTOGRAPH ON PAGE 155

Butterflies

METRIC	AMERICAN
250 g margarine	1 cup margarine
300 g (1½ C) sugar	1½ cups sugar
5 mℓ (1 t) vanilla essence	1 teaspoon vanilla extract
4 eggs	4 eggs
350 g (3 C) flour	3 cups cake flour
15 mℓ (3 t) baking powder	3 teaspoons baking powder
Pinch of salt	Pinch of salt
250 mℓ (1 C) milk	1 cup milk
TOPPING	TOPPING
250 mℓ (1 C) cream	1 cup cream
Strawberry or raspberry jam	Strawberry or raspberry preserves
Icing sugar	Powdered sugar

METHOD Cream margarine and sugar and add vanilla. Add eggs, sifted dry ingredients and milk; beat until smooth. Grease and flour muffin or patty tins; three-quarter fill with batter and bake in 180°C (350°F) oven for 10–15 minutes, or until golden brown. Cool.

Slice tops off cakes and cut in half. Place a spoonful of whipped cream on top of each cake; spoon a little jam along the centre, then press the sliced halves on either side of the jam. Dust with sieved icing sugar (powdered sugar).

Makes 36   PHOTOGRAPH ON PAGE 146

148

Galato Boureka

METRIC	AMERICAN
PASTRY	PASTRY
500 g phyllo pastry	1 lb phyllo pastry
Melted butter for brushing pastry	Melted butter for brushing pastry
FILLING	FILLING
1 ℓ (4 C) milk	4 cups milk
Pinch of salt	Pinch of salt
130 g (⅔ C) sugar	⅔ cup sugar
160 mℓ (⅔ C) semolina	⅔ cup Cream of Wheat
15 mℓ (1 T) butter	1 tablespoon butter
5 mℓ (1 t) finely grated lemon or orange rind	1 teaspoon finely grated lemon or orange rind
3 eggs, separated	3 eggs, separated
SYRUP	SYRUP
200 g (1 C) sugar	1 cup sugar
125 mℓ (½ C) water	½ cup water
Juice of ½ lemon	Juice of ½ lemon
Few whole cloves	Few whole cloves

METHOD First prepare filling. Boil milk with salt and half of the sugar. Add the semolina / Cream of Wheat in a slow stream, stirring constantly with a wooden spoon. Bring to the boil gradually, stirring all the time over low heat until mixture is very thick.

Remove from stove and add the butter. Allow to cool, stirring occasionally to prevent a skin forming on top. Add lemon or orange rind.

Beat egg yolks with remaining sugar until light and creamy. Fold into the mixture. Beat egg whites until stiff and fold in.

TO ASSEMBLE Working on a wooden board, place 3 sheets of phyllo pastry one on top of the other, brushing lightly with melted butter in between each sheet. Cut lengthwise into 3 even strips.

Place a spoonful of filling along the top edge of one pastry strip, 2,5 cm (1 inch) away from the side edges. Fold in the sides and roll up, as for a Swiss roll (jelly roll). Brush with melted butter and place on a greased tray. Repeat this process, using all the filling.

Bake in 180°C (350°F) oven for 30–40 minutes, or until golden brown. Remove from oven and allow to cool on baking tray, then transfer rolls to a deep dish.

SYRUP Boil all ingredients together for 10 minutes. Pour hot syrup over pastries in dish. Turn pastries every now and then. Serve cold.

Makes 12

Mille Feuilles

METRIC	AMERICAN
Melted butter	Melted butter
6–8 sheets phyllo pastry	6–8 sheets phyllo pastry
125 g butter	½ cup butter
Strawberry jam	Strawberry preserves
Whipped cream	Whipped cream
Flaked almonds	Flaked almonds
Maraschino cherries	Maraschino cherries
VANILLA FILLING	VANILLA FILLING
1 package instant vanilla pudding	1 package instant vanilla pudding
200 mℓ (¾ C) cream	¾ cup cream
200 mℓ (¾ C) milk	¾ cup milk
Few drops almond essence	Few drops almond extract
LEMON ICING	LEMON ICING
250 mℓ (1 C) icing sugar	1 cup powdered sugar
15 mℓ (1 T) lemon juice	1 tablespoon lemon juice
Boiling water	Boiling water
GARNISH	GARNISH
Flaked almonds	Flaked almonds
Maraschino cherries	Maraschino cherries

METHOD Brush a baking sheet / cookie sheet (without sides) with a small amount of melted butter. Cover baking sheet with a layer of phyllo pastry. Brush sparingly with melted butter. Repeat the process, layering 6–8 sheets of pastry and brushing in between each layer with melted butter.

Using a sharp knife, cut the pastry breadthwise into 3 even strips. Bake in 180°C (350°F) oven for 10–15 minutes or until golden brown. Turn oven off and allow pastry to dry out for another 15–20 minutes. Remove from oven and allow to cool. Prepare filling and icing.

VANILLA FILLING Combine all ingredients and beat well.

LEMON ICING Combine all ingredients and beat well.

TO ASSEMBLE Run a knife or spatula under the strips of cooled pastry. Place one strip on a serving platter and spread lightly with strawberry jam (preserves). Cover with vanilla filling, then with a layer of whipped cream. Place second strip on top and repeat the jam, vanilla and cream layers. Top with third strip; drizzle with lemon icing and sprinkle with flaked almonds and maraschino cherries. (For individual pastries, cut phyllo strips crosswise into 8 cm (3 inch) sections and assemble individually.)

If you wish to decorate the mille feuilles in the traditional way, make a pattern of lines, using chocolate sauce over the lemon icing. Draw a knife across the top to define the pattern (see photograph on p 154).

CHEF'S TIP Do not assemble the mille feuilles too long before using, as the pastry will become soggy. (I try to do so not more than one hour before serving.) Slice with a serrated knife or, for the best results, with an electric knife.

Serves 8   PHOTOGRAPH ON PAGE 154

Grasshopper Squares

METRIC	AMERICAN
CAKE	CAKE
140 g dark chocolate, diced	¾ cup semi-sweet chocolate chips
175 g butter	¾ cup butter
100 g (½ C) sugar	½ cup sugar
4 eggs, separated	4 eggs, separated
5 mℓ (1 t) vanilla essence	1 teaspoon vanilla extract
Pinch of salt	Pinch of salt
100 g (¾ C) flour	¾ cup cake flour
FILLING	FILLING
35 marshmallows	35 marshmallows
60 mℓ (¼ C) milk	¼ cup milk
60 mℓ (¼ C) Crème de Menthe	¼ cup Crème de Menthe
15 mℓ (1 T) Crème de Caçao	1 tablespoon Crème de Caçao
Few drops green food colouring	Few drops green food color
375 mℓ (1½ C) cream, whipped	1½ cups cream, whipped
GLAZE	GLAZE
45 mℓ (3 T) butter	3 tablespoons butter
30 mℓ (2 T) cocoa powder	2 tablespoons cocoa powder
500 mℓ (2 C) icing sugar	2 cups powdered sugar
1 egg white, unbeaten	1 egg white, unbeaten
GARNISH	GARNISH
Shaved or grated chocolate	Shaved or grated chocolate

METHOD To prepare cake, melt chocolate in a double boiler or microwave and allow to cool. Set aside. Cream butter and half the sugar until light and fluffy. Beat in egg yolks, then add melted chocolate and vanilla.

Beat egg whites very well; add the remaining sugar and continue to beat until very stiff. Using a rubber spatula, stir one third of whites into the chocolate mixture, then pour the chocolate mixture over the rest of the whites. Sprinkle the sifted flour and salt lightly on top. Gently fold the flour into the mixture until no white streaks remain.

Pour batter into two well greased and floured 23 cm (9 inch) square pans and bake in 190°C (375°F) oven for 15–20 minutes. Turn out onto a rack to cool.

FILLING Melt the marshmallows in the milk over a double boiler or in the microwave; allow to cool. Add the liqueurs and beat thoroughly. Add the colouring and stir in well. Beat the cream until stiff, then fold in.

TO ASSEMBLE Line one of the cake pans with foil and place one of the squares in the pan. Spread filling over cake, then top with the second square; press down firmly, ensuring that the filling is spread evenly and flush with the edges of the cake. Cover with plastic wrap and freeze until firm enough to cut into squares.

GLAZE Melt butter with cocoa in a saucepan and stir until well blended. Blend sugar with unbeaten egg white, then add to saucepan with butter / cocoa mixture and stir over low heat just until blended.

TO SERVE Remove cake from pan. Pour glaze over and sprinkle with shaved or grated chocolate. Cut into squares to serve.

Makes 35

Koeksusters

METRIC	AMERICAN
25 g cake yeast	1 oz cake yeast
200 mℓ (¾ C) warm water	¾ cup warm water
600 g (5 C) flour	5 cups flour
5 mℓ (1 t) salt	1 teaspoon salt
100 g (½ C) sugar	½ cup sugar
250 mℓ (1 C) warm milk	1 cup warm milk
125 g margarine, melted	½ cup margarine, melted
2 mℓ (½ t) grated nutmeg	½ teaspoon grated nutmeg
2 eggs, lightly beaten	2 eggs, lightly beaten
Oil for frying	Oil for frying
SYRUP	SYRUP
600 g (3 C) sugar	3 cups sugar
500 mℓ (2 C) water	2 cups water
1 cinnamon stick	1 cinnamon stick

METHOD Liquify yeast by mixing with 5 mℓ (1 teaspoon) sugar. Stir in a little of the measured warm water. Combine flour, salt and sugar in a large bowl. Make a well in the centre and add yeast and all other ingredients except oil. Mix into a dough, then knead in food mixer for approximately 10 minutes. Cover and leave to rise overnight.

Roll out dough to a thickness of approximately 1 cm (½ inch) and cut into strips 20 cm (8 inches) long and 1 cm (½ inch) wide. Fold in half lengthwise and twist. Allow to rise on a lightly floured board for 15–20 minutes.

Deep fry in hot oil until golden brown. Remove and dip into cold syrup. Drain and cool on wire tray.

SYRUP Combine ingredients in a saucepan and simmer without stirring for 10 minutes. Allow to cool thoroughly.

Makes 36   PHOTOGRAPH ON PAGE 147

Nut Squares

METRIC	AMERICAN
4 eggs, separated	4 eggs, separated
250 g (1¼ C) sugar	1¼ cups sugar
140 g (1 C) self-raising flour*	1 cup self-rising flour*
45 mℓ (3 T) oats	3 level tablespoons oats
90 g margarine	6 tablespoons margarine
30 mℓ (2 T) white wine	2 tablespoons white wine
30 mℓ (2 T) crushed cornflakes	2 tablespoons crushed cornflakes
60 g (¾ C) dessicated coconut	¾ cup dessicated coconut
30 mℓ (2 T) chopped pecan nuts	2 tablespoons chopped pecans
Smooth apricot jam	Smooth apricot preserves

GARNISH	GARNISH
Flaked almonds	Flaked almonds

* If using ordinary flour, add 10 mℓ (2 teaspoons) baking powder

METHOD Beat egg yolks very well with 100 g (½ cup) of the sugar. Add flour, oats, margarine and wine. Mix well. Spread into a greased and floured 23 cm (9 inch) square baking pan and refrigerate for 15 minutes.

Whisk egg whites until stiff and gradually add remaining 150 g (¾ cup) sugar, beating all the time. Add cornflakes, coconut and nuts.

Spread apricot jam (preserves) onto cooled dough and top with egg white mixture. Decorate with flaked almonds. Bake in 160°C (325°F) oven for 30 minutes. Cool and cut into squares.

CHEF'S TIP For a variation, add 30 mℓ (2 tablespoons) of grated chocolate to the mixture.

Makes 25

Brownies

METRIC	AMERICAN
60 g chocolate, melted & cooled	¼ cup chocolate, melted & cooled
125 g butter	½ cup butter
2 eggs	2 eggs
200 g (1 C) sugar	1 cup sugar
60 g (½ C) flour, sifted	1 cup all purpose flour, sifted
Pinch of salt	Pinch of salt
5 mℓ (1 t) vanilla essence	1 teaspoon vanilla extract
50 g (½ C) chopped pecans	½ cup chopped pecans

TOPPING	TOPPING
30 mℓ (2 T) cocoa powder	2 tablespoons cocoa powder
500 mℓ (2 C) icing sugar	2 cups powdered sugar
60 g butter	¼ cup butter
Boiling water	Boiling water

METHOD Melt chocolate and butter together; remove from heat and cool. Beat eggs and sugar well. Add cooled chocolate mixture, then add flour and salt. Stir in vanilla and nuts. Pour into a 20 cm (8 inch) square pan. Bake in 180°C (350°F) oven for 25–30 minutes.

TOPPING Combine cocoa and sugar. Pour in boiling water and mix to a smooth spreading consistency. If desired, add a dash of vanilla essence (extract).

Remove brownies from oven; spread topping over them while they are still warm. Cool and cut into squares.

Makes 25

Meringues with Coffee Cream & Walnuts

METRIC	AMERICAN
4 egg whites	4 egg whites
Pinch of salt	Pinch of salt
200 g (1 C) sugar	1 cup sugar
5 mℓ (1 t) vanilla essence	1 teaspoon vanilla extract

FILLING	FILLING
250 mℓ (1 C) cream	1 cup cream
30 mℓ (2 T) icing sugar	2 tablespoons powdered sugar
5 mℓ (1 t) instant coffee powder	1 teaspoon instant coffee powder
5 mℓ (1 t) boiling water	1 teaspoon boiling water
5 mℓ (1 t) vanilla essence	1 teaspoon vanilla extract
Chopped walnuts	Chopped walnuts

METHOD Beat egg whites and salt until foamy. Gradually add sugar and continue beating until stiff and shiny. Add vanilla. Drop by spoonfuls, or pipe into shapes, onto baking sheet lined with foil and bake in 120°C (250°F) oven for 2–3 hours, or until dry.

FILLING Whip cream and sugar until stiff. Mix coffee, boiling water and vanilla together. Cool and fold into cream.

Spread filling on meringues, sprinkle with walnuts and sandwich together.

CHEF'S TIP Piped meringues do not puff up as much, nor are they as light, as those dropped by teaspoonfuls onto a baking sheet. This is because a lot of the air is lost and they are more compressed.

Makes 32

PHOTOGRAPH ON PAGE 154

Lemon Squares

METRIC	AMERICAN
250 g butter	1 cup butter
125 ml (½ C) icing sugar	½ cup powdered sugar
2 ml (½ t) finely grated lemon rind	½ teaspoon finely grated lemon rind
250 g (2 C) flour, sifted	2 cups all purpose flour, sifted

FILLING	FILLING
6 eggs, lightly beaten	6 eggs, lightly beaten
400 g (2 C) sugar*	3 cups sugar
125 ml (½ C) lemon juice	½ cup lemon juice
40 g (⅓ C) flour	⅓ cup flour
7 ml (1½ t) baking powder	1½ teaspoons baking powder
2 ml (½ t) finely grated lemon rind	½ teaspoon finely grated lemon rind

TOPPING	TOPPING
Icing sugar	Powdered sugar

* This measurement differs from the American

METHOD To make pastry crust, cream butter with sugar and lemon rind; add flour. Press into a buttered and floured 33 x 26 x 5 cm (13 x 9½ x 2 inch) pan. Bake in 180°C (350°F) oven for 15 minutes, until light brown. Cool for 20 minutes.

FILLING Mix lightly beaten eggs with sugar and lemon juice. Add sifted flour, baking powder and lemon rind. Pour over cooled crust.

Return to oven and bake at 150°C (300°F) for 20 — 25 minutes, until firm but moist and golden. Cool, sprinkle with icing sugar (powdered sugar) and cut into squares.

Makes approximately 40

Cream Cheese Squares

METRIC	AMERICAN
1 package vanilla cake mix	1 package yellow cake mix
125 g butter, melted	½ cup butter, melted
3 eggs	3 eggs
500 g icing sugar	1 lb powdered sugar
15 ml (1 T) cornflour	1 tablespoon cornstarch
250 g cream cheese	8 oz cream cheese
5 ml (1 t) finely grated lemon rind (optional)	1 teaspoon finely grated lemon rind (optional)

METHOD Combine cake mix, butter and 1 egg. Beat together and spread into a 23 x 33 cm (9 x 13 inch) pan. Mix together remaining ingredients; spread on top of dough.

Bake in 180°C (350°F) oven for 45 minutes. When completely cool, cut into squares.

Makes approximately 40

Greek Doughnuts

METRIC	AMERICAN
120 g (1 C) flour	1 cup all purpose flour
10 ml (2 t) baking powder	2 teaspoons baking powder
15 ml (1 T) sugar	1 tablespoon sugar
Sufficient water to make batter	Sufficient water to make batter
1 l (4 C) oil	4 cups oil
250 ml (1 C) syrup	1 cup golden syrup

METHOD Combine flour, baking powder and sugar. Add sufficient water to make a batter with a dropping consistency.

Pour oil into a small pot and heat. Drop teaspoonfuls of batter into the oil; remove when lightly browned. Drain on absorbent paper and arrange in serving dish.

Heat syrup with 45 ml (3 tablespoons) boiling water and mix well. Pour over the doughnuts.

Makes approximately 30

Lammington Squares

METRIC	AMERICAN
125 g butter	½ cup butter
150 g sugar	¾ cup sugar
2 eggs	2 eggs
180 g (1½ C) flour	1½ cups all purpose flour
Pinch of salt	Pinch of salt
5 ml (1 t) cream of tartar	1 teaspoon cream of tartar
2 ml (½ t) bicarbonate of soda	½ teaspoon baking soda
125 ml (½ C) milk	½ cup milk

CHOCOLATE COATING	CHOCOLATE COATING
300 ml (1¼ C) boiling water	1¼ cups boiling water
75 g butter	5 tablespoons butter
425 ml (1¾ C) icing sugar	1¾ cups icing sugar
10 ml (2 t) vanilla essence	2 teaspoons vanilla extract
45 ml (3 T) cocoa powder	3 tablespoons cocoa powder
Dessicated coconut	Dessicated coconut

METHOD Cream butter and sugar. Add eggs, one at a time, beating well after each addition. Sift together flour, salt and cream of tartar. Dissolve bicarbonate of soda (baking soda) in milk and add to mixture with sifted dry ingredients.

Pour mixture into a greased and floured 20 x 25 cm (8 x 10 inch) pan and bake in 180°C (350°F) oven for 20–25 minutes. Allow to cool and cut into squares.

CHOCOLATE COATING Combine all ingredients in a saucepan and bring to the boil. Dip each cooled square quickly into the hot chocolate mixture. (Do not allow to soak, or they will become soggy.) Roll in coconut.

Makes approximately 24

Biscuits

Chunky Raisin & Walnut Cookies

METRIC	AMERICAN
250 g butter	1 cup butter
100 g (½ C) sugar	½ cup sugar
200 g (1 C) brown sugar	1 cup brown sugar
2 eggs	2 eggs
5 mℓ (1 t) vanilla essence	1 teaspoon vanilla extract
250 g (2 C) flour	2 cups all purpose flour
5 mℓ (1 t) ground cinnamon	1 teaspoon ground cinnamon
300 g (2 C) raisins	2 cups raisins
200 g (2 C) coarsely chopped walnuts	2 cups coarsely chopped walnuts

METHOD Cream butter and sugars. Add eggs and vanilla, then flour and cinnamon. Fold in raisins and nuts.

Drop heaped teaspoonfuls of mixture onto lightly greased baking sheets and bake in 180°C (350°F) oven for 10–12 minutes.

Makes 80

Linzer Cookies

METRIC	AMERICAN
250 g butter	1 cup butter
100 g (½ C) castor sugar	½ cup superfine granulated sugar
4 egg yolks, slightly beaten	4 egg yolks, slightly beaten
2 mℓ (½ t) finely grated lemon rind	½ teaspoon finely grated lemon rind
2 mℓ (½ t) salt	½ teaspoon salt
10 mℓ (2 t) ground cinnamon	2 teaspoons ground cinnamon
Pinch of ground cloves	Pinch of ground cloves
350 g (3 C) flour	3 cups all purpose flour
250 mℓ (1 C) ground almonds or walnuts	1 cup almond meal or ground walnuts
250 mℓ (1 C) raspberry jam	1 cup raspberry preserves or jelly

METHOD Cream butter and sugar. Add egg yolks, lemon rind, salt and spices. Blend in flour and ground nuts to form a dough. Set aside one quarter of the dough for the lattice top. Pat remaining dough onto the bottom and 1 cm (½ inch) up the sides of a greased 40 x 28 cm (16 x 11 inch) pan. Spread jam (preserves) onto dough.

Roll remaining dough into strips and arrange in lattice pattern over the top. Bake in 160°C (325°F) oven for 35 minutes, or until lightly browned. Cut into squares.

CHEF'S TIP These cookies may also be rolled out and cut into shapes such as hearts, triangles, rounds, etc. Using a wet finger, make an indentation in each one and fill with jam (preserves). If using this method, bake the cookies for 10–15 minutes only.

Makes 40   PHOTOGRAPH ON PAGE 155

Marshmallow Nut Delights

METRIC	AMERICAN
1 package vanilla cake mix	1 package yellow cake mix
125 g butter, melted	½ cup butter, melted
1 egg	1 egg
750 mℓ (3 C) miniature marsh-mallows	3 cups miniature marshmallows
TOPPING	**TOPPING**
60 g butter	¼ cup butter
160 mℓ (⅔ C) syrup	⅔ cup corn syrup
5 mℓ (1 t) vanilla essence	1 teaspoon vanilla extract
1 x 180 g packet peanut butter chips or 250 mℓ (1 C) crunchy peanut butter	1 x 6 oz package peanut butter chips or 1 cup crunchy peanut butter
300 g (2 C) salted peanuts	2 cups salted peanuts
500 mℓ (2 C) rice crispies	2 cups rice crispies

METHOD Combine cake mix, melted butter and egg. Spread into a 20 x 28 cm (8 x 11 inch) pan. Bake in 160°C (325°F) oven for 15 minutes.

Remove from oven; cover with marshmallows and return to oven for a further 2 minutes, or until marshmallows are puffed and melted.

TOPPING In a saucepan combine butter, syrup, vanilla and peanut butter chips or peanut butter. Stir over low heat until melted; add peanuts and rice crispies.

Spread over melted marshmallows. Refrigerate until cool and firm, then cut into bars.

Makes 20

Overleaf: (in the foreground, l to r) Mille Feuilles, Chocolate Truffles, Linzer Cookies, Petits Fours Made Easy and Thumbprints. At the back (l to r) Meringues with Coffee Cream & Walnuts, Lemon Upside-down Cake, Quick Orange-glazed Cake and (on the pedestal), Lemon Cheese Gâteau

Chocolate Chip Cookies

METRIC	AMERICAN
250 g butter	1 cup butter
100 g (½ C) sugar*	1 cup sugar
150 g (¾ C) brown sugar	¾ cup brown sugar
5 mℓ (1 t) vanilla essence	1 teaspoon vanilla extract
Pinch of salt	Pinch of salt
2 eggs	2 eggs
250 g (2 C) flour	2 cups all purpose flour
5 mℓ (1 t) bicarbonate of soda	1 teaspoon baking soda
350 g chocolate, coarsely chopped	2 cups chocolate chips
100 g (1 C) walnuts, coarsely chopped	1 cup walnuts, coarsely chopped

* This measurement differs from the American

METHOD Cream butter and sugars until light and fluffy. Add vanilla and salt. Add eggs, then flour and bicarbonate of soda (baking soda). Stir in chocolate and nuts.

Drop spoonfuls of batter onto ungreased baking trays. Bake in 190°C (375°F) oven for 8–10 minutes.

Makes approximately 40

Double Chocolate Chip Cookies

METRIC	AMERICAN
250 g butter	1 cup butter
100 g (½ C) sugar	½ cup sugar
150 g (¾ C) brown sugar	¾ cup brown sugar
2 eggs	2 eggs
5 mℓ (1 t) vanilla essence	1 teaspoon vanilla extract
250 g (2 C) flour	2 cups all purpose flour
30 mℓ (2 T) cocoa powder	2 tablespoons cocoa powder
Pinch of salt	Pinch of salt
5 mℓ (1 t) bicarbonate of soda	1 teaspoon baking soda
200 g (2 C) chopped walnuts or pecan nuts	2 cups chopped walnuts or pecans
350 g dark chocolate, coarsely diced	2 cups semi-sweet chocolate chips

METHOD Cream butter and sugars. Add eggs and vanilla. Sift together flour, cocoa, salt and bicarbonate of soda (baking soda). Add to mixture. Fold in nuts and chocolate.

Drop heaped teaspoonfuls onto 2 lightly greased baking sheets and bake in 180°C (350°F) oven for 10–12 minutes.

CHEF'S TIP For an interesting variation, try using coarsely chopped peppermint chocolates instead of chocolate chips. The peppermint and chocolate colour combination looks most attractive.

Makes 80

Nutty Meringue Fingers

METRIC	AMERICAN
125 g butter	½ cup butter
100 g (½ C) brown sugar	½ cup brown sugar
2 egg yolks	2 egg yolks
5 mℓ (1 t) vanilla essence	1 teaspoon vanilla extract
180 g (1½ C) flour	1½ cups all purpose flour
5 mℓ (1 t) baking powder	1 teaspoon baking powder
Apricot jam	Apricot preserves

TOPPING	TOPPING
2 egg whites	2 egg whites
150 g (¾ C) brown sugar	¾ cup brown sugar
100 g (1 C) chopped nuts	1 cup chopped nuts

METHOD Cream butter and sugar. Add egg yolks and vanilla, then add sifted flour and baking powder. Pat pastry into greased and floured madeleine or finger-shaped éclair tins. Hollow slightly in the middle and fill with apricot jam (preserves).

TOPPING Beat egg whites until stiff. Add brown sugar and beat until creamy, then fold in nuts. Spoon on top of pastry. Bake in 180°C (350°F) oven until lightly browned (about 15–20 minutes).

Makes 24 to 36

Walnut Chocolate Shortbread

METRIC	AMERICAN
175 g butter	¾ cup butter
50 g (¼ C) brown sugar	¼ cup brown sugar
50 g (¼ C) white sugar	¼ cup white sugar
5 mℓ (1 t) vanilla essence	1 teaspoon vanilla extract
75 g (¾ C) walnuts, diced	¾ cup walnuts, diced
175 g dark chocolate, diced	1 cup semi-sweet chocolate chips
250 g (2 C) flour	2 cups all purpose flour

METHOD Cream butter and sugars. Add vanilla, then nuts, chocolate and flour. Pat into greased and floured 30 x 23 cm (12 x 9 inch) pan.

Mark into squares and bake in 160°C (325°F) oven for 25–30 minutes, or until golden brown. Allow to cool before removing from pan. Cut into squares whilst hot.

Makes 28

Caramel Chocolate Squares

METRIC	AMERICAN
125 g butter	½ cup butter
50 g (¼ C) sugar	¼ cup sugar
200 g (1¾ C) flour	1¾ cups all purpose flour

CARAMEL	CARAMEL
125 g butter	½ cup butter
30 mℓ (2 T) syrup	2 tablespoons golden syrup
1 x 396 g tin condensed milk	1 x 14 oz can sweetened condensed milk
150 g (¾ C) castor sugar	¾ cup superfine granulated sugar

TOPPING	TOPPING
125 g chocolate, melted	¾ cup chocolate chips, melted

METHOD Rub butter, sugar and flour together. Press into a greased and floured 39 x 26 x 2 cm (15½ x 10½ x 1 inch) Swiss roll (jelly roll) pan. Bake in 160°C (325°F) oven for 25–30 minutes.

CARAMEL Combine ingredients over heat until melted and allow to simmer over gentle heat for 5 minutes. Pour over biscuit base, spread evenly and allow to cool.

Pour melted chocolate topping over caramel. Cut into squares and serve.

Makes 40

Seven Layer Squares

METRIC	AMERICAN
125 g butter	½ cup butter
250 mℓ (1 C) crushed Marie biscuits	1 cup crushed Graham crackers
250 mℓ (1 C) diced dark chocolate	1 cup semi-sweet chocolate chips
250 mℓ (1 C) diced glacé cherries	1 cup diced glacé cherries
80 g (1 C) dessicated coconut	1 cup dessicated coconut
250 mℓ (1 C) chopped pecan nuts	1 cup chopped pecans
1 x 396 g tin sweetened condensed milk	1 x 14 oz can sweetened condensed milk

METHOD Melt butter in a 23 x 28 cm (9 x 11 inch) baking tin. Sprinkle crushed Marie biscuits (Graham crackers) over butter. Layer diced chocolate or chocolate chips, cherries, coconut and pecans. Pour condensed milk over layers.

Bake in 180°C (350°F) oven for 20–25 minutes. Allow to cool and cut into squares.

Makes 35

Lemon Meringue Bars

METRIC	AMERICAN
125 g butter or margarine	½ cup butter or margarine
100 g (½ C) sugar	½ cup sugar
2 egg yolks	2 egg yolks
5 mℓ (1 t) finely grated lemon rind	1 teaspoon finely grated lemon rind
120 g (1 C) flour	1 cup all purpose flour
Apricot jam	Apricot preserves

MERINGUE	MERINGUE
2 egg whites	2 egg whites
100 g (½ C) sugar	½ cup sugar
15 mℓ (1 T) lemon juice	1 tablespoon lemon juice
75 g (¾ C) chopped pecans or walnuts	¾ cup chopped pecans or walnuts

METHOD Cream butter and sugar. Add yolks and lemon rind. Blend in sifted flour. Spread in a buttered 20 cm (8 inch) square pan. Bake in 180°C (350°F) oven for 20 minutes. Spread a layer of apricot jam (preserves) over pastry.

MERINGUE Beat egg whites stiffly, then gradually beat in sugar. Fold in lemon juice and nuts. Cover pastry with meringue mixture.

Bake for another 25 minutes, until lightly browned. Cool and cut into bars.

Makes 25

Thumbprints

METRIC	AMERICAN
175 g butter	¾ cup butter
100 g (½ C) sugar	½ cup sugar
2 eggs, separated	2 eggs, separated
5 mℓ (1 t) vanilla essence	1 teaspoon vanilla extract
200 g (1¾ C) flour	1¾ cups all purpose flour
Chopped nuts to coat	Chopped nuts to coat
Raspberry & apricot jam	Raspberry & apricot preserves

METHOD Cream butter and sugar. Add egg yolks and vanilla. Add flour, mix into a dough and shape into balls the size of walnuts. Coat with lightly beaten egg whites. Roll in nuts and press a small hollow in the middle of each one.

Place on ungreased baking tray. Fill hollows with jam preserves). Bake in 160°C (325°F) oven for 30 minutes, or until pale gold. Loosen from tray with metal spatula. Fill with more jam if necessary.

Makes 36   PHOTOGRAPH ON PAGE 155

Raspberry Almond Slices

METRIC	AMERICAN
250 g butter	1 cup butter
125 mℓ (½ C) icing sugar	½ cup powdered sugar
2 mℓ (½ t) almond essence	½ teaspoon almond extract
250 g (2 C) flour	2 cups flour
Raspberry jam	Raspberry preserves

TOPPING	TOPPING
125 g butter	½ cup butter
100 g (½ C) sugar	½ cup sugar
60 mℓ (¼ C) milk	¼ cup milk
200 g (2 C) flaked almonds	2 cups flaked or shredded almonds
2 mℓ (½ t) vanilla essence	½ teaspoon vanilla extract

METHOD Cream butter and sugar together. Add almond essence (extract) and mix in flour. Press into a buttered and floured 39 x 26 x 2 cm (15½ x 10½ x 1 inch) pan. Spread with a layer of jam (preserves) and bake in 180°C (350°F) oven for 10 minutes.

TOPPING Melt butter. Stir in sugar and milk. Add nuts and simmer for about 5 minutes. Remove from heat, add vanilla and pour over the pastry.

Return to oven and bake for a further 10–15 minutes. Cool and cut into slices.

Makes 48

Ohio Buckeyes

METRIC	AMERICAN
500 g peanut butter	1 lb peanut butter
250 g butter	1 cup butter
750 g icing sugar	1½ lb powdered sugar

CHOCOLATE DIP	CHOCOLATE DIP
60 g butter or margarine	¼ cup butter or margarine
350 g dark chocolate	2 cups semi-sweet dark chocolate chips

METHOD Beat peanut butter and butter together. Mix in sugar. Shape into balls and press a toothpick halfway through each ball. Chill for 1 hour.

CHOCOLATE DIP Melt butter or margarine and chocolate together. Dip balls into chocolate, leaving a little of the ball uncovered.

Cool on wax paper, remove toothpicks and press an unblanched almond on top of each one.

Makes approximately 70

Date & Nut Spirals

METRIC	AMERICAN
250 g stoned dates, cut up	½ lb pitted dates, cut up
125 mℓ (½ C) orange juice or water	½ cup orange juice or water
25 g (¼ C) chopped nuts	¼ cup chopped nuts
125 g butter	½ cup butter
100 g (½ C) sugar	½ cup sugar
1 egg	1 egg
250 g (2 C) flour	2 cups all purpose flour
Pinch of salt	Pinch of salt
7 mℓ (1½ t) baking powder	1½ teaspoons baking powder

METHOD Cook dates and orange juice or water over medium heat, until mushy. Stir in nuts and allow to cool.

Cream butter and sugar; add egg and beat in. Sift flour with salt and baking powder and add to mixture to form a dough.

Roll out on a lightly floured board into an oblong about ½ cm (¼ inch) thick. Spread with date filling. Roll up as for a Swiss roll (jelly roll). Wrap in foil or plastic wrap and refrigerate overnight.

Cut into slices and bake on a greased and floured baking tray in 180°C (350°F) oven, until slightly golden (about 10–12 minutes).

Makes approximately 48

Crunchy Cookies

METRIC	AMERICAN
250 g butter or margarine	1 cup butter or margarine
150 g (¾ C) brown sugar	¾ cup brown sugar
150 g (¾ C) white sugar	¾ cup white sugar
2 eggs, beaten	2 eggs, beaten
5 mℓ (1 t) vanilla essence	1 teaspoon vanilla extract
180 g (1½ C) flour	1½ cups flour
5 mℓ (1 t) salt	1 teaspoon salt
5 mℓ (1 t) bicarbonate of soda	1 teaspoon baking soda
350 g dark chocolate, grated	2 cups chocolate chips
500 mℓ (2 C) oats	2 cups oats
80 g (1 C) dessicated coconut	1 cup dessicated coconut

METHOD Combine butter or margarine with brown and white sugar. Beat until creamy. Add eggs and vanilla. Sift together flour, salt and bicarbonate of soda (baking soda); add to creamed mixture. Stir in chocolate, oats and coconut.

Drop by teaspoonful onto lightly greased and floured baking sheet. Bake in 180°C (350°F) oven for 10–12 minutes.

Makes approximately 60

Florentine Squares

METRIC	AMERICAN
100 g slab dark chocolate	4 oz semi-sweet chocolate
60 mℓ (¼ C) chopped red, green & yellow glacé cherries	¼ cup chopped red, green & yellow glacé cherries
125 mℓ (½ C) mixed peel	½ cup citrus peel
50 g (½ C) chopped almonds	½ cup chopped almonds
200 mℓ (¾ C) chopped sultanas	¾ cup chopped golden raisins
60 g (½ C) flour	½ cup all purpose flour
125 g butter	½ cup butter
50 g (¼ C) sugar	¼ cup sugar
15 mℓ (1 T) syrup	1 tablespoon syrup
5 mℓ (1 t) lemon juice	1 teaspoon lemon juice

METHOD Melt chocolate and spread onto the bottom of a greased 23 cm (9 inch) square cake pan. Allow to set in refrigerator. Combine fruit and nuts; sprinkle flour over and mix together.

Melt butter and sugar and combine with syrup and lemon juice in a saucepan. Stir in the fruit and flour mixture. Spoon this mixture evenly onto the set chocolate. Bake in a 150°C (300°F) oven for 40–45 minutes, or until golden brown.

Remove from oven and allow to cool for 5 minutes, then carefully mark into 25 squares with a sharp knife. Leave until cold, then lift out of the pan, taking care not to break them.

Makes 25

Aunt Hilda's Crispy Butter Biscuits

METRIC	AMERICAN
125 g butter	½ cup butter
200 g (1 C) sugar	1 cup sugar
550 g (4 C) self-raising flour	4 cups self-rising flour
2 eggs, well beaten	2 eggs, well beaten
125 mℓ (½ C) oil	½ cup oil
5 mℓ (1 t) vanilla or almond essence	1 teaspoon vanilla or almond extract

METHOD Cream butter and sugar very well, until creamy. Add flour alternately with beaten eggs. Stir in oil and vanilla or almond extract. Mix thoroughly until well blended.

Using a cookie maker, press into shapes on an ungreased pan. Bake in 190°C (375°F) oven for 10–15 minutes, or until golden brown.

CHEF'S TIP Should you wish to prepare a double quantity, this dough keeps in the refrigerator for up to 3 weeks.

Makes about 12 dozen

Mandelbrodt

METRIC	AMERICAN
3 eggs	3 eggs
200 g (1 C) castor sugar	1 cup superfine granulated sugar
125 g butter, melted & cooled	½ cup butter, melted & cooled
Approximately 300 g (2½ C) flour	Approximately 2½ cups all purpose flour
Pinch of salt	Pinch of salt
2 mℓ (½ t) almond essence	½ teaspoon almond extract
100 g (1 C) whole almonds with skins	1 cup whole almonds with skins
10 mℓ (2 t) baking powder	2 teaspoons baking powder

METHOD Beat eggs, add sugar and beat well. Mix in remaining ingredients. Divide dough into 4 pieces. Roll each piece into a long, thin strip, approximately 1,5 cm (½ inch) thick and the length of your tray. Pat down and shape into 4 even strips.

Bake in 200°C (400°F) oven for 15 minutes. While still hot, cut strips diagonally at about 2,5 cm (1 inch) intervals, preferably using an electric knife. Place on tray again and return to oven for another 15 minutes.

CHEF'S TIP If you wish, sprinkle the mandelbrodt with icing sugar (powdered sugar) and cinnamon before serving.

Makes approximately 70

Viennese Cookies

METRIC	AMERICAN
250 g butter	1 cup butter
150 g (¾ C) sugar	¾ cup sugar
1 egg, separated & the white beaten lightly	1 egg, separated & the white beaten lightly
250 g (2 C) flour, sifted	2 cups flour, sifted
5 mℓ (1 t) vanilla essence	1 teaspoon vanilla extract

TOPPING	TOPPING
45 mℓ (3 T) icing sugar	3 tablespoons powdered sugar
30 mℓ (2 T) butter	2 tablespoons butter
15 mℓ (1 T) cocoa powder	1 tablespoon cocoa powder
15 mℓ (1 T) flour	1 tablespoon flour

METHOD Cream butter and sugar. Add remaining ingredients, mixing thoroughly. Chill for at least 2 hours.

Roll into small, marble-sized balls. Place on a greased and floured tray. Brush tops of cookies with lightly beaten egg white.

TOPPING Combine all ingredients. Mix together until crumbly. Press on top of unbaked cookies.

Bake in 160°C (325°F) oven for 10–12 minutes.

Makes about 70

Bread & Scones

Pita Bread. 162
Wholewheat Pita Bread 162
Monkey Bread 162
Brie Bread. 162
Zucchini Cheese Bread 163
Stuffed French Toast. 163
Drop Sones 163
Crumpets 163

Pita Bread

METRIC	AMERICAN
10 mℓ (2 t) dried yeast	*2 teaspoons dried yeast*
500 mℓ (2 C) lukewarm water	*2 cups lukewarm water*
500 g (4 C) flour	*4 cups flour*
10 mℓ (2 t) oil	*2 teaspoons oil*
10 mℓ (2 t) salt	*2 teaspoons salt*

METHOD Place yeast in a shallow bowl. Pour over warm water; allow to stand for 10–15 minutes. Measure unsifted flour into a large bowl and make a well in the centre. Stir oil and salt into the yeast, then pour into the well and stir until all the flour has been mixed in.

Knead on a lightly floured board until smooth (about 5 minutes). Cover with a cloth and allow to stand in a warm place until doubled in bulk, or leave overnight.

Punch down, then divide into portions about the size of tennis balls. Roll out until approximately 1,5 cm (about ½ inch) thick and place on a floured baking tray. Cover and allow to stand for another 15–30 minutes. Bake in 230°C (450°F) oven for 12–15 minutes.

Makes 8

Wholewheat Pita Bread

METRIC	AMERICAN
25 g cake yeast	*1 cake yeast*
5 mℓ (1 t) sugar	*1 teaspoon sugar*
375 mℓ (1½ C) lukewarm water	*1½ cups lukewarm water*
200 g (1¾ C) flour	*1¾ cups all purpose flour*
150 g (1¼ C) wholewheat flour	*1¼ cups wholewheat flour*
60 mℓ (¼ C) oil	*¼ cup oil*
5 mℓ (1 t) salt	*1 teaspoon salt*
90 mℓ (6 T) sesame seeds	*6 tablespoons sesame seeds*

METHOD Proof yeast, sugar and 60 mℓ (¼ cup) of the lukewarm water for 10 minutes.

Combine all remaining ingredients. Add yeast mixture and stir until dough forms a ball. Knead for 10 minutes. Divide dough into 6 portions and roll each one into a smooth ball. Using a rolling pin, flatten the balls into rounds ½ cm (¼ inch) thick. Cover with a cloth and allow to rise in a warm place for 45 minutes.

Place rounds on a baking sheet sprinkled with flour. Sprinkle each one with 15 mℓ (1 tablespoon) sesame seeds and bake in a very hot oven (about 240°C / 475 °F) for 12–15 minutes, or until puffed and golden. The bread will deflate and soften after being removed from the oven.

Makes 6

Monkey Bread

METRIC	AMERICAN
300 mℓ (1¼ C) milk	*1¼ cups milk*
125 g butter	*½ cup butter*
100 g (½ C) sugar	*½ cup sugar*
5 mℓ (1 t) salt	*1 teaspoon salt*
40 g cake yeast	*1½ cakes yeast*
2 eggs	*2 eggs*
550 g (4½ C) flour	*4½ cups flour*
1 package instant vanilla pudding	*1 package instant vanilla pudding*
100 g (1 C) chopped pecan nuts	*1 cup chopped pecans*
5 mℓ (1 t) ground cinnamon	*1 teaspoon ground cinnamon*
90 g butter, melted	*6 tablespoons butter, melted*

METHOD Place milk, butter, sugar and salt in a saucepan and heat until butter and sugar have dissolved. Allow to cool to lukewarm.

Liquify the yeast by mixing with 10 mℓ (2 teaspoons) sugar, then adding 15 mℓ (1 tablespoon) lukewarm water. Allow to stand for 10 minutes.

Beat eggs in a separate bowl and set aside. Sift flour into a bowl and make a well in the centre. Add butter / milk mixture, eggs and yeast. Use another 15 mℓ (1 tablespoon) lukewarm water to rinse out the yeast bowl. Mix by hand until blended, then knead in food mixer until smooth. Place in a large covered bowl or airtight container and leave to rise until double in bulk, or leave overnight.

Knead dough for a minute or two, then cut into 32 pieces. Roll each piece into a ball. Combine vanilla pudding, nuts and cinnamon. Dip each piece of dough into melted butter, then into the pudding mixture. Place in layers in a lightly oiled tube tin (pan). Allow to rise until double in bulk. Bake for 25 minutes in 180°C (350°F) oven.

Makes 32

Brie Bread

METRIC	AMERICAN
1 French loaf, halved lengthwise	*1 French loaf, halved lengthwise*
250 g Brie	*8 oz Brie*
2 mℓ (½ t) dried basil	*½ teaspoon dried basil*
1 medium onion, finely diced	*1 medium onion, finely diced*
125 g butter	*½ cup butter*

METHOD Melt butter and sauté onion lightly. Add cheese and basil and stir until melted. Spread over halved French loaf and heat uncovered in 180°C (350°F) oven, until bubbly.

Serves 6 to 8

Zucchini Cheese Bread

METRIC	AMERICAN
180 g (1½ C) white flour	1½ cups white flour
180 g (1½ C) wholewheat flour	1½ cups wholewheat flour
150 g (¾ C) sugar	¾ cup sugar
45 mℓ (3 T) grated Parmesan cheese	3 tablespoons grated Parmesan cheese
15 mℓ (3 t) baking powder	3 teaspoons baking powder
5 mℓ (1 t) salt	1 teaspoon salt
7 mℓ (1½ t) bicarbonate of soda	1½ teaspoons baking soda
250 mℓ (1 C) shredded courgettes (baby marrows)*	1 cup shredded zucchini*
125 mℓ (½ C) melted margarine	½ cup melted margarine
250 mℓ (1 C) buttermilk	1 cup buttermilk
2 eggs	2 eggs
30 mℓ (2 T) grated onion	2 tablespoons grated onion

Shred unpeeled, then squeeze dry in a clean dish towel

METHOD Combine flours, sugar, cheese, baking powder, salt and soda. Add shredded courgettes (zucchini) and mix thoroughly.

In a separate bowl combine margarine, buttermilk, eggs and onion. Beat with electric beater until well combined. Add liquid mixture to flour and mix in thoroughly.

Pour into a well-greased 23 x 12 x 7 cm (9 x 5 x 3 inch) pan and bake at 180°C (350°F) for 55–65 minutes. Leave in pan and allow to cool on a wire rack for 15 minutes, then remove loaf and cool completely on rack.

Makes 1 loaf

Stuffed French Toast

METRIC	AMERICAN
4 thick slices white bread (each approximately 4 cm thick)	4 thick slices white bread (each approximately 1½ inches thick)
3 eggs, beaten	3 eggs, beaten
125 mℓ (½ C) milk	½ cup milk
Butter for frying	Butter for frying

FILLING	FILLING
250 g cream cheese	8 oz cream cheese
30 mℓ (2 T) sugar	2 tablespoons sugar
5 mℓ (1 t) vanilla essence	1 teaspoon vanilla extract
2 mℓ (½ t) ground cinnamon	½ teaspoon ground cinnamon
125 mℓ (½ C) sultanas (optional)	½ cup white raisins (optional)

METHOD Combine all filling ingredients and mix well. Cut a 'pocket' in each slice of bread and fill with some of the cheese mixture.

Combine egg and milk. Dip filled bread into egg mixture, being careful not to squeeze out the filling. Fry on both sides in butter, until golden brown. Serve with jam (preserves) or cinnamon sugar.

Serves 4

Drop Scones

METRIC	AMERICAN
250 g (2 C) flour	2 cups all purpose flour
15 mℓ (1 T) sugar	1 tablespoon sugar
20 mℓ (4 t) baking powder	4 teaspoons baking powder
Pinch of salt	Pinch of salt
90 g butter	6 tablespoons butter
1 egg, beaten	1 egg, beaten
250 mℓ (1 C) sour cream	1 cup sour cream

METHOD Sift dry ingredients together. Cut in the butter with a knife or grate in. Add beaten egg and cream. Drop spoonfuls into patty tins and bake in 200°C (400°F) oven for 10–15 minutes.

Makes 12 to 15

Crumpets (Pancakes)

METRIC	AMERICAN
250 g (2 C) flour	2 cups cake flour
10 mℓ (2 t) cream of tartar	2 teaspoons cream of tartar
5 mℓ (1 t) bicarbonate of soda	1 teaspoon baking soda
10 mℓ (2 t) melted butter	2 teaspoons melted butter
2 eggs, separated	2 eggs, separated
30 mℓ (2 T) syrup	2 tablespoons syrup
250 mℓ (1 C) milk	1 cup milk

METHOD Sift all dry ingredients together. Make a well in the centre and add melted butter, egg yolks and syrup. Add milk gradually while stirring. Stir well until smooth and then add stiffly beaten egg whites.

Drop spoonfuls of batter onto hot, greased griddle. When bubbles appear on surface, turn over. Serve topped with syrup, cream or ice-cream.

CHEF'S TIP For variation, add chocolate chips, diced apple or orange rind to the mixture.

Makes approximately 24

Traditional Jewish Dishes

Kreplach 166
Chicken Soup 166
Baked Perogen (Meat Pies) 166
Fried Perogen 167
Knishes 167
Chopped Herring 167
Sweet & Sour Baked Herring 168
Gefilte Fish 168
Baked Gefilte Fish 168
Pickled Herring in Cream 169
Petzah (Brawn) 169
Flaumen Brisket with Prunes 169
Tzimmes 172
Granny's Knadel 172
Carrot Pudding 172
Potato Kugel 172
Parava Lokshen Kugel 173
Upside-down Noodle Kugel 173
Baked Cheese Blintzes 173
Lokshen Pudding 174
Timberlach (Carrot Sweets) 174
Teiglach 174
My Mother's Cracked Teiglach 175
Orange Preserve (Pomerantzen) 175
Kitke or Challah 175
Bagels 176

PASSOVER
Fat-free Matzo Balls 176
Matzo Knaidlach 176
Geschmertze Matzo (Cheese Matzo) 176
Cheese Cake 177
Passover Chocolate Mousse Cake 177
Passover Apple Cake 177
Topping for Passover Cakes 178
Passover Chiffon Cake 178
Carrot Kugel 178

Kreplach

METRIC	AMERICAN
PASTRY	PASTRY
250 g (2 C) flour	2 cups flour
2 mℓ (½ t) salt	½ teaspoon salt
2 eggs, slightly beaten	2 eggs, slightly beaten
Sufficient cold water to make into dough	Sufficient cold water to make into dough
FILLING	FILLING
2 onions, sliced	2 onions, sliced
30 mℓ (2 T) oil	2 tablespoons oil
250 g cooked flank*	½ lb cooked short ribs*
500 g cooked shin*	1 lb cooked shank*
Pinch of salt	Pinch of salt
Dash of pepper	Dash of pepper
2 mℓ (½ t) sugar	½ teaspoon sugar

* These meats should have been cooked in soup

METHOD Prepare pastry. Sift flour and salt together. Make a well in the centre and add slightly beaten eggs and water. Roll out the dough very thinly on a floured board. Cut into squares.

FILLING Fry onions in oil until golden. Mince (grind) with meat and season to taste with salt, pepper and sugar.

TO COOK Spoon some of the filling onto each pastry square, then pinch closed. Boil in chicken soup for 30 minutes before serving.

Makes approximately 80 PHOTOGRAPH ON PAGE 171

Chicken Soup

METRIC	AMERICAN
500 g sliced shin	1 lb sliced shank
250 g sliced flank	½ lb short ribs
Few chicken portions or giblets	Few chicken portions or giblets
6 whole carrots, peeled	6 whole carrots, peeled
1 whole onion	1 whole onion
2–3 sticks celery	2–3 sticks celery
Few sprigs parsley	Few sprigs parsley
2 turnips	2 turnips
2–3 parsnips	2–3 parsnips
3 leeks	3 leeks
20 mℓ (4 t) salt	4 teaspoons salt
5 mℓ (1 t) celery salt	1 teaspoon celery salt or seed
Dash of pepper	Dash of pepper
5 mℓ (1 t) seasoning salt	1 teaspoon seasoned salt
4 chicken bouillon cubes, crushed	4 chicken bouillon cubes, crushed
Few drops egg yellow	Few drops yellow food color
125 g noodles or lokshen	4 oz noodles or lokshen

METHOD Wash meats very well. Sprinkle with 15 mℓ (1 tablespoon) salt; pour boiling water over to cover. Allow to stand for 10–15 minutes, then drain well.

While meat is soaking, three-quarter fill a very large saucepan with water and bring to the boil. When water boils, add meat, chicken portions or giblets and vegetables. Allow to simmer gently for approximately 5 hours. Add seasonings and bouillon cubes.

Add egg yellow (yellow food color), then strain. Bring to the boil and add noodles or lokshen. Reduce heat immediately to simmer and cook until noodles are tender.

CHEF'S TIP Cleaning the meat very well with water and salt ensures that the soup will be clear, not cloudy.

Serves 12 PHOTOGRAPH ON PAGE 171

Baked Perogen (Meat Pies)

METRIC	AMERICAN
300 g (2½ cups) flour	2½ cups all purpose flour
10 mℓ (2 t) baking powder	2 teaspoons baking powder
5 mℓ (1 t) sugar	1 teaspoon sugar
2 mℓ (½ t) salt	½ teaspoon salt
250 g Holsum or vegetable shortening	1 cup vegetable shortening
1 egg, beaten	1 egg, beaten
200 mℓ (¾ cup) water	¾ cup water
MEAT FILLING	MEAT FILLING
2–3 onions, sliced	2–3 onions, sliced
Oil for frying	Oil for frying
Any left-over meat or chicken*	Any left-over meat or chicken*
5 mℓ (1 t) salt	1 teaspoon salt
1 mℓ (¼ t) pepper	¼ teaspoon pepper
5 mℓ (1 t) concentrated Telma vegetable or chicken soup or ½ Telma cube, crushed	1 teaspoon concentrated Telma vegetable or chicken soup or ½ Telma cube, crushed
45–60 mℓ (3–4 T) chicken soup	3–4 tablespoons chicken soup

* Or use meat that has been cooked in soup

METHOD Sift together dry ingredients and rub in vegetable shortening. Add beaten egg and water and mix into a dough. Knead lightly on a floured board, then roll out and cut into rounds 9 cm (3½ inches) in diameter.

FILLING Fry onions in a little oil for 10–15 minutes. Mince (grind) with meat, then add salt, pepper, concentrated soup or crushed cube and mix well. Add 3–4 tablespoons chicken soup to moisten.

Place a spoonful of filling in each centre, fold over and pinch edges together. Arrange (flat side down) on a greased baking sheet. Brush with beaten egg and bake in 200°C (400°F) oven for 15–20 minutes.

Makes approximately 36

Fried Perogen

METRIC	AMERICAN
PASTRY	PASTRY
250 g (2 C) flour	2 cups all purpose flour
10 mℓ (2 t) baking powder	2 teaspoons baking powder
Pinch of salt	Pinch of salt
10 mℓ (2 t) sugar	2 teaspoons sugar
10 mℓ (2 t) vegetable fat	2 tablespoons vegetable fat
15 mℓ (1 T) chicken fat	1 tablespoon chicken fat
1 egg, beaten	1 egg, beaten
Sufficient water to make a dough	Sufficient water to make a dough
MEAT FILLING	MEAT FILLING
2 onions, sliced	2 onions, sliced
30 mℓ (2 T) oil	2 tablespoons oil
500 g cooked shin*	1 lb cooked shank*
250 g cooked flank*	½ lb cooked short ribs*
2 mℓ (½ t) salt	½ teaspoon salt
Dash of pepper	Dash of pepper
5 mℓ (1 t) sugar	1 teaspoon sugar
30 mℓ (2 T) soup stock	2 tablespoons soup stock

* These meats should have been cooked in soup

METHOD To prepare pastry, sift together flour, baking powder, salt and sugar. Rub in fat with fingertips. Add beaten egg and enough water to form a dough. Roll dough out very thinly. Cut into rounds 7,5 cm (3 inches) in diameter.

FILLING Fry onions in oil until soft; mince (grind) with cooked meats. Add salt, pepper, sugar and soup stock. Mix well together. Adjust seasonings.

TO COOK Place 15 mℓ (1 tablespoon) meat filling on each pastry round. Press edges together to form a ridge on top, then fry in oil on three sides until golden brown. Serve immediately.

Makes approximately 40

Knishes

METRIC	AMERICAN
DOUGH	DOUGH
300 g (2½ C) flour	2½ cups flour
2 mℓ (½ t) salt	½ teaspoon salt
5 mℓ (1 t) baking powder	1 teaspoon baking powder
2 eggs, lightly beaten	2 eggs, lightly beaten
200 mℓ (¾ C) oil	¾ cup oil
30 mℓ (2 T) water	2 tablespoons water
FILLING	FILLING
1 onion, chopped	1 onion, chopped
Chicken fat or butter for sautéing	Chicken fat or butter for sautéing
625 mℓ (2½ C) mashed potato*	2½ cups mashed potato*
Salt & pepper to taste	Salt & pepper to taste
GLAZE	GLAZE
1 egg, beaten	1 egg, beaten
Sesame or poppy seeds	Sesame or poppy seeds

* Or use instant potato mash, cooked according to package directions

METHOD Sift dry ingredients together. Make a well in the centre and add eggs, oil and water. Knead until smooth.

FILLING Sauté onion in chicken fat or butter until golden and mix in remaining ingredients. Roll out pastry thinly and cut into circles 8 cm (3 inches) in diameter. Place 1 teaspoon of filling in each centre. Draw edges together and pinch firmly.

Place on an oiled baking sheet, pinched edges up. Paint with egg and sprinkle with sesame or poppy seeds. Bake at 190°C (375°F) for 25–35 minutes.

Makes 36

Chopped Herring

METRIC	AMERICAN
2 x 350 g jars skinned pickled herring	1 x 1 lb 6 oz jar party herring in wine sauce
3 Granny Smith apples, peeled	3 Granny Smith apples, peeled
4 Marie biscuits	4 Graham crackers
4 hard-boiled eggs	4 hard-boiled eggs
30 mℓ (2 T) matzo meal (or 1 slice stale white bread)	2 tablespoons matzo meal (or 1 slice stale white bread)
2 mℓ (¼ t) pepper	¼ teaspoon pepper
GARNISH	GARNISH
Tomato slices	Tomato slices
Pickled cucumber slices	Pickled cucumber slices

METHOD Drain herring and reserve liquid. Mince (grind) fish with the onion (from the jar), apples, Marie biscuits (Graham crackers) and 3 hard-boiled eggs. Add matzo meal and reserved liquid, then add pepper to taste. Spoon into a serving dish.

Grate the remaining hard-boiled egg. Garnish herring with grated egg, tomato and cucumber slices.

Serves 10 to 12

Sweet & Sour Baked Herring

METRIC	AMERICAN
6 salt herrings	6 salt herrings
250 mℓ (1 C) water	1 cup water
125 mℓ (½ C) vinegar	½ cup vinegar
60 mℓ (4 T) syrup	4 tablespoons golden syrup
125 mℓ (½ C) sultanas	½ cup golden raisins
2 medium onions, sliced	2 medium onions, sliced
10 peppercorns	10 peppercorns
4 bay leaves	4 bay leaves
2 mℓ (½ t) ground ginger	½ teaspoon ground ginger
2 mℓ (½ t) ground cinnamon	½ teaspoon ground cinnamon

METHOD Soak herrings in water overnight. Clean and fillet. Cut into broad slices and arrange in a pyrex dish.

Boil all remaining ingredients together for 10 minutes. Pour over herrings and bake at 180°C (350°F) for 25–30 minutes, until golden brown.

Serves 12

Gefilte Fish

METRIC	AMERICAN
2 kg filleted fish (hake or a combination of hake & line fish)*	4 lb filleted fish (a combination of red snapper & haddock, cod or orange roughy)*
4 medium carrots	4 medium carrots
3 large onions, sliced & fried in 45 mℓ (3 T) oil	3 large onions, sliced & fried in 3 tablespoons oil
45 mℓ (3 T) matzo meal	3 tablespoons matzo meal
4 eggs	4 eggs
10 mℓ (2 t) sugar	2 teaspoons sugar
2 mℓ (½ t) pepper	½ teaspoon pepper
10 mℓ (2 t) salt	2 teaspoons salt
7 mℓ (1½ t) seafood spice	1½ teaspoons old bay seasoning
250 mℓ (1 C) cold water	1 cup cold water

STOCK	STOCK
2–2,5 ℓ water	8–10 cups water
Cleaned bones & skin of fish	Cleaned bones & skin of fish
3 onions, sliced	3 onions, sliced
Salt & pepper to taste	Salt & pepper to taste
Seafood spice to taste	Old bay seasoning to taste
Few drops egg yellow	Few drops yellow food color

Ask for skin and bones and reserve for stock

METHOD Mince (grind) fish with 2 carrots and the lightly fried onions (adding oil in which onions have been fried). Add other ingredients (except 2 remaining carrots) and mix together very well. Shape into balls.

STOCK Place all ingredients in a large pot, bring to the boil and allow to boil for 1 hour. Strain into a clean pot, add 2 carrots, sliced, and the fish balls. Reduce heat and simmer slowly for 1½ hours.

Remove from heat and add egg yellow (yellow food color) to liquid. Allow to cool, then transfer fish balls to a serving dish. Place a slice of cooked carrot on each one, pour strained liquid over and serve.

CHEF'S TIP The fish mixture is also suitable for fish cakes . Shape into balls, sprinkle with crushed cornflakes or matzo meal and fry in oil until nicely browned.

Serves 12   PHOTOGRAPH ON PAGE 170

Baked Gefilte Fish

METRIC	AMERICAN
3 onions, sliced	3 onions, sliced
30 mℓ (2 T) butter	2 tablespoons butter
30 mℓ (2 T) oil	2 tablespoons oil
1,5 kg hake	1 lb red snapper
2 carrots	2 lb haddock, cod or orange roughy
15 mℓ (1 T) flour	2 carrots
30 mℓ (2 T) matzo meal	1 tablespoon flour
3 eggs	2 tablespoons matzo meal
10 mℓ (2 t) salt	3 eggs
Pepper to taste	2 teaspoons salt
5–10 mℓ (1–2 t) seafood spice	Pepper to taste
250 mℓ (1 C) cold water	1–2 teaspoons old bay seasoning
	1 cup cold water

SAUCE	SAUCE
2 small onions, chopped & fried in butter	2 small onions, chopped & fried in butter
1 x 225 g tin button mushrooms, drained	1 x 8 oz can button mushrooms, drained
150 g (1½ C) grated Cheddar cheese	1½ cups grated Cheddar cheese
125 mℓ (½ C) milk	½ cup milk
250 mℓ (1 C) thick or sour cream	1 cup thick or sour cream

METHOD Fry onions in butter and oil. Mince (grind) fish with carrots and fried onions (adding the butter and oil in which the onions have been fried). Add all other ingredients and mix well. Adjust seasoning. Shape into balls and arrange in a greased ovenware dish.

SAUCE Spoon onions and mushrooms over the fish balls, sprinkle with half the grated cheese, then pour over the milk and half the cream.

Bake in 180°C (350°F) oven for 45 minutes. Remove from oven; sprinkle with remaining cheese and pour over the rest of the cream. Serve warm.

Serves 8 to 10

Pickled Herring in Cream

METRIC	AMERICAN
250 mℓ (1 C) thick cream	1 cup sour cream
2 x 350 g jars pickled herring, drained & liquid reserved	1 x 1 lb 6 oz jar party herring in wine sauce, drained & liquid reserved
5 mℓ (1 t) sugar	1 teaspoon sugar
250 mℓ (1 C) mayonnaise	1 cup mayonnaise
Bay leaves & peppercorns	Bay leaves & peppercorns

METHOD Mix together cream, reserved liquid from herrings, sugar and mayonnaise.

Arrange alternate layers of herring, cream mixture, bay leaves and peppercorns in a serving dish. Refrigerate for 2 hours before serving.

Serves 12

Petzah (Brawn)

METRIC	AMERICAN
1 cow's heel (hoof removed by butcher)	1 cow's heel (hoof removed by butcher)
2 onions	2 onions
4 bay leaves	4 bay leaves
8 peppercorns	8 peppercorns
10 mℓ (2 t) salt	2 teaspoons salt
2 mℓ (½ t) pepper	½ teaspoon pepper
Dash of ground ginger	Dash of ground ginger
1 chicken bouillon cube	1 chicken bouillon cube
2 slices beef shin	2 slices beef shank
3 chicken legs	3 chicken legs
2–3 cloves garlic, crushed	2–3 cloves garlic, crushed
Few drops egg yellow	Few drops yellow food color
3 hard-boiled eggs	3 hard-boiled eggs

METHOD Place cow's heel, bay leaves, peppercorns, salt, pepper, ginger and bouillon cube in a large pot; cover with water and simmer slowly for approximately 6–8 hours, until soft. Add shin (shank) and simmer for a further 1½–2 hours. Add chicken legs and cook for 1½ hours, or until liquid is reduced by half.

Remove bones; mince or grind cow's heel only and place in large bowl. Pour over strained stock. Skin chicken legs and dice flesh. Add chicken and meat to mixture. Stir in garlic and egg yellow (yellow food color).

Arrange a layer of sliced hard-boiled eggs in 1 oblong and 1 square dish. Gently pour mixture over egg slices. Allow to cool and set in refrigerator. Cut into diamond shapes and serve with the egg side up.

Serves 20

Flaumen Brisket with Prunes

METRIC	AMERICAN
3 kg fresh, deboned brisket	6 lb fresh, deboned brisket
750 mℓ (3 C) water	3 cups water
1 onion, halved	1 onion, halved
1 carrot, halved	1 carrot, halved
5 mℓ (1 t) ground ginger	1 teaspoon ground ginger
10 mℓ (2 t) salt	2 teaspoons salt
½ chicken bouillon cube	½ chicken bouillon cube
2 mℓ (½ t) seasoning salt	½ teaspoon seasoned salt
2 mℓ (½ t) crushed garlic powder	½ teaspoon garlic powder
1 mℓ (¼ t) pepper	¼ teaspoon pepper
Approximately 25 prunes	Approximately 25 prunes
Juice of 1 lemon	Juice of 1 lemon
45–60 mℓ (3–4 T) golden syrup	3–4 tablespoons cane syrup
10 mℓ (2 t) gravy powder or 10 mℓ (2 t) cornflour mixed to a paste with cold water	2 teaspoons gravy mix or 2 teaspoons cornstarch mixed to a paste with cold water
About 6 potatoes, halved & parboiled	About 6 potatoes, halved & parboiled

METHOD Simmer brisket with water, vegetables, seasonings and spices until tender (approximately 3 hours). Add more water as required, 250 mℓ (1 cup) at a time. Add prunes, lemon juice and syrup, then potatoes.

Simmer for approximately 15 minutes, until liquid is reduced. Spoon off the excess fat and thicken the sauce with gravy powder (gravy mix) or cornflour (cornstarch) paste.

Serves 12 to 15   PHOTOGRAPH ON PAGE 171

Overleaf: (in the foreground) *Upside-down Noodle Kugel and Flaumen Brisket with Prunes,* (behind) *Gefilte Fish and Chicken Soup with Kreplach and* (at the back), *Teiglach and Kitke or Challah*

Tzimmes

METRIC	AMERICAN
500 g brisket	1 lb brisket
8–10 carrots	8–10 carrots
2 potatoes, cubed	2 potatoes, cubed
7 mℓ (1½ t) salt	1½ teaspoons salt
1 mℓ (¼ t) pepper	¼ teaspoon pepper
1 mℓ (¼ t) ground ginger	¼ teaspoon ground ginger
1 large slice of pumpkin, peeled & cut into a few pieces	1 large slice of pumpkin, peeled & cut into a few pieces
1 mℓ (¼ t) ground cinnamon	¼ teaspoon ground cinnamon
½ chicken bouillon cube	½ chicken bouillon cube
1 sweet potato, peeled & cubed	1 yam, peeled & cubed
30 mℓ (2 T) brown sugar	2 tablespoons brown sugar
10 mℓ (2 t) cornflour, mixed to a paste with cold water	2 teaspoons cornstarch, mixed to a paste with cold water

METHOD Place brisket and carrots in a saucepan; cover with water and boil for approximately 1 hour. Add remaining ingredients, except sugar and cornflour (cornstarch).

Continue to cook over gentle heat until the vegetables are tender and the water has reduced to a quarter of the original volume. Add the brown sugar and thicken with cornflour (cornstarch) paste. Spoon into a casserole dish, place in 180°C (350°F) oven and allow to brown.

CHEF'S TIP This dish can be prepared the day before required and browned just before serving.

Serves 15 to 20

Granny's Knadel

(To be made with Tzimmes)

METRIC	AMERICAN
45 mℓ (3 T) schmaltz or chicken fat	3 tablespoons schmaltz or chicken fat
20 mℓ (4 t) sugar	4 teaspoons sugar
1 egg	1 egg
120 g (1 C) flour	1 cup all purpose flour
2 mℓ (½ t) salt	½ teaspoon salt
2 mℓ (½ t) pepper	½ teaspoon pepper
1 mℓ (¼ t) ground ginger	¼ teaspoon ground ginger
2 mℓ (½ t) ground cinnamon	½ teaspoon ground cinnamon
15 mℓ (1 T) mealie meal	1 tablespoon corn meal
5 mℓ (1 t) baking powder	1 teaspoon baking powder
30–45 mℓ (2–3 T) water	2–3 tablespoons water

METHOD Beat together fat, sugar and egg; add remaining ingredients and mix into a dough. Shape into a thick roll, using a little additional flour, add to tzimmes and cook for a further 30–40 minutes.

CHEF'S TIPS Thicken tzimmes after knadel has cooked and brown in oven.

Knadel may also be used for dumplings. Drop spoonfuls of the mixture into the stew when almost done. Cook for a further 20–30 minutes.

Serves 8

Carrot Kugel

METRIC	AMERICAN
175 g margarine	¾ cup margarine
150 g (¾ C) brown sugar	¾ cup brown sugar
2 eggs	2 eggs
300 g (2½ C) flour, sifted	2½ cups all purpose flour, sifted
10 mℓ (2 t) baking powder	2 teaspoons baking powder
7 mℓ (1½ t) salt	1½ teaspoons salt
5 mℓ (1 t) bicarbonate of soda	1 teaspoon baking soda
30 mℓ (2 T) water	2 tablespoons water
500 mℓ (2 C) grated carrots	2 cups grated carrots
5 mℓ (1 t) vanilla essence	1 teaspoon vanilla extract
10 mℓ (2 t) lemon juice	2 teaspoons lemon juice
Fresh breadcrumbs	Fresh breadcrumbs

METHOD Cream margarine and sugar together. Add eggs, one at a time. Sift together dry ingredients (except breadcrumbs) and mix in. Add water, carrots, vanilla and lemon juice. Mix well.

Grease a bundt pan and sprinkle with breadcrumbs. Spoon mixture into pan and bake at 180°C (350°F) for approximately 1 hour. Serve as a side dish with poultry.

Serves 8

Potato Kugel

METRIC	AMERICAN
5 medium potatoes	5 medium potatoes
1 onion	1 onion
3 eggs, beaten	3 eggs, beaten
30 mℓ (2 T) matzo meal	2 tablespoons matzo meal
45 mℓ (3 T) schmaltz	3 tablespoons schmaltz (chicken fat)
5 mℓ (1 t) salt	1 teaspoon salt
1 mℓ (¼ t) pepper	¼ teaspoon pepper
5 mℓ (1 t) sugar	1 teaspoon sugar

METHOD Grate potatoes and onion and drain off liquid. Add beaten eggs, matzo meal, schmaltz, seasonings and sugar. Stir well.

Pour into a well-greased pyrex dish, or into a greased muffin pan. Bake at 180°C (350°F) for 30–40 minutes.

Serves 10 to 12

Parava Lokshen Kugel

METRIC	AMERICAN
500 g broad lokshen	1 lb noodles
5 eggs, lightly beaten	5 eggs, lightly beaten
2 x 113 g tins apricot nectar	2 x 4 oz cans apricot nectar
100 g (½ C) sugar	½ cup sugar
30 mℓ (2 T) syrup	2 tablespoons syrup
125 g margarine or butter	½ cup margarine or butter
1 sachet Orley Whip*	½ cup non-dairy whipping
1 cooking apple, peeled & grated	cream*
	1 tart apple, peeled & grated

* If preferred, use 125 mℓ (½ cup) cream instead

STREUSEL TOPPING	STREUSEL TOPPING
50 g (¼ C) sugar	¼ cup sugar
5 mℓ (1 t) ground cinnamon	1 teaspoon ground cinnamon
250 mℓ (1 C) crushed corn-flakes	1 cup crushed cornflakes
30 mℓ (2 T) margarine, melted	2 tablespoons margarine, melted

METHOD Bring to the boil a large pot of water, to which 5 mℓ (1 teaspoon) salt has been added. Add lokshen (noodles) and boil for 20–30 minutes, until tender. Drain. Add remaining ingredients to the lokshen and mix lightly until blended. Pour into a greased, oblong ovenware dish.

STREUSEL TOPPING Combine all ingredients. Mix well and sprinkle over noodle mixture. Bake in 190°C (375°F) oven for 30 minutes. Cut into squares to serve.

CHEF'S TIP This kugel makes a delicious accompaniment to meat or poultry.

Serves 10 to 12

Upside-down Noodle Kugel

METRIC	AMERICAN
60 g margarine	4 tablespoons margarine
100 g (½ C) brown sugar	½ cup brown sugar
8 slices canned pineapple, drained	8 slices canned pineapple, drained
8 glacé cherries	8 candied cherries
500 g broad, flat noodles	1 lb broad flat noodles
5 eggs, beaten lightly	5 eggs, beaten lightly
50 g (¼ C) white sugar*	½ cup white sugar
125 mℓ (½ C) raisins (optional)	½ cup raisins (optional)
250 g margarine, melted	1 cup margarine, melted
2 mℓ (½ t) salt	½ teaspoon salt
1 x 113 g tin apricot nectar	1 x 4 oz can apricot nectar

* This measurement differs from the American

METHOD Melt margarine in a 23 cm (9 inch) square or round ovenware dish or pan. Sprinkle with brown sugar. Arrange pineapple rings on top of sugar mixture and place a cherry in each centre.

Cook noodles in salted water until tender. Drain well and mix with remaining ingredients. Spoon over the pineapple rings. Bake in 180°C (350°F) oven for 40–45 minutes. Allow to cool and invert carefully onto a serving platter.

Serves 12   PHOTOGRAPH ON PAGE 170

Baked Cheese Blintzes

METRIC	AMERICAN
4 eggs	4 eggs
500 mℓ (2 C) milk	2 cups milk
120 g (1 C) flour	1 cup flour
Pinch of salt	Pinch of salt
Oil for frying	Oil for frying
FILLING	FILLING
500 g smooth cottage cheese	2 cups cottage cheese (smooth & creamy style)
2 eggs	2 eggs
30 mℓ (2 T) flour	2 tablespoons flour
Sugar to taste	Sugar to taste
125 mℓ (½ C) sour cream	½ cup sour cream
SAUCE	SAUCE
Cinnamon & sugar to taste	Cinnamon & sugar to taste
Butter	Butter
60 mℓ (¼ C) milk	¼ cup milk
60 mℓ (¼ C) cream	¼ cup cream

METHOD Combine eggs and milk and beat well. Add sifted dry ingredients. Beat until smooth. Grease pan with oil, heat and pour in a thin layer of batter. Fry on one side only until done. Continue until all the batter has been used, stacking the cooked blinis one on top of the other.

FILLING Combine all ingredients gently by hand. Press through a sieve.

TO BAKE Spoon 15 mℓ (1 tablespoon) filling onto each blini. Fold over into squares and arrange in buttered pyrex dish. Sprinkle generously with cinnamon and sugar; dot with butter.

Pour over 60 mℓ (¼ cup) milk and the same amount of cream. Bake in 180°C (350°F) oven until piping hot. Serve immediately.

Makes 24

Lokshen Pudding

METRIC	AMERICAN
250 g thick ribbon noodles	½ lb thick ribbon noodles
60 g butter, melted	4 tablespoons butter, melted
125 mℓ (½ C) cream	½ cup cream
150 g (¾ C) sugar	¾ cup sugar
15 mℓ (1 T) syrup	1 tablespoon syrup
60 g cream cheese	4 tablespoons cream cheese
2 mℓ (½ t) cinnamon	½ teaspoon cinnamon
2 eggs	2 eggs
250 mℓ (1 C) milk	1 cup milk

METHOD Boil noodles in salted water until tender (about 10–15 minutes). Drain well. Combine with butter, cream, sugar, syrup, cream cheese and cinnamon.

Beat eggs and milk together; stir into noodle mixture. Pour into a buttered pyrex dish and bake at 180°C (350°F) for 45 minutes.

Serves 8

Imberlach (Carrot Sweets)

METRIC	AMERICAN
3 ℓ (12 C) cleaned & grated carrots	12 cups cleaned & grated carrots
1,6 kg (8 C) sugar	8 cups sugar
2 whole oranges, minced or chopped finely in food processor	2 whole oranges, ground or chopped finely in food processor
Juice of 1 lemon	Juice of 1 lemon
20 mℓ (4 t) ground ginger	4 teaspoons ground ginger

METHOD Boil carrots and sugar together in a large uncovered pot for approximately 1 hour, stirring frequently with a wooden spoon to prevent burning.

Add oranges, lemon juice and ginger. Reduce heat and allow to cook for 1–2 hours, until mixture is thick. To test for readiness, spoon a little onto a plate and allow to cool. If it sets, it is ready.

Wet a large board with a little cold water. Using a knife, spread mixture over the board to a thickness of about 1 cm (½ inch). If necessary, use a damp rolling pin to smooth it out.

Allow to stand for a few hours, then cut diagonally into pieces. Leave to dry out on a wire tray.

Makes about 80

Teiglach

METRIC	AMERICAN
8 extra large eggs	8 extra large eggs
60 mℓ (4 T) oil	4 tablespoons oil
Finely grated rind of 1 orange	Finely grated rind of 1 orange
15 mℓ (1 T) ground ginger	1 tablespoon ground ginger
250 g (2 C) cake meal	2 cups cake meal

SYRUP	SYRUP
1 x 1 kg tin syrup	1 x 2 lb can imported golden syrup
800 g (4 C) sugar*	5 cups sugar
1 ℓ (4 C) water	4 cups water
30 mℓ (2 T) ground ginger	2 tablespoons ground ginger

* *This measurement differs from the American*

METHOD Place eggs, oil, orange rind and ginger in electric mixer bowl and beat for approximately 5 minutes. Sift about three-quarters of the cake meal over the egg mixture; fold in with a spatula.

Using some of the remaining meal, sift 15–30 mℓ (1–2 tablespoons) onto a large wooden board. Place mixture on the board and knead for a short time, adding more meal if dough is too soft. (The consistency should be correct when you have used all but 2 tablespoons - or a little less than 2 - of the cake meal.)

Roll into balls about the size of walnuts. Make holes in the centres with the handle of a wooden spoon.

SYRUP Combine syrup, water and sugar in a large pot over medium heat. Stir occasionally until the sugar dissolves and then allow to boil. (The syrup must be boiling vigorously when you put the teiglach into it.)

TO COOK Immerse teiglach in the boiling syrup. Cover and cook on high for approximately 12 minutes, then turn heat down to medium and allow to cook undisturbed for a further 15 minutes (do not uncover the pot at all for the first 25 minutes).

Remove lid, stir quickly with a wooden spoon, then cover again and continue to cook, stirring every 10–15 minutes. Reduce heat to low when necessary.

When nicely browned, lift one out of the syrup; if it does not fall back easily they are done, otherwise allow to cook longer. (Teiglach usually take about 1¼ hours to cook.) Just before removing from syrup, stir in the additional 30 mℓ (2 tablespoons) ginger.

Remove teiglach with a slotted spoon and roll in crushed post toasties, coconut or finely chopped nuts. Cool on a cooling rack.

Makes approximately 30 to 40 PHOTOGRAPH ON PAGE 170

My Mother's Cracked Teiglach

METRIC	AMERICAN
9 extra large eggs	9 extra large eggs
5 egg yolks	5 egg yolks
90 mℓ (6 T) oil	6 tablespoons oil
Grated rind of 1 orange	Grated rind of 1 orange
15 mℓ (1 T) ground ginger	1 tablespoon ground ginger
15 mℓ (1 T) sugar	1 tablespoon sugar
500 g (4 C) flour*	3¾ cups all purpose flour
60 g (½ C) Passover cake meal	½ cup Passover cake meal

SYRUP	SYRUP
1,5 ℓ (7 C) water*	5 cups water
1,2 kg (5 C) sugar*	6 cups sugar
1,5 kg syrup	3 lb imported golden syrup

TO ADD	TO ADD
250 mℓ (1 C) boiling water	1 cup boiling water
30 mℓ (2 T) ground ginger	2 tablespoons ground ginger

COATINGS	COATINGS
Dessicated coconut	Dessicated coconut
Flaked almonds	Flaked almonds
30–45 mℓ (2–3 T) sugar mixed with 5 mℓ (1 t) ground ginger	2–3 tablespoons sugar mixed with 1 teaspoon ground ginger

*	These measurements differ from the American

METHOD Beat together eggs, yolks, oil, orange rind, ginger and sugar for 3–4 minutes in a stainless steel or porcelain mixing bowl (do not use plastic). Sift together flour and cake meal. Set aside approximately 125 mℓ (½ cup) of the sifted mixture and add remainder to eggs. Mix into a medium soft dough.

Sprinkle a little additional flour on a wooden board and knead the dough until smooth, using the reserved flour if necessary. Roll into balls and use the handle of a wooden spoon to make a hole in each centre. (If you wish, shape some of the dough into rolls and form into a knot.)

Leave the teiglach in a sunny place for 1 hour, turn over and leave for another hour. This will result in cracked teiglach; for ordinary teiglach, simply omit this step.

SYRUP Bring the water, sugar and syrup to the boil. When liquid is boiling very fast, add the teiglach, cover and cook on high for 20 minutes. Stir quickly, replace lid and turn down to medium heat. Boil for another 40 minutes, until done.

When ready, add the 250 mℓ (1 cup) boiling water mixed with the 30 mℓ (2 tablespoons) ground ginger. Stir quickly, being very careful not to get burnt by rising steam. Cook for a further 5–10 minutes.

Reduce heat to low and remove teiglach from syrup with a slotted spoon, taking out a few at a time. Roll lightly in coconut, flaked almonds or ginger sugar. Cool on wire trays.

TO USE SYRUP AGAIN Add 4 cups sugar and 6 cups water (metric measurements) or 4 cups sugar and 5 cups water (American measurements); boil together as before .

Makes about 50

Orange Preserve (Pomerantzen)

METRIC	AMERICAN
7 large oranges	7 large oranges
1,2 kg (6 C) sugar	6 cups sugar
250 mℓ (1 C) water	1 cup water
Chopped almonds	Chopped almonds

METHOD Grate rind of oranges. Place oranges in pot of boiling water and boil until soft (but not pulpy). Remove from pot and cut into quarters.

Combine sugar and water in a pot and bring to the boil. Drop quartered oranges into pot and allow to boil until liquid becomes syrupy.

Transfer fruit to a large platter and allow to cool. Cut into smaller pieces and sprinkle with chopped almonds to serve.

Serves 10 to 12

Kitke or Challah

METRIC	AMERICAN
750 g (6 C) flour	6 cups all purpose flour
50 g cake yeast	2 cakes yeast
50 g (¼ C) sugar	¼ cup sugar
5 mℓ (1 t) salt	1 teaspoon salt
125 mℓ (½ C) oil	½ cup oil
625 mℓ (2½ C) warm water	2½ cups warm water
2 eggs	2 eggs
Poppy or sesame seeds	Poppy or sesame seeds

METHOD Liquify yeast by mixing with 15 mℓ (1 tablespoon) of the sugar. Add all remaining ingredients except seeds. Knead well with dough hook for 5 minutes. Cover and allow to rise for 3 hours or longer.

Roll dough into 3 strips and braid. (If you would prefer to make two small loaves rather than one large one, divide the dough in half.) Leave in a warm, draught-free place for 45 minutes.

Brush with additional beaten egg and sprinkle with poppy or sesame seeds. Bake in 190°C (375°F) oven for 45 minutes, until golden.

Makes 1 very large or 2 small loaves	PHOTOGRAPH ON PAGE 170

Bagels

METRIC	AMERICAN
40 g cake yeast	1½ cakes yeast
625 mℓ (2½ C) warm water	2½ cups warm water
750 g (6 C) flour	6 cups all purpose flour
15 mℓ (1 T) sugar	1 tablespoon sugar
10 mℓ (2 t) salt	2 teaspoons salt
2 eggs	2 eggs
30 mℓ (2 T) oil	2 tablespoons oil

METHOD Dissolve yeast in a little of the warm water. Combine remaining ingredients, add yeast mixture and knead well. Cover and allow to rise until double in bulk (about 4–5 hours) or leave overnight.

Shape into bagels on floured board and leave to rise for 30 minutes. Bring a large pot of water to the boil, adding to it 15 mℓ (1 tablespoon) sugar and 5 mℓ (1 teaspoon) salt. Drop bagels, a few at a time, into boiling water and cook for 1–2 minutes.

Remove with a slotted spoon and transfer to a well-greased baking tray. Bake in a hot oven (230°C / 450°F) for 10–15 minutes, or until golden brown.

Makes 40

Fat-free Matzo Balls

METRIC	AMERICAN
4 eggs	4 eggs
120 g (1 C) matzo meal	1 cup matzo meal
5 mℓ (1 t) salt	1 teaspoon salt
2 mℓ (½ t) black pepper	½ teaspoon black pepper
2 mℓ (½ t) ground cinnamon	½ teaspoon ground cinnamon

METHOD Mix together all ingredients. Drop spoonfuls into boiling, salted water (as for dumplings). Cover and cook for 15–20 minutes.

Makes 6 to 8

Matzo Knaidlach

METRIC	AMERICAN
2 eggs	2 eggs
200 mℓ (¾ C) water	¾ cup water
45–60 mℓ (3–4 T) schmaltz, melted	3–4 tablespoons schmaltz (chicken fat), melted
2 mℓ (½ t) salt	½ teaspoon salt
1 mℓ (¼ t) pepper	¼ teaspoon pepper
1 mℓ (¼ t) ground cinnamon	¼ teaspoon ground cinnamon
5 mℓ (1 t) sugar	1 teaspoon sugar
150 g (1¼ C) matzo meal	1 cup matzo meal

METHOD Beat together eggs, water and schmaltz. Add seasonings, cinnamon, sugar and matzo meal. Allow to stand for 2–3 hours.

Shape into balls and drop into rapidly boiling salted water, then reduce heat and simmer for 30 minutes.

Serves 12 to 14

Geschmerte Matzo (Cheese Matzo)

METRIC	AMERICAN
500 g smooth cottage cheese	1 lb cottage cheese (smooth & creamy style)*
100 g (½ C) sugar	½ cup sugar
1 egg, lightly beaten	1 egg, lightly beaten
30 mℓ (2 T) thick cream	2 tablespoons heavy cream
30 mℓ (2 T) matzo meal	2 tablespoons matzo meal
30 mℓ (2 T) sugar mixed with 5 mℓ (1 t) cinnamon	2 tablespoons sugar mixed with 1 teaspoon cinnamon

* Blend in food processor until smooth and creamy

METHOD Mix cheese, sugar, egg, cream and matzo meal together by hand (do not beat). Wet 2½ matzos quickly under cold water tap and place on greased baking sheet. Spread with cheese mixture and sprinkle with cinnamon sugar.

Bake in 190°C (375°F) oven for 20 minutes. Cut into squares when cool.

Serves 8 to 10

Cheese Cake

METRIC	AMERICAN
DOUGH	DOUGH
125 g butter	½ cup butter
100 g (½ C) sugar	½ cup sugar
1 egg	1 egg
5 mℓ (1 t) grated lemon rind	1 teaspoon grated lemon rind
15 mℓ (1 T) oil	1 tablespoon oil
150 g (1¼ C) cake meal	1¼ cups cake meal
60 mℓ (¼ C) potato starch	¼ cup potato starch
CHEESE FILLING	CHEESE FILLING
500 g creamed cottage cheese	1 lb cottage cheese (smooth & creamy style)*
100 g (½ C) sugar	½ cup sugar
15 mℓ (1 T) lemon juice	1 tablespoon lemon juice
2 eggs, beaten	2 eggs, beaten
15 mℓ (1 T) cake meal	1 tablespoon cake meal
45 mℓ (3 T) thick cream	3 tablespoons thick cream

*   Blend in food processor until smooth and creamy

METHOD Cream butter and sugar; add egg, lemon rind and oil. Mix in dry ingredients to form a dough. Chill in fridge for 1 hour (this dough should be fairly soft).

Combine filling ingredients and mix together by hand. Pat dough into a 23 cm (9 inch) pie dish. Pour in cheese mixture.

Bake in a 200°C (400°F) oven for 10 minutes, then turn oven down to 150°C (300°F) and bake for a further 20 minutes.

CHEF'S TIP This dough may also be used for apple tarts.

Serves 10 to 12

Passover Chocolate Mousse Cake

METRIC	AMERICAN
6 eggs, separated	6 eggs, separated
200 g (1 C) sugar	1 cup sugar
250 g butter or margarine	½ lb butter or margarine
250 g dark chocolate, melted	8 oz semi-sweet chocolate, melted
50 g (½ C) chopped almonds	½ cup chopped almonds
60 mℓ (¼ C) brandy, rum or Grand Marnier	¼ cup brandy, rum or Grand Marnier
60 mℓ (4 T) cake meal	4 tablespoons cake meal
TOPPING	TOPPING
250 mℓ (1 C) cream	1 cup cream
5 mℓ (1 t) vanilla essence	1 teaspoon vanilla extract
15 mℓ (1 T) sugar	1 tablespoon sugar

METHOD Beat egg yolks for approximately 15 minutes, until thick and very creamy. Set aside 90 mℓ (6 tablespoons) of the sugar, then add remaining sugar to egg yolks. Add softened butter or margarine; stir in cooled, melted chocolate. Mix for a further two minutes and set aside.

Whip egg whites until frothy. Add reserved sugar gradually, until whites peak but are not dry. Fold into egg yolk mixture. Measure 250 mℓ (1 cup) of this mixture and refrigerate until required. Fold chopped nuts and brandy, rum or Grand Marnier into remaining mixture, then fold in cake meal.

Line a well-greased 23 cm (9 inch) springform pan with wax paper; grease again before pouring in batter. Bake in 180°C (350°F) oven for 45 minutes, or until cake shrinks away from the sides. Cool in container for 15 minutes.

Remove sides of cake pan. Allow to cool completely before inverting onto a platter. Remove wax paper. Spread reserved chocolate mixture on top. Cover and refrigerate for 6–8 hours, or overnight.

TOPPING Whip cream until thick, then fold in vanilla and sugar. Use to decorate top of cake.

Serves 8

Passover Apple Cake

METRIC	AMERICAN
2 eggs	2 eggs
100 g (½ C) sugar	½ cup sugar
45 mℓ (3 T) oil	3 tablespoons oil
1 mℓ (¼ t) salt	¼ teaspoon salt
60 g (½ C) matzo meal	½ cup matzo meal
20 mℓ (4 t) potato starch	4 teaspoons potato starch
15 mℓ (1 T) cake meal	1 tablespoon cake meal
2–3 cooking apples, peeled, cored & sliced	2–3 cooking apples, peeled, cored & sliced
30 mℓ (2 T) cinnamon & sugar mixture	2 tablespoons cinnamon & sugar mixture

METHOD Beat eggs and sugar together. Add oil, mix in all other ingredients except apples and cinnamon / sugar mixture and blend well.

Place sliced apples in greased 23 cm (9 inch) baking dish. Sprinkle with sugar and cinnamon, pour batter over and bake at 180°C (350°F) for 25–30 minutes.

Serve warm or cold.

Serves 8 to 10

Topping for Passover Cakes

METRIC	AMERICAN
45 mℓ (3 T) sugar	3 tablespoons sugar
45 mℓ (3 T) cocoa powder	3 tablespoons cocoa powder
45 mℓ (3 T) Kosher wine	3 tablespoons Kosher wine

METHOD Combine ingredients in a saucepan. Dissolve over low heat, then bring slowly to the boil. Remove from heat and add 15 mℓ (1 tablespoon) butter or margarine. Pour over cooled cake.

Passover Chiffon Cake

METRIC	AMERICAN
30 mℓ (2 T) cocoa mixed with 30 mℓ (2 T) sugar	2 tablespoons cocoa mixed with 2 tablespoons sugar
30 mℓ (2 T) boiling water	2 tablespoons boiling water
90 g (¾ C) cake meal	¾ cup cake meal
125 mℓ (½ C) potato starch	½ cup potato starch
5 mℓ (1 t) salt	1 teaspoon salt
300 g (1½ C) sugar	1½ cups sugar
8 extra large eggs, separated	8 extra large eggs, separated
125 mℓ (½ C) oil	½ cup oil
125 mℓ (½ C) orange juice	½ cup orange juice

SEVEN MINUTE FROSTING	SEVEN MINUTE FROSTING
300 g (1½ C) sugar	1½ cups sugar
160 mℓ (⅔ C) water	⅔ cup water
Pinch of cream of tartar	Pinch of cream of tartar
2 egg whites	2 egg whites

METHOD Combine cocoa / sugar mixture with the boiling water and set aside. Sift together cake meal, potato starch, salt and 150 g (¾ cup) of the sugar. Make a well in the centre and add egg yolks, oil and orange juice. Mix well.

Beat egg whites stiffly. Gradually add the remaining sugar, beating until stiff and shiny. Fold into the flour mixture.

Pour one third of the batter into a chiffon cake tin (tube pan). Add the cocoa mixture to half of the remaining batter and mix in lightly but thoroughly. Pour the chocolate batter over batter in tin; top with remaining yellow batter. Zig-zag through the layers with a knife.

Bake in 180°C (350°F) oven for 1 hour. Reduce temperature to 150°C (300°F) and bake for a further 10 minutes. Remove cake from oven and invert onto a cooling rack. Allow to cool in the tin.

When cool, loosen edges and centre with knife and turn out. Loosen the bottom of the pan and remove. Ice top and sides of cake with Seven Minute Frosting.

SEVEN MINUTE FROSTING Place sugar, water and cream of tartar in a saucepan. Stir over low heat until sugar has dissolved. Beat egg whites stiffly. Allow mixture in saucepan to boil gently until sugar spins a thread, then pour slowly onto stiffly beaten egg whites. Beat until mixture has a good spreading consistency.

Serves 12

Carrot Pudding

METRIC	AMERICAN
4 eggs, separated	4 eggs, separated
100 g (½ C) sugar	½ cup sugar
250 mℓ (1 C) grated carrots (tightly packed)	1 cup grated carrots (tightly packed)
½ Granny Smith apple, peeled & grated	½ Granny Smith apple, peeled & grated
5 mℓ (1 t) finely grated lemon rind	1 teaspoon finely grated lemon peel
Juice of ½ lemon	Juice of ½ lemon
80 mℓ (⅓ C) potato starch	⅓ cup potato starch
60 mℓ (¼ C) red wine	¼ cup red wine

METHOD Beat egg yolks with sugar until light and creamy. Add grated carrot, apple, lemon rind and juice, potato starch and wine. Blend well. Beat egg whites until stiff and fold in.

Pour into a deep, well-greased casserole dish and bake at 190°C (375°F) for 30–35 minutes, or until well done. Serve hot or cold as a dessert.

Serves 6

Weights & Measures

In this book quantities are given in metric and American measurements. Included for the convenience of British users are the following approximated metric/Imperial equivalents:

Weight		Liquid capacity	
Metric	*Imperial equivalent*	*Metric*	*Imperial equivalent*
25 g	1 ounce	25 mℓ	1 fl ounce
50 g	2 ounces	50 mℓ	2 fl ounces
75 g	3 ounces	125 mℓ	4 fl ounces
100 g	4 ounces	150 mℓ	¼ pint
150 g	5 ounces	300 mℓ	½ pint
200 g	7 ounces	450 mℓ	¾ pint
250 g	9 ounces	600 mℓ	1 pint
450 g	16 ounces (1 lb)	1 000 mℓ (1 ℓ)	1¾ pints
500 g	1 lb 2 ounces		
750 g	1 lb 10 ounces		
900 g	2 lb		
1 kg	2,2 lb		

Metric measurements

Mass is given in grams (g) and kilograms (kg). Volume is given in millilitres (mℓ) and litres (ℓ). The equivalent amount in metric cups (C), tablespoons (T) and teaspoons (t) is given in brackets afterwards.

Approximate metric volume equivalents

0,5 mℓ = ⅛ teaspoon		60 mℓ = ¼ cup	
1 mℓ = ¼ teaspoon		80 mℓ = ⅓ cup	
2 mℓ = ½ teaspoon		125 mℓ = ½ cup	
5 mℓ = 1 teaspoon		200 mℓ = ¾ cup	
7 mℓ = 1½ teaspoons		250 mℓ = 1 cup	
10 mℓ = 2 teaspoons		375 mℓ = 1½ cups	
15 mℓ = 1 tablespoon		500 mℓ = 2 cups	
30 mℓ = 2 tablespoons		750 mℓ = 3 cups	
45 mℓ = 3 tablespoons		1 litre = 4 cups	

Approximate weights per 250 mℓ (1 C)

Breadcrumbs (fresh) 60 g
Breadcrumbs (dry) 120 g
Cheese (Cheddar, grated) 100 g
Flour (self-raising) 140 g

Flour (plain) 120 g
Raisins 150 g
Sugar (granulated) 200 g
Sugar (icing) 130 g

Oven temperatures	°C	°F	*Gas Mark*
Very cool	100 – 120	200 – 250	¼ – ½
Cool	140 – 150	275 – 300	1 – 2
Warm	160 – 180	325 – 350	3 – 4
Moderate	190 – 200	375 – 400	5 – 6
Hot	220 – 230	425 – 450	7 – 8
Very hot	240 – 260	475 – 500	9 – 10

Index

A

Aioli dip 12
Almond
  peach pie 140
  slices, raspberry 158
Appetizers
  cold 12–17
  hot 18–30
Apple/s
  and rhubarb cobbler 97
  baked with caramel sauce 96
  cake, Passover 177
  cheese and mon tart 137
  cream tart, brandy 136
  custard crêpes 102
  pie, Dutch 136
  strudel 137
Apricot
  chutney 88
  glaze 125, 132, 148
Artichoke/s
  and crab stuffed in mushrooms 21
  and mushroom salad 90
  and shrimp casserole 24
  dip 18
  Italian-style 24
  lettuce and Parmesan salad 91
  pie, and Ricotta cheese 29
Asparagus
  and crab crêpes 30
  and tuna pie 29
  fresh
    in spaghetti primavera 87
    with mushroom sauce 82
    with sesame seeds 82
  tart 28
Aubergine Parmesan 82
Avocado
  and citrus salad 92
  and orange salad 90
  and shrimp salad 93

B

Baby marrows *see* Courgettes
Bagels 176
Baked bean casserole 83
Baking tips 114
Banana
  cream pie 140
  fritters 97
  loaf 115
Barley and bean soup 36
Bean/s
  and barley soup 36
  baked, casserole 83
  green, with almonds 83
  Lima, with braised lamb chops 77

Béarnaise sauce 66
Beef
  braised, in red wine 70
  brisket
    barbecued 68
    tzimmes 172
    with prunes 169
  corned
    glazed 70
    pickling solution for 69
  en croûte with Béarnaise sauce 66
  fillet chasseur 68
  goulash 70
  mince, hot 'n spicy 73
  rib roast with green peppercorn sauce 66
  ribs, barbecued 68
  roast 67
  short ribs, barbecued 68
  steak
    marinades for 69
    Diane 67
    on a stick 69
  stew with dumplings 71
Beetroot
  Harvard beets 84
Berries
  and cream with marshmallow ring 108
  see also Blueberry; Cranberry; Gooseberry;
    Raspberry; Strawberries; Youngberry
Berry jelly 104
Biscuits 145, 153–9
Bisque, lobster 32
Black Forest cherry cake 130
Blintzes, cheese, baked 173
Blueberry sour cream cake 117
Boerewors, quick spaghetti bolognaise 73
Bolognaise, spaghetti, quick 73
Bombe, chocolate mint 103
Brandy
  Alexander gâteau 129
  apple cream tart 136
  cake, Cape 125
Brawn 169
Breads 161–3
Brie bread 162
Brisket *see under* Beef
Broccoli
  and mushroom soup, cream of 36
  in spaghetti primavera 87
  salad, nutty 92
  with mushroom sauce 82
Brownies 151
Butter
  biscuits, crispy 159
  cheese cake 124
  grenadilla cake 117
  roses 114
  sponge cake 133

Butter-cream filling 148
Butterflies (small cakes) 148
Butternut soup, curried 37

C

Cabbage
  and pineapple slaw 91
  stir-fried 83
  stuffed 72
Caesar salad 91
Cake/s
  chocolate mousse 111
  decorations 114
  for Passover 177–8
  recipes 113-33
  small 145,148–52
Canneloni, spinach-stuffed, with tomato
  cream sauce 87
Cape brandy cake 125
Caper sauce 45
Caramel
  chocolate squares 157
  crème 110
  crunch cake 116
  sauce 96
Carrot
  and grape mélange 83
  cake 115
  kugel 172
  pudding 178
  sweets 174
Casserole
  artichoke and shrimp 24
  baked bean 83
  grits 85
  tuna crêpe 25
  veal and mushroom 75
Challah 175
Cheese
  apple and mon tart 137
  blintzes, baked 173
  bread, zucchini 163
  crêpes with strawberry sauce 101
  dumplings, Ukranian 84
  gâteau, lemon 125
  matzo 176
  pastries, Greek 21
  Ricotta, and artichoke pie 29
  strata 22
Cheese cake 177
  butter 124
  custard 123
  Israeli 123
  marble 124
  with sour cream topping 123
Cherries jubilee 97

Cherry cake, Black Forest 130
Chestnuts, water
  and mushrooms with wild rice 86
  and spinach salad 93
Chicken
  apricot 56
  breasts Normandy 56
  Chinese stir-fried 58
  curried, in phyllo 28
  fingers, Polynesian 21
  gumbo 32
  honey-glazed 56
  livers, peri-peri 23
  marinade for 58
paprikash, Hungarian 57
  Parisienne 58
  peri-peri, with pineapple 59
  soup 166
  tandoori 59
  teriyaki 57
  wings, Cantonese 23
  with zucchini and tarragon 57
Chiffon
  cake, Passover 178
  pie, pumpkin 143
Chilli, hot 'n spicy Texas 73
Chinese soup 36
Chocolate
  cake 130
    coconut 122
    delicious 131
    white 130
  caramel squares 157
  chip cookies 156
  coating 152
  cream torte, Viennese 132
  decorations 114
  gâteau 128
  glaze 129, 132, 133
  lychees, Chinese 112
  meringue 110
  mint bombe 103
  mocha cake 132
  mocha cream cake 131
  mousse 128
    marbled 109
    rich 109
    with raspberry sauce 108
    cake, fancy 111
    cake, Passover 177
  pastry 141
  pie Alaska 101
  roulade, raspberry/strawberry 129
  shortbread, walnut 156
  soufflé 100
  torte, triple 133
  truffles 112
Chowder
  clam 33
  corn 37
Chutney
  apricot 88
  cranberry, spicy 88
Citrus and avocado salad 92

Clam
  chowder 33
  sauce and spaghetti 53
Cobbler
  fruit, crunchy 96
  rhubarb and apple 97
Coconut
  cake supreme 122
  chocolate cake 122
Coeur à la crème 109
Coffee cream and walnuts with
  meringues 151
Coleslaw, cabbage and pineapple 91
Cookies see Biscuits
Corn chowder 37
Corn meal see Mealie meal
Corn pudding 85
Corned beef
  glazed 70
  pickling solution 69
Cottage pie 72
Courgettes
  cheese bread 163
  fried 84
  nut cake 116
  with chicken and tarragon 57
Crab
  and artichoke stuffed in mushrooms 21
  and asparagus crêpes 30
  salad, tarragon 16
  soup 32
Cranberry chutney, spicy 88
Crayfish
  grilled 48
  see also Lobster
Cream
  cake, Devonshire 133
  puff ring, lemon 105
Cream cheese
  dip, vegetable 12
  icing 115
  mould and smoked salmon 17
  squares 152
Crème caramel 110
Crêpes
  apple custard 102
  cheese, with strawberry sauce 101
  crab and asparagus 30
  souffléd, with custard 103
  Suzette 102
  tuna, casserole 25
Croquettes, salmon, with
  mushroom sauce 22
Crudités 12
Crumpets 163
Crunchy cookies 158
Cucumber/s
  pickled 88
  sauce 16
Curly dessert cups 104
Curry
  Madras, simple 76
  puffs 20
Custard

and souffléd crêpes 103
apple, crêpes 102
cheese cake 123
creams, fried 100
crème caramel 110
flowers, tapioca 112

D

Date and nut spirals 158
Desserts
  cold 103–112
  hot 96–103
Devonshire cream cake 133
Dips
  aioli 12
  artichoke 18
  eight-layer Mexican 18
  spinach and vegetable 12
  vegetable cream cheese 12
Dough 166, 167
  tart 136, 137
  see also Pastry
Doughnuts, Greek 152
Drop scones 163
Duck
  à l'orange 61
  in clay 61
  Montmorency 60
  with figs 60
Dumplings
  cheese, Ukranian 84
  for beef stew 71

E

Egg mould with sour cream and caviar 17
Eggplant Parmesan 82
Escalopes, à la crème 74
Escargots in mushroom caps 23

F

Fettucini
  Alfredo 87
  with pesto 88
Fillet see under Beef
Fish 40–53
  barbecued 41, 44
  en croûte 44
  gefilte 168
  pickled, Cape Malay 46
  pineapple ginger 45
  whole, baked or barbecued with
    herbs 41
Five-cup salad, special 90
Flan, walnut 141
Florentine
  lemon 105
  squares 159
Fondant glaze, quick 148
French
  silk tart 141
  toast, stuffed 163

Friandises 112
Fricadelles 72
Fritters
  banana 97
  sweetcorn 83
Frosting
  mocha 132
  seven minute, for cakes 178
  see also recipes given with specific cakes
Fruit
  cobbler, crunchy 96
  salad, frozen 104
  tart 142
Fruitcake, boiled 121

G

Galato boureka 149
Gâteau *see under* Cakes
Gefilte fish 168
Geschmerte matzo 176
Ginger
  Macadamia and pineapple delight 120
  pineapple cake 120
Glazes
  apricot 125, 132, 148
  chocolate 129, 132, 133
  fondant, quick 148
  *see also recipes given with specific cakes
  and tarts*
Gooseberry, sour cream cake 117
Goulash
  beef 70
  veal, with spaetzle 76
Grape and carrot mélange 83
Grasshopper squares 150
Gravilax 46
Grenadilla
  cake, butter 117
  ice-cream 103
Grits casserole 85
Guacamole 13, 73
Gumbo, chicken 32

H

Haddock pie 44
Halibut, broiled 40
Hazelnut gâteau 128
Herb
  butter 40
  sauce 67
Herring
  chopped 167
  pickled, in cream 169
  sweet and sour baked 168
Hors d'oeuvres
  cold 12–17
  hot 18–30
Horseradish sauce 67
Hummous 12

I

Ice-cream
  fried 100
  grenadilla 103
  orange pineapple nut 104
  peanut crisp 104
Ice mould 12
Icing
  lemon 149
  see also recipes given under specific cakes
Imberlach 174
Italian salad 90

J

Jam cake 124
Jambalaya, Bombay prawn 52
Jelly (jello), berry 104
Jewish dishes 165–78

K

Kentucky Derby pie 143
Kingklip, broiled 40
Kitke 175
Knadel 172
Knaidlach, matzo 176
Knishes 167
Koeksusters 150
Kreplach 166
Kuchen, plum 122
Kugel
  carrot 178
  potato 172
  upside-down noodle 173

L

Lamb
  barbecue, en croûte 80
  chops, braised with Lima beans 77
  in mustard sauce 80
  shaslik 80
  spring, roast rack of 77
Lammington squares 152
Lemon
  cheese gâteau 125
  cream puff ring 105
  Florentine 105
  icing 149
  meringue bars 157
  sauce 100
  sponge pie 140
  squares 152
  upside-down cake 120
Lychees, chocolate, Chinese 112
Lentil soup, Koppel 37
Lettuce, artichoke and Parmesan salad 91
Lima beans with braised lamb chops 77
Linzer cookies 153
Liver/s
  chicken, peri-peri 23
  pâté 13

Lobster

Lobster
  Américaine 52
  and prawn thermidor 49
  bisque 32
  cocktail 16
  see also Crayfish
Lokshen
  kugel, parava 173
  pudding 174
Lox and cream cheese mould 17

M

Macadamia, pineapple and
  ginger delight 120
Mandelbrodt 159
Mango mousse 108
Marinade
  for barbecued chicken 58
  for barbecued fish 44
  for steak 69
Marrows, baby *see* Courgettes
Marshmallow
  nut delights 153
  ring, with cream and berries 108
Matzo
  balls, fat-free 176
  geschmerte/cheese 176
  knaidlach 176
Mealie meal
  casserole 85
  spoonbread souffle 24, 102
Meat
  pies
    curried 71
    perogen 166, 167
  recipes 66–80
Mélange, carrot and grape 83
Melktert 142
Meringue/s 128, 130
  chocolate 110
  fingers, nutty 156
  Greek 105
  lemon, bars 157
  Pavlova, foolproof 110
  with coffee cream and walnuts 151
Mille feuilles 149
Minestrone, easy 36
Mint sauce 77
Mississippi mud pie 143
Mocha
  chocolate cream cake 131
  dark chocolate cake 132
  frosting 132
Mon, apple and cheese tart 137
Monkey bread 162
Moulds
  cream cheese and salmon 17
  egg 17
  ice 12
  salmon 16
Moules marinière 49

Mousse
  chocolate 128
    marbled 109
    rich 109
    fancy cake 111
    with raspberry sauce 108
  chocolate cake, Passover 177
  mango 108
Muffins, potato, crispy 85
Mushroom/s
  and artichoke salad 90
  and broccoli soup, cream of 36
  and water chestnuts with wild rice 86
  caps and escargots 23
  in French loaf 19
  sauce 22, 82
  stuffed with crab and artichokes 21
Mussels, moules marinière 49
Mustard sauce and lamb 80

N

Noodles
  kugel, upside-down 173
  see also Pasta
Nut/s
  and date spirals 158
  and raisins with curried rice 86
  cake, zucchini 116
  marshmallow delights 153
  orange pineapple ice-cream 104
  squares 151
Nutty meringue fingers 156

O

Ohio buckeyes 158
Orange
  and avocado salad 90
  pineapple cake 121
  pineapple nut ice-cream 104
  preserve 175
  sponge layer cake 116
Orange-glazed cake, quick 117
Oyster/s
  soup, crusted creamy 33
  supreme 23

P

Pancakes *see* Crêpes
Pancakes (crumpets) 163
Parava lokshen kugel 173
Parmesan salad, with lettuce
  and artichokes 91
Passover recipes 176–8
Pasta *see* Canneloni; Fettucini; Lokshen;
  Noodles *or* Spaghetti
Pastry
  chocolate 141
  puff 20
  see also Dough

Pâté
  liver 13
  salmon, pink 16
  salmon, smoked 13
  shrimp 13
Pavlova, foolproof 110
Peach/es
  almond pie 140
  and cream dessert 96
  'n cream pie 141
Peanut butter, Ohio buckeyes 158
Peanut crisp ice-cream slab 104
Pear tart, caramelized 142
Peas, Oriental 82
Peppercorn, green, sauce 66
Perogen
  baked 166
  fried 167
Pesto with fettucini 88
Petits fours 148
Petzah 169
Phyllo, curried chicken in 28
Pickling solution for corned beef 69
Pie/s
  asparagus and tuna 29
  haddock 44
  meat
    curried 71
    perogen 166, 167
  Ricotta cheese and artichoke 29
  sweet 135–43
Pineapple
  and cabbage slaw 91
  ginger cake 120
  Macadamia and ginger delight 120
  orange cake 121
  orange nut ice-cream 104
Pita
  bread 162
    wholewheat 162
  chips, toasted 93
Pizza
  loaf, quick 'n easy 19
  Mexican 19
Plum kuchen 122
Pomerantzen 175
Poppy-seed
  apple and cheese tart 137
  cake 121
Potato
  kugel 172
  muffins, crispy 85
  pudding, Israeli 84
  salad 93
  sole aux pommes 41
Poultry 56–71
Praline 114
Prawn/s
  and lobster thermidor 49
  brochette 52
  garlic 53
  jambalaya, Bombay 52
  sweet and sour 47
  with Chinese vegetables 48

  see also Shrimps
Preserve, orange 175
Puddings, sweet *see under* Desserts
Puff pastry 20
Pumpkin
  chiffon pie 143
  loaf 115

Q

Quiche, Terry's fabulous 28

R

Raisin/s
  and nuts with curried rice 86
  and walnut cookies, chunky 153
Raspberries and cream, with
  marshmallow ring 108
Raspberry
  almond slices 158
  chocolate roulade 129
  glaze 132
  pudding, hot baked 97
  sauce 109
    with white chocolate mousse 108
Rhubarb and apple cobbler 97
Rice
  Chinese fried 86
  curried, with nuts and raisins 86
  spicy 86
  wild, with mushrooms and
    water chestnuts 86
Roulade, chocolate raspberry/
  strawberry 129
Roux 32

S

Salads and salad dressings 89–93
Salmon
  croquettes with mushroom sauce 22
  gravilax 46
  mould
    with cream cheese 17
    with cucumber sauce 16
  pâté
    pink 16
    smoked 13
  poached 45
  roll, savoury 25
Samoosas 22
Sauce
  Béarnaise 66
  caper 45
  caramel 96
  clam, with spaghetti 53
  cucumber 16
  green peppercorn 66
  herb 67
  horseradish 67
  lemon 100

mint 77
mushroom 22, 82
mustard 80
raspberry 108, 109
seafood 24
strawberry 101, 102
taco 18
tomato cream 87
Sausage
quick spaghetti bolognaise 73
rolls 20
Scallops
broiled 47
with spaghetti 47
Scones, drop 163
Seafood 40–53
marinated 49
sauce 24
soup, creamy 33
Seven-layer squares 157
Shashlik 80
Shortbread walnut chocolate 156
Shrimp/s
and artichoke casserole 24
and avocado salad 93
creole 48
pâté 13
Schezuan 53
with Chinese vegetables 48
see also Prawns
Slaw, cabbage pineapple 91
Snails see Escargots
Snoek and sweetcorn soufflé 30
Sole
aux pommes 41
Véronique 41
Soufflé
chocolate 100
spoonbread 24, 102
tuna 30
Souffléd crêpes with custard 103
Soups 32–7, 166
Sour cream
cake, gooseberry/blueberry 117
topping on cheese cake 123
Spaetzle and veal goulash 76
Spaghetti
bolognaise, quick 73
primavera 87
with scallops 47·
with white clam sauce 53

Spinach
and vegetable dip 12
and water chestnut salad 93
stuffed canneloni with tomato
cream sauce 87
Sponge
cake 148
butter 133
layer cake, orange 116
lemon, pie 140
Spoonbread, soufflé 24, 102
Steak see under Beef
Stew, beef, with dumplings 71
Stir-fried
cabbage 83
chicken, Chinese 58
Strawberries and cream, with
marshmallow ring 108
Strawberry
chocolate roulade 129
sauce 101, 102
Strudel
apple 137
fish 29
Sweetcorn
and snoek soufflé 30
fritters 83
Swordfish, broiled 40

T

Taco sauce 18
Tandoori chicken 59
Tapioca custard flowers 112
Tart dough 136, 137
Tarts
asparagus 28
sweet 135–43
Teiglach 174, 175
Teriyaki chicken 57
Thumbprints (biscuits) 157
Tomato cream sauce 87
Tomatoes, scalloped 83
Tongue, pickling solution for 69
Topping
for Passover cakes 178
see also under recipes for specific cakes
Tostados 73

Trout
almondine 40
stuffed, Southern style 40
Truffles, chocolate 112
Tuna
and asparagus pie 29
crêpe casserole 25
melt 18
roll, savoury 25
soufflé 30
strudel 29
Turkey, smoked 59
Tzimmes 172

V

Veal
and mushroom casserole 75
chops, quick 'n easy 74
chops, tasty 75
délicieuse 75
escalopes à la crème 74
goulash with spaetzle 76
Myrna 74
Vegetable/s 82–5
and spinach dip 12
Chinese, with prawns 48
cream cheese dip 12
Vichyssoise 37
Viennese cookies 159

W

Waldorf salad, exotic 92
Walnut/s
and coffee cream with meringues 151
and raisin cookies, chunky 153
chocolate shortbread 156
flan 141
Water chestnuts
and mushrooms with wild rice 86
and spinach salad 93

Y

Yorkshire pudding 67, 85
Youngberry pudding, hot baked 97